The age of upheaval

The age of upheaval provides an in-depth yet concise study of one of the most intense and formative periods of modern British political history. The years 1899–1914 witnessed a fundamental challenge to many Victorian values and institutions. Free Trade, the New Poor Law, the House of Lords, the Irish Union – all were under attack while organised labour and the feminist movement displayed an unprecedented assertiveness and aggression.

Drawing on a wide variety of sources, David Brooks examines what made these years the most politically turbulent between the Chartist era and today. The author emphasises the long shadow cast by the South African War, and the challenges to national identity posed by imperialism and by the Irish nationalist movement. Full consideration is also given to the 1906 Liberal landslide and the way in which this aroused expectations that could not always be fulfilled. New perspectives are offered on the leading figures of the day – Chamberlain, Balfour, Lloyd George, Asquith and Churchill. While the emphasis of the book is political throughout, the author also sets his discussion within the broad context of social and economic change.

The study will provide a thorough and up-to-date textbook for undergraduate students of Edwardian history and their lecturers.

David Brooks is Lecturer in History at Queen Mary & Westfield College, University of London.

NEW FRONTIERS IN HISTORY

series editors

Mark Greengrass
Department of History, Sheffield University

John Stevenson
Worcester College, Oxford

This important new series reflects the substantial expansion that has occurred in the scope of history syllabuses. As new subject areas have emerged and syllabuses have come to focus more upon methods of historical enquiry and knowledge of source materials, a growing need has arisen for correspondingly broad-ranging textbooks.

New Frontiers in History provides up-to-date overviews of key topics in British, European and world history, together with accompanying source material and appendices. Authors focus upon subjects where revisionist work is being undertaken, providing a fresh viewpoint which will be welcomed by students and sixth-formers. The series also explores established topics which have attracted much conflicting analysis and require a synthesis of the state of the debate.

Published titles

C. J. Bartlett   Defence and diplomacy: Britain and the Great Powers, 1815–1914

Jeremy Black   The politics of Britain, 1688–1800

Keith Laybourn   The General Strike of 1926

Panikos Panayi   Immigration, ethnicity and racism in Britain, 1815–1945

Daniel Szechi   The Jacobites: Britain and Europe, 1688–1788

Forthcoming titles

Paul Bookbinder   The Weimer Republic

Joanna Bourke   Production and reproduction: working women in Britain, 1860–1960

Michael Braddick   The nerves of state: taxation and the financing of the English state, 1558–1714

Ciaran Brady   The unplanned conquest: social changes and political conflict in sixteenth-century Ireland

David Carlton   Churchill and the Soviets

Carl Chinn   Poverty and the urban poor in the nineteenth century

Barry Coward   The Cromwellian Protectorate

Conan Fischer   The rise of the Nazis

Neville Kirk   The rise of Labour, 1850–1920

Tony Kushner   The Holocaust and its aftermath

Alan O'Day   Irish Home Rule

John Whittam   Fascist Italy

The age of upheaval

Edwardian politics, 1899–1914

David Brooks

Manchester University Press
Manchester and New York
Distributed exclusively in the USA and Canada by St. Martin's Press

Published by Manchester University Press
Oxford Road, Manchester M13 9NR, UK
and Room 400, 175 Fifth Avenue, New York, NY 10010, USA

Distributed exclusively in the USA and Canada
by St. Martin's Press, Inc., 175 Fifth Avenue, New York,
NY 10010, USA

British Library Cataloguing-in-Publication Data
A catalogue record for this book is available from the British
Library

Library of Congress Cataloging-in-Publication Data applied for

Brooks, David, 1947–
    The age of upheaval : Edwardian politics, 1899–1914 / David
Brooks.
        p.   cm.
    Includes bibliographical references (p.   ) and index.
        ISBN 0–7190–3695–X (hardback). —— ISBN 0–7190–3696–8
(paperback)
        1. Great Britain——Politics and government——1901–1910.   I. Title.
    DA570.B76   1995
    320.941′09′041—dc20   94–36786
ISBN 0 7190 3695 X *hardback*
    0 7190 3696 8 *paperback*

First published 1995

99 98 97 96 95   10 9 8 7 6 5 4 3 2 1

Typeset in Linotron Palatino
by Northern Phototypesetting Co. Ltd, Bolton

Printed in Great Britain
by Bell & Bain Ltd, Glasgow

Contents

Acknowledgements

Many people have assisted in the preparation of this book; to all of them I would like to express my gratitude. John Stevenson from the start has provided valuable encouragement and advice; and the staff of Manchester University Press, and all those associated with the book's production, have proved unfailingly helpful and considerate. My colleagues and students at Queen Mary and Westfield College in the University of London have afforded frequent stimulation, and I was greatly assisted by the grant of a sabbatical term's leave. Finally I would like to thank my wife, Gill, who has been a constant source of inspiration and support.

D.B.

To Gill,
to my mother
and to the memory of my father

Introduction

The Edwardian era – a convenient if not entirely accurate designation of the period covered by this book – contains many elements of paradox. In popular imagination it remains the last brilliant phase and expression of a golden age of peace and prosperity, stretching well back into Victorian times, an Indian summer of stability and imperial splendour before the cataclysm of the first world war and all the problems that would follow in its wake. The reality, as it appeared to many at the time, was very different. Certainly these were years of prosperity, but, as so often, they carried a price with them in the form of inflated expectations and a heightened jealousy between classes of society, each eager to extract a maximum advantage. In the decade and a half before the first world war, the British people felt the ground shifting beneath their feet to a degree hardly experienced since the 1830s and 1840s. Traditional values and constraints on behaviour appeared to be breaking down under the impact in particular of militant feminism and trade unionism. Social reform, energetically promoted by governments of different hues, looked likely to create as many new problems as to solve old ones. The constitution itself seemed to be imperilled in the violent controversies over the House of Lords and Irish home rule. Truly, the fifteen years or so before the first world war constituted an age of upheaval, and not only in domestic terms. They can indeed aptly be identified as the interval between the outbreak of two wars, one in south Africa and one in Europe, both of which were to have a major impact on Britain's political system and society, and which were to leave the country with a lasting anxiety as to its power and status in the world.

The first chapter will examine the political effects in Britain of the conflict in the southern hemisphere. This is a subject which has been much neglected by historians, although there are numerous accounts of actual hostilities in the field. As so often in this period, the element of paradox is to the fore. The Unionist administration of the day was arguably as incompetent in managing a war as any British government in modern times, yet for various reasons it survived and even contrived to win a second landslide victory at the polls. But in so doing it offered significant hostages to fortune, by promising to win both the war and the ensuing peace. Herein lay the seeds of future disaster for the Unionists, a development apprehended by Joseph Chamberlain, the most commanding figure in their ranks, whose mind under the impact of war began to conceive new schemes for averting possible catastrophe for both his party and his country.

Chapter 2 more or less coincides with Balfour's term of office as prime minister. Its theme is the squandering of a substantial political inheritance, hitherto accumulated by one of the more effective of Britain's coalition governments. Rivalry between Balfour and Chamberlain now replaced their one-time successful partnership. A continuing influence at work was the shadow cast by the south African war even during the years after it officially had ended. The problems of Balfour's administration began well before the opening of Chamberlain's tariff reform campaign, but it was this that most obviously altered the balance between the parties and changed the terms of the political debate, for instance by questioning the economic and social status quo. As part and parcel of the imperial preoccupations of the time, it also raised the whole issue of Britain's national identity, rather as does membership of the European Union today, and it had a similarly disruptive effect on the unity and cohesion of British Conservatism.

Chapter 3 is concerned with the period 1906–10, the last years of Liberal majority government in Britain. The 1906 election represented the Liberals' final decisive triumph at the polls, but its true significance has perhaps never been sufficiently appreciated. In particular, it is important to see it as as much a victory for traditionalism as a harbinger of change, and as as much a repudiation of Balfour as of Joseph Chamberlain. Likewise, Campbell-Bannerman's relatively short administration has rarely had full justice done to it, though in many ways it represented a successful expression of long-standing Liberal beliefs. Historians have shown much greater interest in the apparent transition from an older to a newer Liberalism, which began with the government's attempts to combat a severe downturn in its popularity. The reasons for this downturn have often been ascribed to the House of Lords and its obstructive influence, but it is important also to stress economic factors and the Liberals' failure to fulfil some of the expectations which they had aroused. The people's budget provoked one of the most spectacular confrontations of twentieth-century British political history. But it was to prove by no means an unqualified success for Liberalism. The ensuing January 1910 election, though fought on ground apparently favourable to the Liberals, ended their secure hold on power. It is necessary to explore the reasons for this conundrum, which has an important bearing on the potential viability of Liberalism in the years to come.

The fourth and final chapter deals with the years immediately before the first world war, years of hung parliaments and of great political and constitutional uncertainty. This was to prove a severely testing time for all four parties, including also Labour and the Irish Nationalists, and indeed it was to be as much a critical period for the future of Conservativism as for Liberalism. As the continuing government of the day, though holding power somewhat on sufferance, the Liberals faced a welter of problems associated partly with their minority status and dependence on heterogeneous support, and partly with an over-crowded legislative timetable which the apparent triumph of the 1911 Parliament Act had not done much to remedy. The country also seemed threatened with a degree of ungovernability, as feminist and trade union militancy challenged the workings of the system. For their part, the Conservatives or Unionists faced severe internal disunity, a leadership crisis, and the loss of many of the foundations of traditional Britain, such as a well entrenched House of Lords and union with Ireland. The December 1910 election was a bad setback for the Unionist party. It is important to get the problems of the day, faced by all political parties, into a proper perspective. The country experienced a rising level of disorder, but that stopped well short of anything that could be called revolutionary, and certain protagonists, such as the militant suffragettes, rather defeated their own ends. Ireland, which dominated so much of the politics of this period, posed a serious threat to both main parties, but developments on the eve of war did perhaps offer some hint of a solution. Industrial unrest, which was such a feature of these years, was partly a response to government policies, but it was also in some measure a mark of disillusion with the Labour party. Indeed all of the four principal parties faced an individual crisis of identity in these years, but it is the Liberal party which has most preoccupied historians, and indeed its destiny has become a kind of metaphor for that of Edwardian Britain as a whole. The chapter will conclude with a résumé of the political situation at that most intriguing of times, the year before the outbreak of the first world war. All through, the emphasis will be very much on domestic rather than on external policies and concerns.

1

Politics and war, 1899–1902

The long Victorian peace ended in October 1899. On the 9th of that month, the two Boer republics in south Africa, the Transvaal and the Orange Free State, issued an ultimatum demanding the immediate withdrawal of British troops. On Britain's failure to comply, their forces invaded Natal on 12 October, thus bringing to a dramatic end a lengthy period of diplomatic confrontation. Boer aggression took Britain more or less united into war, with the exception of the Irish Nationalist party and a handful of left-wing radicals. An amendment, moved in October by Dillon and Labouchere and blaming Britain for the outbreak of hostilities, received only 54 votes as against 322, and in the same month only 28 MPs opposed the granting of war credits. Controversy over responsibility for the war in all its aspects was not however stilled for long. The south African conflict was Britain's first serious war against a power of European standing since the Crimea, and it proved more prodigal of blood and treasure than any armed quarrel in which it had been engaged since Waterloo. More than most wars, it tested Britain's institutions and raised serious questions about its imperial identity which had occasioned the outbreak of the war. The conflict with the Boers also exposed Britain's international isolation, forcing it to adopt a new approach in foreign policy, and helping to develop a neurosis about national decline which has never quite gone away. In sum, it brought to an end the Victorian era of confidence, and helped to usher in the Edwardian age of political upheaval and reform. Its shadow remained over the country at least until 1914.

5

The government which took Britain into war in 1899 was a coalition composed of Conservative and Liberal Unionists. Gradually, this would emerge, both in and out of office, as a more unified political formation, and it will be convenient in these pages to refer to it by its collective name of Unionist. Under Salisbury's leadership, the coalition had won a landslide majority in 1895, mainly on domestic issues, though its subsequent tenure of power is sometimes seen as Britain's imperial zenith. This was not quite how matters seemed at the time, for Salisbury was much criticised for his apparent willingness to appease both the United States and Russia, in South America and China respectively. His government's greatest success came in 1898, with the overthrow of the Mahdi's regime in the Sudan and the diplomatic triumph over France at Fashoda, but these events only temporarily reinforced the popularity of his administration, which found itself once again losing by-elections in the following year. Apart from Salisbury himself, other senior figures in the cabinet were Devonshire, the leader of the Liberal Unionist peers, and Hicks Beach, the rigorous-minded chancellor of the exchequer. Among younger ministers, Balfour, Salisbury's nephew, was the coming man on the Conservative side, but the statesman most in the public view was the colonial secretary, Joseph Chamberlain.

Chamberlain was, and has remained, the most controversial political figure of his generation. His responsibility for the war in south Africa was widely alleged at the time, and has been much debated since. This is not the place to examine the diplomatic background to a conflict whose origins went back several decades. But so often has it been described as Chamberlain's war that some elucidation of his role should be attempted. Chamberlain by 1899 was in an unusual position, as both a triumphant and a disappointed politician. His oratorical, not to say demagogic, talents, both inside and outside parliament, had made him one of the commanding figures in the government, but, at the same time, his career lacked a substantial measure of achievement. His secession from the ranks of Liberalism had helped deny him the chance to effect a really large instalment of domestic reform. Since 1895, he had sought to carve out a new sphere of operations for himself as colonial secretary, with responsibility for the development of what he called Britain's overseas estates. Here he had hardly enjoyed conspicuous success, but in southern Africa the Transvaal beckoned as the greatest prize of all. The larger of the two Boer republics, it had been briefly ruled by Britain prior to the first Boer war of 1880–81. Since then it had become enormously rich, due to the discovery of massive gold deposits, whose exploitation had been rendered possible largely thanks to the industry of the Uitlanders, predominantly English settlers in the Transvaal who were, however, denied political rights there. In Britain itself, the Uitlanders had a mixed reputation, being regarded either as emissaries of empire or as cosmopolitan riff-raff. But to Chamberlain they represented a Trojan horse which could be used to prise control of the Transvaal away from the Boers and bring it back within the British empire. During most of 1899, Chamberlain endeavoured to browbeat Kruger, the Transvaal's president, into conceding the franchise to the Uitlanders on generous terms. This was work for which Chamberlain was well suited, for it combined his new-found enthusiasm for the empire with his former role as the arch-exponent of democracy.

Chamberlain probably did not intend to have to go to war in south Africa. He was a politician of cautious instincts, for all his fierce rhetoric and dynamic temperament, and he seems to have long believed that Kruger could be bluffed into submission. However, his general record in south African affairs made him something of a marked man, and one unlikely to achieve a settlement broadly satisfactory to all sides. His exact role in the Jameson Raid, a pirating expedition against the Transvaal launched by Rhodes in 1895–96 in an endeavour to raise an Uitlander revolt, has never been satisfactorily explained. Earlier still, Chamberlain had been a member of the Liberal government which had signed two conventions virtually acknowledging the independence of the Transvaal in 1881 and 1884; and it was well known that he was keen to repudiate all aspects of his Gladstonian past. Both episodes made him an object of the deepest suspicion to the Boers, who guessed that Chamberlain's ambitions were not confined simply to gaining the franchise for the Uitlanders. There was also the manner of Chamberlain's negotiations with the Boers, which rather resembled the war of attrition which he had conducted inside the Liberal party in 1886 and 1887. Chamberlain repeatedly shifted his position. He stressed the importance of the franchise

question, and, when Kruger showed some flexibility, he concentrated instead on demanding the abrogation of the 1881 and
1884 conventions. Throughout, he never made it entirely clear
exactly what the British government wanted from the Boers.
Chamberlain was on record as saying that war between Boers and
Britons in south Africa would be a disaster akin to that of civil
war. He was certainly a more moderating influence than Milner,
the British high commissioner in south Africa, who probably bore
more responsibility than anyone else on the British side for the
outbreak of war. But somehow he managed to give the opposite
impression. Chamberlain's hectoring and sometimes brutal
rhetoric, especially the speech at a garden party in August 1899,
where he described Kruger in unflattering terms, helped to pre-
cipitate the final crisis by making the Boers feel that they had no
alternative but to fight.

The second Boer war of 1899–1902 was a conflict of several
dimensions. In one sense, it represented the most intense phase
of the long-running struggle for supremacy between Dutch and
British in southern Africa, a stuggle which, militarily or politically, was to endure for a century and a half. The two peoples had
clashed intermittently throughout the nineteenth century, but
each derived different lessons from the experience. Britain felt
confident that it could crush the Boers once it really decided to do
so. The Boers believed that Britain would always lack the will to
prevail against their stubborn independent-mindedness. For
Britain, south Africa had long held a strategic significance, as a
vital link to its other colonial possessions. But recent developments had greatly enhanced the imperial dimension. The grab for
Africa had brought European rivals, and in particular Germany,
uncomfortably close to British territory at the southern end of the
continent. Gold discoveries had turned the Transvaal into a mag-
net which threatened to suck other colonies out of Britain's orbit.
The British empire, which ultimately rested on prestige, could
not afford to ignore these challenges. The war which broke out in
1899 represented the most serious imperial crisis since the Indian
Mutiny.

War in south Africa rapidly transformed the political situation
in Britain. A few months earlier, the government's popularity
had not stood very high. In June and July 1899, it had lost three
urban seats at by-elections, one at East Edinburgh and two at

Oldham. Two of the defeated Unionist candidates, Wauchope and the young Winston Churchill, had names which would become famous through fighting in south Africa, but they were little enough to conjure with in mid-1899. The government had enjoyed striking diplomatic and military successes in the Nile valley in late 1898, but for much of the following year this had availed it little with an electorate suspicious of its apparent inclination to favour the interests of countryside over town. Now, with the outbreak of fighting against Britain's traditional enemy, the Boers, everything changed. The first demonstration came at an east London by-election, held at Bow and Bromley in late October 1899. This had been a Liberal seat in 1885 and 1892, but now it saw a doubling of the Conservative majority to over two thousand. Unionist spokesmen rammed home the message, declaring that defeat for their candidate would give aid and comfort to Britain's foes, whether Boers, or Irish, or unsympathetic European powers. The lesson of Bow and Bromley was repeated at subsequent by-elections, whatever the fortunes of war. At York, previously a marginal seat, a by-election contest early in 1900 witnessed a striking increase in the Unionist majority.

The fortunes of war, however, did not favour British arms as 1899 turned into 1900. The Boers had begun the fighting with distinct advantages, partly because of the way in which the crisis in Anglo-Boer relations had developed. The British government had tried to put increasing diplomatic pressure on the Transvaal in the course of 1899, but at the same time had feared to send out sufficient troops to south Africa in case this provoked Kruger into an early declaration of hostilities. Consequently the Boers had begun the war with a numerical ascendancy, for they were easily able to call into the field the bulk of their adult male population, a highly mobile citizen army composed of men who from an early age had learnt to shoot and ride. The Boers were also better prepared for conflict than their opponents. The Jameson Raid had revealed to them what they believed to be Britain's real intentions in south Africa, and in the interval they had used the wealth of their goldfields to re-equip their forces with the most modern weaponry, including artillery from Krupp and Creusot and the Mauser magazine rifle. These were superior to anything on the British side: the Boer artillery easily outranged the British, and the Mauser was more fast-loading than the Lee-Enfield. The British also made the mistake of underestimating their opponents. Many had not expected the Boers to fight anyway, believing that Kruger would back down under pressure as he had done in earlier diplomatic confrontations in 1894 and 1897; and they were also caught somewhat by surprise when the Orange Free State, with which Britain had no immediate quarrel, threw in its lot with the Transvaal. Once the fighting had started, it was possible to predict a relatively easy victory for Britain's well-trained infantry, after it had been assembled in sufficient numbers. But the British army had hardly faced a European foe since 1815. Its experience had been gained mainly in colonial combat, as for instance against the Dervishes at Omdurman in 1898, when its method of fighting had been to deploy at 800 yards distance from the enemy, and advance in a series of rushes interspersed with volley fire. But such tactics were not well suited to use against the Boers, all of whom were mounted troops, who combined a maximum of mobility with a defensive capability based on expert marksmanship, superior weapons, and knowledge of the terrain.

The Boer armies quickly captured the initiative at the war's outset. Working on internal lines, and enjoying an initial superiority of numbers, they invaded neighbouring British territory and besieged the towns of Mafeking, Kimberley and Ladysmith. In the long run this would prove a mistake. Arguably the Boers should have bypassed such places and sought to press on to the coast, raising a revolt against British rule amongst their numerous Dutch compatriots in Cape Colony, and capturing the seaports at which reinforcements from Britain had to land. But the Boers' citizen armies were reluctant to march too far from home, and they were confident that, as in 1881 and 1896, a bloody nose or two would suffice to make their enemies give up. For the moment at least, the British were indeed forced to dance somewhat to the Boers' tune. The three besieged towns rapidly took on the status of household names in Britain, requiring early efforts at relief, and it was in trying to break through the cordons surrounding them that British forces sustained their worst shocks of the war. These were the three defeats of Stormberg, Magersfontein and Colenso, all occurring within a few days of each other between 10 and 15 December 1899. Famous infantry regiments – of the Guards, Highland and Irish Brigades – were involved; and though the casualties, amounting in all to some three thousand, would seem modest enough by the standard of 1914–18, they seriously dismayed opinion back in Britain, which had rarely experienced anything on such a scale since 1857.

Black Week, as it soon came to be known, shook the country out of whatever complacency still remained. At last Britain was stimulated into taking the war, and the new conditions of fighting, seriously. On 16 December 1899 a meeting of the cabinet decided on a number of emergency measures. In its desperate need for men, it now looked well beyond the ranks of the regular army. Britain already possessed three kinds of auxiliary forces, dating back to the days of the French invasion scares of the late eighteenth and early nineteenth centuries: the Militia, Yeomanry, and Volunteers. Traditionally their role had been limited to that of home defence, but the cabinet now allowed their members to opt for service in south Africa. In particular, the cabinet welcomed the raising of a 10,500-strong detachment of Yeomanry, now renamed the Imperial Yeomanry, which it was proposed to use in south Africa as mounted infantry; and to this end also it now willingly accepted colonial contingents, not only mounted infantry raised from the loyal areas within south Africa itself, but also offers of help much further afield from Canada, Australia and New Zealand. Finally, the cabinet overhauled the British command structure in south Africa. Lord Roberts of Kandahar was sent out to be commander-in-chief, accompanied as chief of staff by Lord Kitchener of Khartoum. This double appointment, of two men whose names and titles evoked the military glories of the Victorian age greatly reassured public opinion.

Three points of wider significance here deserve emphasis. In looking to raise large numbers of mounted troops, the authorities acknowledged the vital importance of mobility in a country with few railways, of the size of a sub-continent, like south Africa. This was to be almost the last major conflict in which horses would play an outstanding role, thereby suggesting a dubious precedent for 1914. Horses posed one of the larger logistical problems of the war, for the army remount department was geared to providing 2,500 horses a year, and eventually it had to find 518,794 for south Africa, from places as far apart as Argentina and Australia. Horses supplied the longest casualty list of the war: over 13,000 horses died on the voyage to south Africa, and a further 347,000 were 'expended' out there. Of much more long-term significance was the imperial dimension of the south African conflict. This was the first of Britain's wars in which an important contribution was made by her self-governing colonies, with no less than 52,000 recruits being supplied by Natal and Cape Colony, 16,715 by Australia, 6,400 by New Zealand, and 6,000 by Canada. (Offers of aid also came from the non-white subjects of the empire – including Maoris, Malays, Indian princes, West Indians, Nigerians, Pathans, and Canadian Indians – but for political reasons could not be accepted.) Opinion in Britain was deeply touched by the loyalty and new-found unity of the wider British world, and among politicians Chamberlain was sufficiently inspired to launch a political crusade on this basis in 1903.

The south African war was significant in a further sense in that it directly touched so many different classes of society. Previously Britain's wars had been fought in the main by recruits drawn from the lower social strata and from Scotland and Ireland, but the south African conflict drew on much wider sections of society, as represented by the Yeomanry, Militia, and Volunteers. The latter in particular were predominantly middle-class, and they signalled a new departure in military organisation, beyond the immediate control of the war office. Their most famous unit, the City Imperial Volunteers, for example, were raised from the counties of London, Middlesex, Essex and Surrey, and paid for by the livery companies of the City of London; and other units, both of Volunteers and Yeomanry, were funded by charitable contributions. In all, no less than 242,808 new recruits joined the Volunteers in wartime, and though only a small proportion of them would actually serve in south Africa, they contributed significantly to home defence, making possible the transfer of many regular army regiments to the southern hemisphere. The number of those who experienced the war at least at second hand was thus considerable, with no less than one-seventh of the entire adult male population of military age being in uniform at this time.[1]

Whatever the response of public opinion in Britain's hour of need, the government itself seemed unable to rise fully to the occasion. This was especially so with regard to ministerial speeches made outside parliament, which almost entirely failed to provide the country with any inspiration or leadership. Chamberlain, at Leicester in November 1899, delivered one of his least opportune orations, abusing France for allowing its press to publish a scurrilous caricature of Queen Victoria – so far had the old republican changed – and celebrating the apparent improvement in Britain's relations with Germany and the United States almost in terms of a triple alliance. This was hardly in accordance with the facts, and the only result was to compound Britain's sense of isolation and cause general resentment all round. Balfour's speeches at this time were among the most unfortunate of his career, especially those at Manchester in January 1900, where he implied that everybody was to blame for the military crisis in south Africa except the government. According to Balfour, unhelpful parliamentary and public opinion in the wake of the Jameson Raid had inhibited the government from making warlike preparations much earlier, and had obliged it to prolong the negotiations over the Transvaal franchise simply as a device to postpone war until Britain was ready. This was a classic case of *qui s'excuse s'accuse*, and amounted to a sorry confession on the government's part of confusion, double-dealing, and want of leadership. Salisbury added to the lamentable impression with a maundering speech at the reopening of parliament, blaming British defeats on treasury civil servants, whom he claimed had starved the intelligence services of sufficient funds. Only Devonshire, with his habitual common sense, retained a degree of proportion in his public speeches. At York, in mid-December 1899, he urged his countrymen to forego party bickering and xenophobia, and to look to the positive gains of the war in promoting national and imperial unity.[2]

Parliament reconvened in late January 1900, shortly after another costly reverse, at Spion Kop. British casualties amounted to 1,200, greater than in any previous engagement. Once again Boer marksmanship, adaptability and knowledge of the terrain, had prevailed against a British force superior in numbers but deficient in generalship, which had been trying to break through to the relief of Ladysmith. The war's conduct had now become the burning political question of the hour. Since the reign of Queen Anne, every major war in which Britain has been involved, with one exception, has provoked a change of government. The exception is the south African war of 1899–1902, and it is justifiable to ask why this did not have the same political consequences as in 1915–16 and 1940. Comparison with the circumstances of the Crimean war of nearly half a century earlier appears especially instructive. On the face of it, the similarities seem striking. In 1855, as in 1900, a coalition government stood accused in the House of Commons of having gone to war without sufficient preparation, and for having dispatched the best regiments in the British army thousands of miles away to a distant shore without adequate equipment and without even a properly considered plan of campaign. As in 1900 also, in 1855 the war office had faced the strongest indictment, being presided over on both occasions by a reputedly inefficient aristocratic grandee. Lord Lansdowne in 1900 was the target which the Duke of Newcastle had been in 1855. At least, the British army in the Crimea had started the war with three victories, whatever state it had been left in after that to face the Russian winter; yet this had not saved Aberdeen's government from one of the severest defeats inflicted in the nineteenth-century House of Commons. At the beginning of 1900, Salisbury's government had no such military successes to its name; and it was virtually unprecedented for the British army to have begun a campaign with no less than four successive disasters.

Here however the similarities end. Salisbury's coalition in 1900 was to prove politically much stronger than Aberdeen's had been. No one in 1900 was willing to break up the government from within, as Lord John Russell had done earlier; nor was anyone waiting in the wings to assume the premiership like Palmerston in 1855, Lloyd George in 1916 or Churchill in 1940. The key to the situation lay with Chamberlain, whose restless energy might in other circumstances have made him wish to grasp the lead. As colonial secretary he bore considerable responsibility for the outbreak of the war, but not for the military mess that had ensued. But Chamberlain was hardly a likely choice as prime minister, even if he had wished to be at this time, and there is no evidence that he did. His political base in the House of Commons was too small. A good number of Conservatives still regarded him with suspicion for his radical past, whereas to the Liberals and Irish Nationalists he remained a political pariah because of his desertion of their cause in 1886. The terms of the attack mounted by the Liberals immediately after parliament's reassembly merely reinforced Chamberlain's sense of identification with the government, for they sought to focus not only on the current conduct of the war but also on the whole course of policy since the Jameson Raid in which Chamberlain had been so intimately involved.

The main Liberal challenge came in the form of Fitzmaurice's amendment to the address, moved at the outset of the 1900 session of parliament. This stood in the name of a former Liberal under-secretary of state for foreign affairs, and it expressed regret 'at the want of knowledge, foresight and judgement displayed by Her Majesty's advisers, alike in their conduct of south African affairs since 1895 and in their preparations for the war now proceeding'. It occasioned the most prolonged parliamentary trial of strength of the war, with debates stretching over several days, but it was one which the Liberals would have done better to avoid, for it served only to emphasise their own internal differences rather than those of their opponents. The amendment derived from Campbell-Bannerman's attempt to paper over the cracks which had appeared in Liberal unity due to the war. As Stanhope's motion of October 1899 had already shown, when it expressed strong disapproval of the handling of the negotiations which ended in hostilities, the Liberals were basically split three ways. The largest section, including Campbell-Bannerman himself, believed the war to be 'an unnecessary and wanton business', for which the government was substantially to blame, but which, once begun, had better be carried through to a conclusion.[3] Another section agreed with Rosebery, Asquith, Grey and other Liberal Imperialists that the war was one of legitimate self-defence, forced on Britain by a corrupt Boer oligarchy which persecuted those Britons under its control. Only a tiny section of Liberals, on the other hand, pushed their uncompromising opposition to the war so far as to demand recognition of the complete independence of the Boer republics and to oppose wartime votes of credit. There were only about half a dozen of them – MPs like Dr G. B. Clark, Bryn Roberts, H. J. Wilson, and Sir Wilfrid Lawson – but they could count on Irish Nationalist support in the lobbies, and they assumed a disproportionate significance since Chamberlain in particular used them as a stick with which to beat the whole Liberal party.

The fault of the Fitzmaurice amendment was that it attempted to include too much. Only one or two Unionists, like Sir Edward Clarke, were prepared to break ranks and support its interpretation of the war's causes, no doubt influenced by dislike of Chamberlain. There was considerable unease on the Unionist backbenches – especially, as in 1940, amongst members of military background – at the government's actual conduct of the war, and the apparent mismangement of operations. But such men had little patience with an attempt to rake over all the past controversies of 1895–99, and, in any case, they could see little alternative to the government presently in office, as the Liberal party did not seem to know its own mind on the issue. They were easily rallied by speeches from their own side, by Wyndham, the eloquent under-secretary of state for war, and especially by Chamberlain, who at this juncture made one of the most statesmanlike parliamentary interventions of his career. Apart from noting the Liberals' inconsistency in both condemning the war as unjust and demanding that it be prosecuted more efficiently, Chamberlain uncharacteristically avoided displays of party rancour and instead went out of his way to stress the most positive aspects of the war, the ways in which it had promoted a much greater sense of imperial pride and unity and would force to a conclusion the old antagonism of Boer and Briton, thus making possible an eventual reconciliation of all the races in south Africa. The end of the debate saw the Unionists rewarded with a decisive majority of 352:139.[4]

Shortly afterwards, the fortunes of war abruptly changed in south Africa, permanently as it would later prove. The new leadership of Roberts and Kitchener had sought to put Britain's long-term military advantages to good use. Reinforcements had been arriving from all over the empire throughout the autumn and early winter, and by February 1900, over and above all the British troops holding their positions elsewhere, a fully equipped field force of 37,000 men had been mobilised on the western frontier of the Orange Free State. Equally important, nearly one-third, some 11,500 men, were mounted, thus providing the precious element of mobility that had been lacking earlier. As the Boers still clung obstinately to the sieges of Mafeking, Kimberley and Ladysmith, Roberts had the initiative and the ability to decide exactly where to strike. He disguised his intentions until the last moment, and then released French's cavalry, which in a massive onrush broke through the Boer lines to relieve Kimberley. French then advanced further, and trapped the main Boer force under Cronje between himself and Roberts's infantry at Paardeberg. Cronje was a lacklustre and elderly commander who had failed to preserve his freedom of manoeuvre, partly as he was encumbered by wagons full of women and children, one of the hallmarks of a citizen army. For a time he beat off Kitchener's costly frontal assaults, which caused more British casualties than in any of their earlier defeats. Then Roberts, with his more patient style, took back charge of the battle, and after surrounding Cronje obliged him to surrender with some 4,000 men. The Orange Free State now lay wide open, and its capital, Bloemfontein, was occupied by British forces in mid-March. Over in Natal, thanks partly to the withdrawal of Boer troops to confront the threat from Roberts, Buller had at last been able to raise the siege of Ladysmith at the end of February.

These events ensured that Britain could now hardly lose the war. But they also established a pattern of events that would tend to become recurrent over the following two years. Major British successes raised expectations of an imminent end to hostilities which were all too often disappointed. Thus the capture of Bloemfontein did not, as anticipated, knock the Orange Free State out of the war. Instead it delivered leadership into the hands of a young and energetic commander, De Wet, who determined to replace the Boers' defensive tactics with guerilla warfare, and who scored early successes at Sannah's Post and Reddersburg. Meanwhile Roberts was forced to halt for a month and a half at Bloemfontein in order to regroup his forces for an assault on the Transvaal. Here defective supplies and medical arrangements caused a severe outbreak of typhoid or enteric fever, which in the course of the war was to kill far more British soldiers than did the Boers. Roberts himself could do no wrong so far as British public opinion was concerned, but after these setbacks the call was heard increasingly for the disciplining of those commanders who failed in their duties, and comparisons were drawn with the much more rigorous standards that seemed to prevail in the navy. Some of the criticisms not unnaturally attached themselves to the government, and ministers sought to defuse them by putting blame on particular generals. An example of this was the unedifying affair of the Spion Kop dispatches, when, months after the actual event, the government published severe reflections on Buller's generalship. Buller may have had his faults, but he had gone on to relieve Ladysmith, and it made little sense to reprimand him publicly and still leave him in his command. Opposition speakers took the government to task in parliamentary debates in May 1900, charging it with inconsistency and favouritism, for it had neither censured nor retired other generals such as Lord Methuen, who could be held accountable for the disaster at Magersfontein.

However, by this time, Roberts's army was on the move again, and seemed likely to achieve conclusive victory. With the advantage in numbers, and possessing sufficient cavalry, Roberts defeated the Boers at Doornkop, the site of Jameson's surrender a few years earlier. The occupation of Johannesburg and Pretoria swiftly followed in late May and early June; but arguably Roberts now lost the chance of securing peace with the increasingly war-weary Boers by not immediately following up these successes and by insisting on unconditional surrender. Evidently he believed that occupation of the enemy's capitals would suffice, as it had in Afghanistan two decades earlier, but delay allowed De Wet and the Free Staters to put pressure on the Transvaalers to continue fighting. However all these events were dwarfed in the public imagination back home in Britain by news of the relief of Mafeking, which had come about on 16 May 1900. Far away from the main battlefields, on the Transvaal's western frontier, Mafeking was a military sideshow. But its long survival against odds, defended by amateur soldiers and colonial police, under the enterprising leadership of Baden-Powell, had made besieged Mafeking the supreme symbol of the empire in its hour of need.

The stage was now set for a general election, which in many ways would prove the most hollow since that of 1865. Arguably the parliament elected five years earlier was by now played out. The government's domestic programme, such as it was, had more or less stalled with all the din of battle raging in south Africa. The only legislation of note to emerge from the 1900 session of parliament was that creating the Commonwealth of Australia, which added further to the kudos of the colonial secretary, Chamberlain. Otherwise the only parliamentary achieve-

ment had been that of Hicks Beach, the chancellor of the Exchequer, whose budget, for the time being, had succeeded in
financing the war by a judicious mixture of loans and moderate
tax increases all round. This vindication of the free-trade system
won general approval, except from the protectionist wing of his
own party. Judged by the by-elections, at which the war was still
the topic of the hour, the government remained popular. Contests in the Isle of Wight, and especially in South Manchester, in
late May saw large increases in the Unionist majorities. After this,
an early dissolution of parliament was very much on the cards,
although, apart from confirming the existing government in
office, it seemed unlikely to turn on any fundamental issues. No
crucial difference of policy divided the two main political parties.
Both accepted the annexation of the Boer republics as more or less
inevitable, the Unionists more wholeheartedly than many
Liberals. Both professed a desire for army reform and a stable
settlement of south Africa without specifying very much what
was meant by either of these things. Otherwise, issues which had
for years divided Unionists and Liberals seemed in 1900 to be
strangely in abeyance. Home rule, which had so dominated
previous general elections, was now largely absent from the
hustings; and indeed Ireland as a whole figured less than in any
election campaign since 1865. Domestic issues generally failed to
excite much interest. Partly because of widespread prosperity,
the country was not in a reform-minded mood; and, though
Campbell-Bannerman made some play with social concerns such
as housing, education and temperance, most Liberals were now
happy to dispense for the time being with the more radical
commitments of the 1891 Newcastle programme. The fact that so
large a number of seats remained uncontested – 243 all told – lent
a further air of unreality to the proceedings; indeed the 1900
election saw more unopposed returns than on any occasion since
1865. Not surprisingly, the electoral contest mainly resolved itself
into a classic confrontation between Ins and Outs, with actual
policies at a discount, and personal acrimony and recrimination
very much to the fore. The choice for the electorate was not a
particularly edifying one. The Liberal opposition continued to
appear divided and ineffective, whereas the Unionist government, although supported by the strongest majority in both
houses of parliament ever seen in modern times, was, according

to one observer, perhaps the weakest in purpose which had administered public affairs since the first Reform Act.

The dying months of Queen Victoria's fourteenth parliament, from June to August 1900, certainly confirmed this diagnosis. Once again the government bungled the presentation of its case before the House of Commons. Public concern over the typhoid epidemic, which had killed nearly 1,000 British soldiers at Bloemfontein earlier in the year, was brought to a head by a letter written to *The Times* by Burdett-Coutts, a disgruntled Unionist backbencher who, having recently returned from investigating conditions for himself in south Africa, put the blame once again on war office complacency and maladministration. The matter was raised by speakers on all sides in the House of Commons, and provoked the usually languid Balfour to uncharacteristic outbursts of ill temper. He accused the opposition of making party capital out of soldiers' sufferings, and of undermining the authority of generals in the field, rather an odd argument on the part of one who had published the Spion Kop dispatches. In the end he was forced to concede the appointment of a special war hospitals committee to look into the affair, but this drew further adverse comment on the grounds that it was composed of a majority of medical experts who could not be trusted to judge their own profession objectively. Late in July, the Liberals cut an even sorrier figure in the House of Commons when they split three ways in the vote on Sir Wilfrid Lawson's motion to reduce the colonial secretary's salary. This was not of course either the first or the last occasion on which the Liberals suffered serious parliamentary embarrassment during the south African war, but this incident, in particular, severely impugned their leader's credibility. In the interests of party unity, Campbell-Bannerman urged his fellow-Liberals to walk out of the chamber rather than vote on a motion which was of little more than symbolic significance, and 35 of them heeded his advice. But 31 Liberals, including prominent figures such as Bryce, Labouchere, Lloyd George and Reid, could not resist the opportunity of registering a further protest against the man they held chiefly responsible for the war and for the policies of the 'freebooter, filibuster, burglar and Boxer' that went with it; while on the other hand no less than 40 Liberals voted with the governemnt. The case for the latter group was put by Grey, who argued that the issue now was no longer that of the merits of the war but rather that of the future imperial settlement of south Africa, and here the government might justifiably have to take strong measures involving not only the annexation of the Boer republics but also the suspension of the Cape constitution and the disfranchisement of rebels.[5]

Chamberlain and Balfour therefore pressed further for an early general election which would not only capitalise on victory but also catch the Liberals at a serious disadvantage. Many Unionist backbenchers added their voices, sensing that the opposition would not be able to find candidates for many constituencies, and hopeful also that after an election would come a ministerial reshuffle in which there might well be opportunities for promotion all round. Salisbury for a time resisted the pressure, for reasons which may be divined. Apart from his habitual pessimism, he may have feared that a premature dissolution would appear to the electorate as a piece of sharp political practice, a breach with tradition. It was virtually unprecedented for a government, undefeated in the House of Commons, to go to the country a full two years before its parliamentary mandate would legally expire. Doubtless Salisbury recalled how Gladstone had tried to put one over, so to speak, by calling a snap general election in 1874, and had had his nose bloodied as a result. And there was one other material consideration. An early dissolution would not add anything to the government's strength. It already possessed a more than adequate parliamentary majority, on which it could hardly expect to improve much at the polls. And any appreciable reduction in the size of that majority might undermine the government's standing and thus make it more difficult to bring the war in south Africa to a conclusion.

Events in a very different part of the world for a time compounded Salisbury's instinctive caution. The summer of 1900 witnessed a major popular upheaval in Imperial China, whose society and institutions were crumbling under the impact of modernisation and foreign intervention. As on other occasions in Chinese history, both before and since, popular insurrection assumed a fiercely anti-Christian and xenophobic character. The Righteous and Harmonious Fists – or Boxers, as the Chinese rebels were generally known in the west – murdered the German ambassador and besieged the European community in its Legations in Peking. Here was a crisis to drive south Africa, and thoughts of a general election, from the front pages of the British press. Even Chamberlain acknowledged that it would be unwise to dissolve parliament at a time when news might arrive at any moment of mayhem and massacre in the far east. Doubtless he recalled the furore over General Gordon's death in 1885, and he knew that public opinion would call the government to account for any serious loss of British lives in China, a part of the world which many considered to have shown up Salisbury's foreign policy at its weakest in recent years. But, speedily enough, the situation was resolved. In mid-August 1900, an international force fought its way through to Peking, relieved the Legations, and ruthlessly suppressed the Boxer uprising. Once again the times seemed propitious for an early appeal to the country, all the more so as the first half of September witnessed a sudden favourable turn of events in south Africa. After months of comparative stalemate, some severe Boer setbacks made it seem that the war was at last virtually at an end. In what was to prove the last set-piece battle of the war, at Bergendal, Buller's infantry stormed the Boer position, and the remaining territorial redoubt of the eastern Transvaal, with its vital railway link to the sea, fell into British hands. Roberts felt confident enough to proclaim the annexation of the Transvaal as a whole. Kruger, president of the erstwhile South African Republic, fled into exile.

Parliament, at Westminster, was dissolved on 17 September 1900. The stage was set for a general election during the first half of October, for, in the years before 1918, pollings usually stretched over a period of between two and three weeks. The Liberals got off to a bad start when Herbert Gladstone, their chief whip, admitted that they could hardly expect to gain from their opponents the 160 seats that would enable them to form a government. This was not the first unfortunate intervention of Herbert Gladstone's in his political career. Fifteen years earlier, he had seriously embarrassed his father with the Hawarden Kite, a premature disclosure to the press concerning Irish home rule. Arguably he was now doing no more than stating the obvious. The Liberals were indeed badly handicapped in 1900 by their general demoralisation and their inability to find sufficient candidates. They were forced to leave Unionists unopposed in no less than 163 constituencies, enjoying the same advantage in only 22 of their own. Not since the 1860s had a political party made such an outright gift of seats to its opponents. Still, it was hardly good politics for Herbert Gladstone to give his side out, as was said, before a ball had been bowled. On the other hand, it has to be admitted that Salisbury's contribution to the electoral process was not much more inspired. Once again, in time of war, he failed to rise to the occasion. Published as an open letter, his appeal for votes warned somewhat despondently against mass abstention and complacency. *The Times* thought it the most curious manifesto ever put forth by a statesman in high office, and wondered what use Pitt or Palmerston might have made of a similar opportunity.[6]

Salisbury however was no longer a major performer on the hustings. Among Unionist speakers, the most conspicuous figure was of course Joseph Chamberlain. Indeed, the 1900 election was seen as his election in much the same way as the war was described as 'Chamberlain's war'; and it is necessary to consider in what senses this may have been true. Chamberlain, the most hard-hitting of orators, is usually blamed for infusing the whole campaign with a mood of vulgar jingoism. The most notorious example of this was to be found in a letter of support, sent by him to the Unionist candidate at Heywood in Lancashire, in which, apparently quoting the mayor of Mafeking, he declared that 'a seat gained by the Liberals is a seat lost to the Boers' (Doc. 1). Telegraphic error unfortunately amended this to 'a seat sold to the Boers'. Chamberlain never put it quite like this in any of his platform speeches, but it was very much the implication behind what he had to say. Especially in the first half of the election campaign, he made pointed reference to the so-called Pretoria correspondence. This consisted of letters written by politicians sympathetic to the Boers, which had come to light at the time of the British occupation of Pretoria. Among them were letters from two Liberal backbenchers, Labouchere and Dr Clark, advising Kruger on the best course to follow in the difficult negotiations of the summer of 1899, especially with a view to humbling the colonial secretary. Chamberlain used the Pretoria letters as a stick with which to beat the whole Liberal party. Why, he demanded to know, had not the Liberal leader, Campbell-Bannerman, repudiated the actions of followers who were so evidently determined to put party before country? 'Nothing more factious', he declared, 'had been done by a British minister (*sic*) since Charles

Fox in his private letters rejoiced at the defeat of his countrymen and the success of Napoleon'. By failing to support the government's diplomatic stance during the summer months of 1899, the Liberals had largely contributed, in Chamberlain's view, to the outbreak of hostilities. 'Rather than Mr. Kruger himself, they had the guilt of war upon their shoulders.'[7]

The Pretoria letters, and the venom which they injected into the election campaign, had an additional significance. Chamberlain was one of the most thin-skinned of politicians, and it is possible that his exploitation of them was provoked by Liberal insinuations that his own relatives had enriched themselves during the war by supplying munitions to the government through the armaments firm of Kynochs. Lloyd George in particular made much of this, with trenchant observations such as 'the more the empire expands, the more the Chamberlains contract'. Liberals were pleased to be able to pay Chamberlain out for the attacks which he had made on the supposed corruption of Rosebery's administration in 1895. The 1900 election was thus strongly affected by the long-running feud which had divided the two branches of Liberalism since they had split apart in 1886. Nothing is so unforgiving as a family quarrel.

Chamberlain had always been at his most effective politically in exposing divisions within the ranks of his erstwhile party. Years previously, he had played on its uncertainties and inner frictions over the Newcastle programme and home rule. One of his main arguments had been that extremists had supplanted the moderates within the Liberal party, thus leaving it unfit to govern. Now that imperialism had become the leading question of the hour, Chamberlain found this argument to be even more fully confirmed. The Liberal party was still evidently at sixes and sevens, as witness its three-way split over Lawson's amendment in July 1900. Though Chamberlain disagreed most profoundly with those whom he labelled Pro-Boers, he reserved his particular scorn for the so-called Liberal Imperialists, moderate Liberals whose views in many ways approximated to his own, but whom he regarded as lacking the courage of their convictions and as liable to confuse the issue before the electorate. Of what use, he demanded to know, had the self-professed Liberal Imperialists been to the cause of empire during the south African war. They had failed to denounce the authors of the Pretoria

letters, or indeed those fellow Liberals, admittedly only a handful, who had opposed the voting of war credits in October 1899
and February 1900. The bulk of the Liberal party had clearly not
been converted to genuine imperialism. Indeed Chamberlain
claimed in his speeches that no less than two-thirds of all Liberal
MPs desired Britain's humiliation in the south African war and
were opposed to the annexation of the Transvaal and the Orange
Free State.[8] Worst of all perhaps, the Liberal Imperialists had
encouraged the rest of their party to sail under false colours, and
to adopt a 'sham imperialism' for the purpose of securing re-
election (Doc. 1).

Chamberlain's role in the 1900 election campaign naturally
commands attention, but it would be wrong to over-emphasise it.
The Unionist victory in 1900 was a team effort, the last major
success of the combination of parties which would in the end
dominate domestic politics for twenty years. England, it has been
said, does not love coalitions; but this proposition has been
proved untrue at least as often as it has been proved true. Where
coalitions have provided successful, or at least stable, government, they have almost invariably been re-elected, and usually
by a decisive margin. Such was the case in 1865, 1918 and 1935;
and it was certainly the case also in 1900. The Unionist government in 1900 was still composed of household names, in sad
contrast to the state of affairs a few years later. It comprised major
national figures, both Tory and Liberal Unionist, who commanded widespread confidence and even affection. Salisbury,
the prime minister and foreign secretary, took little active part in
the election campaign, but he was a symbol of national unity
during the south African war, and his presence provided
reassurance that Britain would not lightly enter into foreign
adventures or seek to quarrel with the rest of the world. Hicks
Beach, at the Treasury, despite his abrasive manner, was also a
reassuring figure, in the sense that he was firmly opposed to any
departure from financial or economic orthodoxy. His management of affairs during the south African war had generally won
praise, and the 1900 election was notable among other things for
being the first for over a generation in which finance was not a
serious issue. The Duke of Devonshire, who made a number of
interventions in the campaign, retained his valued reputation for
moderation and common sense. But, apart from Chamberlain

himself, undoubtedly the most important speaker on the Unionist side was Arthur Balfour. Indeed, his contribution to the campaign was in some ways more significant than Chamberlain's. For, whereas the latter hardly ventured beyond the three midlands counties of Warwickshire, Worcestershire and Staffordshire, Balfour carried the fight much more into the enemy's territory, campaigning extensively in the north of England and in Scotland, where no doubt he deserved some of the credit for the Unionists' strong showing.

The 1900 election represented a final triumph for one of the more effective political partnerships of modern British history. Balfour and Chamberlain were an unlikely duo in some ways, the feline Scot and scion of the British aristocracy allying with the bulldog-like spokesman of urban and industrial England. But, with their complementary qualities, they had for a decade successfully harried the forces of radicalism and home rule. Their mutual co-operation had preserved the Unionist alliance through difficult times and had contributed substantially to the Liberal debacle of 1895. The 1900 election victory represented a further joint achievement, and one in which Balfour's role was arguably as great as Chamberlain's. Though his speeches used many of the same arguments as did Chamberlain, they were less acrimonious, and included their own distinctive points of emphasis. Whereas Chamberlain belaboured Campbell-Bannerman and the Pro-Boers, Balfour reserved his thrusts for Rosebery, whom he described as remaining in a political penumbra, 'neither belonging to a party nor not belonging to a party'. In particular, Balfour attacked the record of Rosebery's previous government, when the Liberals had more or less failed to implement any of the 'musty items' of the by now half-forgotten Newcastle programme. By contrast, Balfour went out of his way to defend the legislative record of the Unionist government since 1895, regarding workmen's compensation, education, rating reform, and the protection of agricultural tenants. Essentially Balfour's point was that the Liberal party did not stand for anything any more. Its old cries were gone, and the best that it could offer now was a mixture of crankiness and small points of controversy like dog-muzzling. If it were ever to regain office, it would be dependent on Irish support; and, more than any other Unionist in 1900, Balfour continued to warn against allowing the Nationalists to hold the balance of power again at Westminster.[9]

Faced with the big guns of Unionism, what resources did the Liberals have at their disposal? Their leader, Campbell-Bannerman, was an energetic campaigner who probably covered more ground than any other candidate, but his efforts arguably left him little cause for satisfaction. Throughout his speeches there ran two fairly consistent notes of apology and complaint. He spent too much time trying to justify the Pretoria letters, and indeed protesting against their use, although this was clearly playing to the Unionists' strength. He complained about the timing of the election, on a stale electoral register, and he continued to harp on the iniquity of the Jameson Raid, although this was a matter that was fast becoming ancient history. With some justice, Campbell-Bannerman claimed that the Liberal reforms of 1870–71 had produced the military system which had eventually triumphed in south Africa, and he called for further army reform which he believed that only a Liberal government could provide. But he remained unclear as to the nature of such reform, nor was he any clearer as to the character of any future Liberal settlement of southern Africa. More positively, Campbell-Bannerman did put forward proposals for certain domestic reforms in Britain. Almost alone among leading Liberals, he laid stress on the need for measures regarding education, temperance, the housing of the working classes, and taxation of land values. Of the younger Liberals, arguably only Grey improved his reputation nationally. Campaigning mainly in the north-east of England, he concentrated on the weaknesses in the government's record, especially its failure either to stand up to Russia in the far east or to anticipate the coming of war in southern Africa, both by reforming the British army and by preventing the arming of the Transvaal.

The one-time champions of Gladstonian Liberalism were not much in evidence in 1900. Harcourt, it is true, fought a typically rumbustious campaign in which he laid about the Unionist record since 1895 with gusto. But his efforts were confined to Monmouthshire, in the neighbourhood of his constituency; and, as he tended to dwell on themes dear to his heart, such as finance and the dangers of ritualism in the Church of England, his words did not greatly influence the national debate. John Morley was another leading Liberal orator whose services, for reasons of health, were not available in 1900. He did however issue two manifestes to his Montrose constituents, sufficient to ensure his re-election, which warned against adding 'another and far more dangerous Ireland to the dominions of the Queen', as well as transforming her 'ancient realm' into 'a boasting military empire, inevitably to be supported by military conscription, and with an imperial customs union thrown in'. With still greater prescience, Morley added that 'our real and deep danger is the loss of our commercial supremacy', a line of argument hardly heard in 1900, which would become a staple of Unionist speechmaking in the years to come.[10]

Amongst the Liberal old guard, the most egregious contribution came from Rosebery. Although no longer leader of the party, he enjoyed the status of a former prime minister whose administration, at least in terms of foreign policy, had arguably been no more deficient than the present one. Besides, Rosebery's imperialist views and general support for the south African war made him seem a possible alternative premier at a time of national emergency. Throughout his career, however, Rosebery disappointed those who looked to him for decisive leadership; and his one intervention in the 1900 election campaign proved entirely characteristic. Despite being pressed to put his considerable powers of oratory to the service of Liberalism, Rosebery limited himself to issuing a letter in support of Captain Hedworth Lambton, one of the two Liberal candidates in the double constituency of Newcastle-upon-Tyne. Admittedly Lambton was in some ways an appropriate choice. As a minor war hero, who had served in the defence of Ladysmith, he seemed the ideal embodiment of respectable patriotic Liberalism. And certainly Rosebery's supporting letter pulled no punches, castigating Salisbury's administration for being the weakest that he could remember, with its bungling in the far east and southern Africa and its neglect of education, temperance, housing, and military reform.[11] Rosebery however left himself open to the retort from Balfour that he himself as prime minister had done nothing to forward any of these objectives, and that, as a part-time politician, he was in little position to do so in the future. In addition, Newcastle was hardly the ideal constituency for Rosebery's gesture, for Lambton was there teamed with a fellow

28

Liberal called Storey, whose views were a mixture of radicalism and protectionism. Running together in harness, the two candidates showed up their party's divided state; and, embarrassingly, Lambton came bottom of the poll, some 5,000 votes behind the second Tory candidate.

Newcastle was in many ways the keynote individual contest of the 1900 general election. It demonstrated clearly which way things were going, just as Derby had done in 1895 or Manchester was to do in 1906. It also marked the point at which the election moved decisively in the Unionists' favour. Pollings had begun on 1 October 1900, and had briefly seemed to favour the Liberals, who after a couple of days had gained 10 seats against their opponents' 7. But these were mainly in the medium-sized boroughs of the English north and midlands, which had often enough proved favourable ground for Liberalism. Soon enough the returns from the larger centres of population, including New-castle, began to make their influence felt. A feature of the 1900 election was the pronounced increase in Unionist majorities in most of the leading cities of the land. As *The Times* put it, 'it is where the working men are strongest that the Unionist vote is overwhelming'.[12] In London as a whole the Unionists' poll increased by 4,357 votes, whereas the Liberals' decreased by 12,404; and, at the same time, the Unionists were able to strengthen their hold on the main provincial centres. Of the ten largest cities in Britain, the Unionists won a majority of the seats in all but one, the exception being Edinburgh, whose repre-sentation stayed evenly divided. A particularly striking Unionist success came in Glasgow, where the Liberals lost their last 2 remaining seats of Blackfriars and Bridgeton by large majorities, involving a turnover of 1,000 votes in each case. (Bonar Law first entered parliament at this point of time as MP for Blackfriars.) Glasgow's 7-seat representation had been entirely Liberal in 1885; now it was entirely Unionist. Three days after the start of polling, the Unionists led the Liberals in the register of gains by 21 seats to 13; though, over the next week and a half, the pendulum swung gradually back again as the Liberals picked up agricultural con-stituencies in the south-west of England and in east Anglia. Probably this reflected, in certain areas, the continuance of agricultural depression. Wheat farming in particular, which was heavily concentrated in the eastern counties, was an exception to the otherwise nationwide prosperity of 1900. Wheat acreage had fallen back drastically in the mid-1890s, and, after a brief rally in 1898 and 1899, had just retreated once again. Pollings in the 1900 election came to an end in mid-October with a flurry of Unionist gains in northern Scotland, including, as a rare event, the capture of Orkney and Shetland. All in all, the Unionists recorded a total of 37 gains as against 35 for the Liberals.

How should one assess the outcome of the 1900 election? On the face of it, the Unionists had won a resounding triumph. They had successfully defended the already hefty majority which had been theirs in the previous parliament. Indeed, in slightly improving on the number of seats held at the dissolution, they had become the first party in office actually to increase their majority since 1865. Even this probably understated their real level of support, for, across the country, the Unionist vote went up substantially. In Britain as a whole, it increased by 93,904, as against 36,196 for the Liberals. But the increase tended to be concentrated in areas where there was little scope for winning additional seats, for instance in London, where the Unionists were unable to improve on the 54:8 advantage which they had enjoyed since 1895. However in 1900 the Unionists did tap new reserves of support, most notably in Scotland, where, for the first time since 1832, the Liberals' majority of seats was overturned. Indeed the Unionists' vote there went up by 24,427, whereas the Liberals' declined by 5,510. Scotland's case was instructive, for, unlike the other three realms of the British isles in 1900, the overwhelming majority of its 72 seats were actually contested, by Liberals and Unionists alike. In addition, it helped to sustain the case for continued coalition government; for the Liberal Unionists did particularly well north of the border, gaining 6 seats and retaining the 11 which they already held. In Britain as a whole they won 2 seats overall, thereby demonstrating their continuing viability as part of the Unionist coalition.

The Liberal party's own performance, by contrast, appeared mediocre. It managed to win only 184 seats in 1900 as against the Unionists' grand total of 402. True, the difference in votes was much less pronounced, with the Liberals garnering 1,572,000 as against the Unionists' 1,768,000 but this did not take account of the much greater number of seats left uncontested by the Liberals. Only in Wales did the Liberal party improve its position, probably in reaction to a markedly poor showing in 1895; and there it gained 4 seats and polled an additional 11,867 votes. (The Unionists' vote decreased by 2,181 in the principality, partly as they chose not to contest 11 seats.) Across the greater part of Britain, the Liberals manifestly failed in 1900 to exploit the government's weaknesses: its indifferent legislative record, its lack of preparedness in southern Africa, and the disasters which had marked the initial stages of the war. Instead the Liberals found attention to be concentrated on their own divisions and uncertainties, with their party standing accused of not knowing its own mind on the leading issues of the day. In the short term, the 1900 election did little to resolve this problem. By *The Times*'s calculations, the number of Liberals Imperialist MPs had increased from 63 to 81; but the Liberal party as a whole was still split into discordant groups whose antipathies were liable to be made worse by recrimination over defeat.[13]

The election of 1900 has long been known as the 'khaki election' (Doc. 2). In some ways this is a misnomer. Of course the political mood of the country was deeply influenced by the war, but in a complexity of ways. The Liberal party did not so much fail the test of patriotism as the test of ability to govern. This is borne out by the success of many of the so-called Pro-Boers in holding on to their seats. Two of the three MPs involved in the affair of the Pretoria letters, Labouchere and Ellis, were re-elected, and the third, Dr Clark, was defeated not by a Unionist but by an independent Liberal. Casualties there were among the government's critics, for instance Stanhope and Sir Wilfrid Lawson, both of whom had moved resolutions hostile to the war. But others who had spoken in much the same sense, such as Morley, Bryce, Reid, S. T. Evans and Lloyd George, survived. This was in marked contrast to what had happened in 1857, in a general election also called on an issue of patriotism, when Palmerston had made practically a clean sweep of the representation of the Manchester School, including its leaders, Cobden and Bright. In 1900, however, the Liberal party did face a serious test of its identity. It seemed to have little distinct to say or offer to the electorate. With the country enjoying an apparently unprecedented surge of prosperity in 1899 and 1900, there seemed little scope for criticism of the prevailing political and social system. The Liberals had discarded most of the radical items of the former Newcastle programme, without finding anything to put in their place. The abandonment of home rule as a leading article of their faith had cost the Liberals the support of many Irish people resident in Britain, who were otherwise tempted to vote Unionist on the issue of state aid to Catholic education. In particular, this seems to have been a factor north of the border, where Campbell-Bannerman summed up his party's overall performance as follows:

> The wretched result in Scotland is due partly to bread-and-butter influences in the Clyde district where warlike expenditure is popular; partly to the turnover of the Catholic vote, which was the main cause of my diminished majority; partly to khaki; and partly to our own factions which have taken some of the heart out of us.[14]

Ireland nonetheless provided a silver lining for the Liberals in 1900. As even the Duke of Devonshire observed, the Irish members had now 'been definitely struck off the strength of the Liberal party'.[15] For years the Liberal–Nationalist alliance had been a factor in politics, though arguably it had done the Liberals little good with British public opinion. Now that alliance was to all intents and purposes dissolved. Apart from a handful of Liberal MPs, the Irish Nationalists were the real Pro-Boer party. Their outspoken attacks on the British army, and refusal to vote war credits, had put them beyond the pale so far as the mass of Liberal opinion was concerned. In distancing themselves from the cause of home rule, the Liberals lost a powerful contingent of support at Westminster, but put themselves in a better position to appear as the party of purely British, and not least English, interests. This was all the more significant as Ireland seemed likely to remain a thorn in the Unionists' side. Indeed it represented the one conspicuous failure of Unionism in the 1900 general election.

If ever the Unionists had an opportunity to reverse the electoral tide against them in Ireland, outside Ulster, it was in 1900. Significant influences were in their favour. The Unionist government had conferred undoubted benefits on Ireland, in the form of land purchase and elected county councils, in pursuit of its policy of killing home rule with kindness. The Irish Nationalists, for their part, though nominally reunited in 1900, were still wracked by divisions, and fought each other in a dozen seats at the general election. The gain of Galway city by a Catholic Unionist at this time showed what might have been accomplished. Even the war, unpopular with many politicians, was by no means unpopular with the people of Ireland. Famous Irish regiments were involved in the fighting in south Africa, and the Irish Guards were established in celebration of the relief of Ladysmith. A visit of Queen Victoria herself to Dublin in 1900 provoked considerable enthusiasm. But the Unionists squandered such advantages as they had by internal squabbling, and at the general election this even cost them one of the few seats which they had held outside Ulster, in South Dublin.

Britain, however, ensured that the Unionists won in 1900 by a landslide. But it was in one sense a close-run thing. Under a statute of 1797, were the sovereign to die at any point between the dissolution of one parliament and the state opening of the next, the intervening general election would be declared null and void, and the old parliament would reassemble for six months. Had Queen Victoria's death come, not in January 1901, but three months earlier, the country would have had to go to the hustings again in the middle of the following year. For their part, the Liberals would soon enough have cause not to regret losing the 1900 general election. In their quest for victory at the polls, the Unionists had given some hostages to fortune. They had raised expectations, not least among their own supporters, a number of whom now looked for promotion in a rejuvenated administration. But Salisbury's autumn cabinet reshuffle, though it retired respected figures like Goschen and Ridley, found room for few exciting new appointments. Its most notable feature was the promotion of Lansdowne to be foreign secretary, even though his administration of the war office was widely blamed for Britain's early setbacks in south Africa. Salisbury's other nephew, Gerald Balfour, was also retained in the cabinet, although his previous tenure of the Irish chief secretaryship was largely credited with the demoralisation among Unionists in Ireland. As the prime minister also made his son-in-law, Selborne, first lord of the admiralty, he could not unjustly be accused of favouritism towards his relatives. One disgruntled backbencher complained of the predominance of 'souls, Cecils, sycophants and socialists'. Far more serious hostages to fortune, however, were those which the Unionists had given during the 1900 election in the form of promises of army reform and of an early termination of the war.

Unionist candidates had insisted that the government's triumphant re-election would finally persuade the Boers to lay down their arms. In fact the reverse was to prove true. The return of summer in south Africa in late 1900 brought also a strong renewal of guerilla activity, this time as much in the Transvaal as in the Orange Free State. Botha and De la Ray would soon match De Wet's exploits as guerilla leaders. The war itself changed gear. Instead of the British attempting to storm the citadels of the Boer republics, the Boers now sought to wrest these two newly annexed colonies from Britain's grasp. The field of conflict actually widened, as Boer commandos invaded Cape Colony in an effort to raise their fellow-countrymen there against British rule. Kitchener replaced Roberts in overall command in late 1900, and began a vast counter-insurgency operation which was to prove both costly and controversial. Determined to wear the Boers down and curtail their freedom of manoeuvre, he set about establishing an immense system of blockhouses to fence in all the disaffected areas of south Africa. Eventually they would number 8,000, garrisoned by 50,000 men, and between them mobile British columns scoured the country in an endeavour to corner the elusive Boer commandos.

Kitchener also sought to carry the war to the Boer civilian population, in order to wear the guerillas down by cutting them off from support from their homes and families. The policy of farm-burnings, begun by Roberts as a form of reprisal upon Boer civilians who gave aid and comfort to their menfolk still in the field, was greatly extended. And, most notoriously of all, Kitchener determined to uproot as many Boer women and children as possible and concentrate them in encampments under British military control, partly for their own protection but mainly to prevent them from communicating with the enemy. This was to prove the bitterest legacy of the war, with emotional scars that remain in south Africa to this day. The British army had no experience of dealing with large numbers of civilians, and the Boer women and children, used to the open spaces of the veldt, were ill adapted to subsisting on a vitamin-deficient diet in over-crowded and insanitary camps. In consequence, mortality was very high, amounting in the course of the war to the combined battle casualties on both sides. Some 28,000 Boers, it has been calculated, died in the camps, including 4,000 adult women and 22,000 children, a total which amounted to about one-seventh of the entire white population of the two former republics. Not surprisingly, many Boers came to see this as part of a deliberate attempt to exterminate their race.

The concentration camps, as they soon came to be called, aroused bitter controversy in Britain. Lloyd George was the most outspoken of a group of Liberal backbenchers who raised the matter regularly, in both parliament and the country, and in consequence he was almost lynched when he tried to address a meeting at Birmingham in December 1901. In subsequent years, the Liberals were to benefit considerably from the sense of outrage generated over various aspects of the south African war, but not in 1901 and on this issue. It sounded too much like attacking the good name of the British army while it was fighting in the field. When Lloyd George moved for an adjournment of the House of Commons to discuss the matter in June 1901, he carried with him the party leader, Campbell-Bannerman, and 149 Liberal and Irish MPs, but another fifty or so Liberal MPs abstained. It was in this month that Campbell-Bannerman first used the expression 'methods of barbarism' to describe the policy of farm-burnings and concentration camps in south Africa; but instead of giving a lead to his party, he succeeded only in emphasising its continuing divisions. This was made clear in two major speeches delivered in the autumn of 1901 by the two main rivals for the leadership of Liberal opinion. At Stirling, in a more eloquent address than usual, Campbell-Bannerman defended his use of the phrase about methods of barbarism and warned of the legacy of hatred which the concentration camps would leave in south Africa. Britain, he declared, risked creating 'a new Ireland in the southern seas to be a weakness and a difficulty to the empire'. At Chesterfield, on the other hand, Rosebery defended the use of concentration camps, which he described as a result of the necessity of clearing the country, and asserted that whatever horrors they might involve were dwarfed by deliberate Boer inhumanity to British wounded, native Africans, and emissaries of peace. But he also urged that every effort should be made to achieve reconciliation in south Africa, even if it meant offering the Boers the most generous financial terms in return for laying down their arms. No avenue should be left unexplored. As he somewhat quaintly put it, 'some of the greatest settlements in the world's history have come with an apparently casual meeting of travellers at a wayside inn'.[16]

Britain's increasing war-weariness as 1901 drew to a close was reflected in both these speeches, for October had marked the second anniversary of the outbreak of hostilities. But peace seemed no nearer on the horizon. At Middelburg, in February–March 1901, Kitchener had offered the Boers more generous terms than those formerly conceded to the Jacobites or to the Confederate states of America. But the Boers had rejected them, ostensibly because they did not provide also for an amnesty for their kinsmen who had rebelled against British rule in neighbouring Cape Colony. Evidently they still counted on European intervention or an eventual weakening in Britain's resolve. In these circumstances, Chamberlain remained the most effective spokesman of the government's determination to fight the war through to a successful finish. As in 1900, he blamed the Liberals for the prolongation of the war, on the grounds that the Pro-Boer minority had encouraged the enemy in his resistance, and he defended his earlier assertion that a seat won by the Liberals was a seat gained by the Boers.

Otherwise, Chamberlain had few ideas to offer about ending the war, though he did at one point propose using Indian or native African troops against the Boers thereby eliciting a horrified reaction from the Irish benches. At a speech in Edinburgh, in October 1901, he hinted at yet sterner measures, declaring that Britain could look for examples in the methods of warfare lately practised 'in Poland, the Caucasus, Almería, Tongking, Bosnia, and in the Franco-Prussian war'.[17] Chamberlain saw himself as the heir of Chatham and Pitt in standing at bay against the rest of Europe, but his habit of lashing out generally against European criticism only underlined Britain's international isolation during the south African war. His other main target was the Irish Nationalist party, which he virtually described as a treasonable organisation at Westminster. Chamberlain's proposed remedy was a redistribution measure that would effect a drastic reduction in Irish representation at Westminster, on the pretext of Ireland's declining population. But this was to promise more than the Unionists would be able to deliver in the existing parliament. Many feared giving the

Liberals an excuse to call in question other anomalies in the electoral system such as plural voting.

Unionist ministers gained few laurels in 1901. As in 1900, Hicks Beach was one of the few leading Conservatives whose reputation actually improved during the war. His 1901 budget represented something of a parliamentary triumph, even though it increased taxation all round to meet the spiralling cost of hostilities. Beach raised income tax and added to the sugar duty, and he also placed an exceptional levy on the export of coal. This was a controversial yet enterprising measure. It seemed to challenge free-trade orthodoxy, but Beach was able to argue that Peel's government had had recourse to such a levy, that mineowners were gaining fat profits from the war, and that it made sense generally to try to conserve Britain's natural resources. The Liberals had no answer to this, and one of their leading figures, John Morley, even voted with the government on the grounds that the budget would provoke a review of the whole subject of the distribution of taxation.

There were no other Unionist successes in the parliamentary arena. As in 1896, just after a previous electoral triumph, the government brought in an Education Bill, and, as in 1896, it was forced to abandon it in mid-session. If the government had any reforming mandate at all as a consequence of the khaki election, it was to overhaul the structure and administration of the British army. To this effect, Brodrick, the new secretary of state for war, brought forward proposals in early 1901 to establish six new army corps, which he believed necessary if Britain were ever again to confront simultaneously a crisis in the empire and a direct threat of invasion from Europe. But, like those of subsequent years, his proposals encountered opposition from both sides of the House of Commons, and indeed army reform was to remain the most conspicuous failure of the 1900–1905 parliament. Britain, it seemed, despite the war, was still in many ways an anti-militarist society. A fundamental lesson of the war was that the mother country was immune from invasion so long as the British navy remained supreme. This being the case, even Conservative backbenchers questioned the need to spend money adding another tier to a military bureaucracy which had hardly covered itself with glory in the south African conflict. Brodrick's proposals did not address the key problems of military planning and coordination,

as was made clear when Lansdowne clashed with the commander-in-chief, Wolseley, in the House of Lords in March 1901. In
any case, they got off to a bad start when it was found necessary
to sack Buller for making a political speech, shortly after his
appointment to command the first army corps at Aldershot.

By-elections in 1901 reflected the uncertainty of a public
opinion that was not particularly enthusiastic about the government, but was even less enamoured of the opposition. The
Liberals looked anxiously for some sign of a turn of the political
tide in their favour, but they were to remain largely disappointed
during the year. The by-election which probably gave them most
cheer was at Saffron Walden in June, where the Liberal candidate
increased the majority from 110 to 792. This was the kind of
constituency in which the Liberals had done quite well even in
1900. Agricultural questions were much to the fore, and considerable concern was expressed at the impact of the increased sugar
duty on low wages in the countryside. But one swallow did not
make a summer. By-elections in other largely rural seats, such as
Oswestry and Stratford-upon-Avon, actually saw an increase in
Unionist majorities. The Liberals failed to win Monmouth,
despite local resentment of the coal export duty, and in
September they suffered the humiliation of losing a seat at North
East Lanark, where a Liberal Imperialist and a lib–lab candidate
opposed each other on the question of the war and thus let in the
Conservative. Liberal embarrassment was further compounded
at the opening of the 1902 parliamentary session, when two
backbenchers, Cawley and McKenna, moved what Balfour called
another 'many-coloured amendment'. This blamed the government for the continuation of the war and urged it to pursue
negotiations, but at the same time demanded that the war be
prosecuted more effectively. Designed to offer something to each
section of the Liberal party, this composite motion, like
Fitzmaurice's amendment two years earlier, opened up too wide
an area of debate, and merely succeeded in exposing Liberal
divisions further. Some Liberals were preoccupied with the
morality of the war, and others with the best way of winning it,
while others again were chiefly concerned about the recent
imposition of martial law in Cape Colony. Eventually the amendment was defeated 333:123. Lloyd George was so disgusted with
his party's shilly-shallying that he refused to support it, and

instead voted for an Irish Nationalist amendment condemning the methods of barbarism allegedly being practiced in south Africa.[18]

The war, which had been going on for two and a half years, showed little sign of ending by the spring of 1902. To meet its spiralling costs, the chancellor of the exchequer brought in a budget raising income tax by a further penny and imposing a duty on imported corn of 3d per hundredweight. This was an event of considerable significance. Taxing the people's bread, even on a temporary basis, seemed a blatant departure from the tenets of free trade, although Hicks Beach, with his reputation for orthodoxy, was able to get away with it, partly by demonstrating that even Gladstone had found such a duty acceptable, for purely revenue purposes, at least down to 1869. For all his protestations, however, the budget did afford considerable encouragement to the protectionist wing of the Conservative party, which still hankered for a return to something like the old system of the Corn Laws and Navigation Acts. This sentiment naturally found an echo amongst ministers, and in November 1902 the cabinet tentatively agreed on the need to continue the corn import duty into peacetime, though with full remission and thereby preferential treatment for colonial produce. This proposal was, however, successfully blocked by Hicks Beach's successor, Ritchie, with consequences which would come to dominate the political history of the following year, and beyond.

For the first half of 1902, however, the focus of national attention remained on the battlefront. In March, the Boers scored a considerable success when they captured a general, Lord Methuen, along with 600 men at Tweebosch in the western Transvaal. To many in Britain, the war seemed as far away from finishing as ever. But, ironically, success proved harmful to Boer illusions, by revealing that they could make but little use of it. They had no means of retaining so many prisoners, and they had scant ability to supply their own men and horses, let alone their children and womenfolk. Kitchener's protracted war of attrition had taken its toll, his counter-insurgency methods had steadily become more effective. In contrast to the Boers', British resources seemed limitless. The dominions in 1902 offered further reinforcements, and there were two particularly disturbing new developments for those Boers still in the field. Many of their own people, anxious perhaps to escape internment in a concentration camp, had now taken up arms against them, enrolled in the British army as national scouts. To augment his forces further, Kitchener was also increasingly putting arms into the hands of native black Africans, some of whom had felt sufficiently encouraged by this to effect a massacre of around 50 Boer civilians at Holkrantz. The rebel Boers, still numbering about 21,000, risked becoming outcasts in their own land, for Milner's system of government was gradually taking hold of wider and wider areas. For his part, Kitchener was also keen to bring the fighting to an end. He had his eye on the chief command in India, and political success, added to his military laurels, would do no harm to his prospects of promotion. He had developed a respect for the Boers as fighting men, and judged that, if once reconciled, they might become a surer foundation for British power than the money-grubbing Uitlanders. In these circumstances, a settlement at last seemed possible. At Vereeniging, in May 1902, Kitchener allowed an amnesty for rebels in Cape Colony. He promised three million pounds of financial assistance, recognition of the Dutch language, and an eventual return to internal self-government, with no provision for a non-white franchise in the meantime. In return, the Boers accepted the sovereignty of the king, and incorporation in the British empire. South Africa had been secured for the wider British world, in which it would remain for fully half a century and more. The cost in lives, particularly for the Boer and black populations, had been high, and the memory of the concentration camps would never disappear. On the other hand, south Africa became an area of comparative stability and calm. No major war has been fought over its surface since 1902, in sharp contrast to the experience of most other parts of the continent.

Notes

1   T. Pakenham, *The Boer War* (London, 1979); P. Warwick ed., *The South African War* (Harlow, 1980); M. Glover, *Warfare from Waterloo to Mons* (London, 1980).
2   *The Times*, 1 and 15 December 1899, 9 January 1900.
3   Hamilton Diary, 6 October 1899, BL Add. Mss 48675.
4   4 *Hansard* LXXVIII 609ff. (5 February 1900).
5   *Ibid.* LXXXVII 1164ff. (25 July 1900).

6 *The Times*, 24 September and 1 October 1900.

7 Speeches at Bilston and Stourbridge, *The Times*, 29 September and 10 October 1900.

8 Speeches at Birmingham and Oldham, *The Times*, 24 and 26 September 1900.

9 Speeches in Manchester, *The Times*, 25 and 27 September 1900.

10 *The Times*, 24 September and 5 October 1900.

11 *The Times*, 28 September and 5 October 1900.

12 *The Times*, 3 October 1900; *Annual Register*, pp. 206–8.

13 *The Times*, 19 October 1900.

14 Campbell-Bannerman to H. Gladstone, 22 October 1900. BL Add. Mss 45987.

15 Speech at Bradford, *The Times*, 24 September 1900.

16 *The Times*, 26 October and 17 December 1901.

17 *The Times*, 26 October 1901.

18 4 *Hansard* CL 324ff. (20 January 1902).

2

The Unionist debacle, 1902–1905

Peace in south Africa opened a new phase in British domestic politics. So long as the war had continued, a patriotic presumption had operated in the government's favour. With the safety of the empire at stake, it was unlikely that the country would shift its support to a party as uncertain and divided in its opinions and loyalties as the Liberals. Now all this began to change. Emphasis shifted to the accumulated problems left behind by the war, to the dragon's teeth, as it were, sown in its wake. Here the government was to find itself much more exposed. It had to meet the greatly increased expenditure occasioned by the war, to soothe public anxieties concerning Britain's military system and institutions, and to clear up the messy aftermath of hostilities in southern Africa. The change in popular mood and expectations was signalled in a series of by-elections in mid-1902, which witnessed the first serious government defeats since the last months of peace some three years earlier. In May 1902 the Unionists lost Bury, largely, it was thought, due to resentment with the corn duty included in the recent budget. A few months later, there came a much more dramatic defeat at North Leeds, a seat which had never previously since its creation in 1885 returned a Liberal. Now a Tory majority of 2,517 was transformed into a Liberal majority of 758, the result being attributed, in some considerable part, to resentment at the Education Bill currently before parliament in a northern stronghold of nonconformity. In August 1902 the rot seemed to spread to the Unionists' southern heartland when their majority at Sevenoaks

fell from 4,812 to 891. In October, the Unionists had the con-
solation of gaining Devonport by 28 votes, but in November the
round of defeats resumed with the loss of Orkney and Shetland.
The impression was gaining ground of an administration which
had been in power too long, and which, well before the tariff
reform controversy of the following year, was already using up
its popularity and authority.

The close of the south African war brought also a more immediate and direct result in a change of prime minister. Salisbury,
though with an increasing sense of weariness following his wife's
death in 1899, had stayed on as head of government for the
duration of hostilities. His presence served to reassure the
country at a time of partisan bitterness and international isolation. But, soon after Vereeniging, in July 1902, he took the opportunity to retire, and his timing was additionally significant in that
it coincided with Chamberlain's temporary incapacitation in a
traffic accident. Naturally this eased the succession of Salisbury's
nephew, Arthur Balfour, who in any case had the best claim as
leader of the largest party in the House of Commons, but it also
bruised the feelings of Chamberlain and Devonshire, older men
who felt that they had at least a right to be consulted, and thus
helps to account for their behaviour in the following year.
Salisbury's departure, therefore, served to loosen the bonds of
the coalition government which had ruled the country in comparative ease since 1895. As significant in its way was the current
departure of the chancellor of the exchequer. Sir Michael Hicks
Beach had held this office for seven years in succession, longer
than anyone since Gladstone in the 1860s. He was a figure of
authority, effective in cabinet, and highly respected on both sides
of the House of Commons for his fiscal orthodoxy and devotion
to economy. His absence would be sorely felt on the government
benches in the ensuing years, as the ship of state encountered the
rough seas of financial and economic controversy.

Balfour's accession, nonetheless, promised a new look for the
Unionist administration. He was the first Conservative prime
minister in the House of Commons since 1876, and he was clearly
far more committed than his predecessor to accomplishing major
legislative changes in the broad field of social policy. Balfour's
forte indeed was measures rather than men, as he demonstrated
right at the start of his administration. For it could be argued that

Balfour then forfeited an ideal opportunity to revive the Unionists' flagging fortunes. What the administration needed was an infusion of new blood to offset the departure of elder statesmen like Salisbury and Beach. Instead Balfour provided no new faces, and only a reshuffling of the ministerial middle order. Public opinion found little to enthuse over in the elevation of the unremarkable Ritchie to the chancellorship of the exchequer, or of the party wire-puller, Akers-Douglas, to the home secretaryship. Clearly the old gang was still very much in place at cabinet level, and much the same was true of the minor appointments, where almost the only promising development was Bonar Law's promotion to an under-secretaryship. There was not much here likely either to impress the country or to appease the increaingly restless spirits on the Unionist back benches, among them rising stars like Lord Hugh Cecil, Seely, and Winston Churchill. It is intriguing to speculate what might have been the political history of the next few years if Balfour had offered the young and ambitious Churchill office in 1902. No doubt he recalled the earlier rivalry of Hatfield and Blenheim, and the effect of Churchill's own father's erratic genius.

Salisbury, as prime minister, had on the whole preferred to let sleeping dogs lie. His successor, for all his languid manner, was prepared to push certain reforms through against powerful vested interests. His administration established the much increased legislative tempo of the Edwardian period, its first substantial achievement being the Education Act of 1902. This dealt with one of the most thorny subjects in English public life, one thoroughly enmeshed in political and religious controversy. Leaving aside the independent or so-called public schools, the great mass of English and Welsh schoolchildren received their elementary education, under the Act of 1870, at the hands of either voluntary or board schools. The former were religious foundations, for the most part Anglican, but including also Wesleyan and Catholic institutions, which endeavoured to educate children in the spirit of a particular denomination. They were funded partly by religious endowments and partly by national taxation, the latter having made possible the abolition of school fees in 1891. The voluntary schools numbered some 14,000 in all, and they accommodated three million pupils. They were particularly prevalent in rural areas, where the parochial system of the

Church of England was strongest. The board schools, on the other hand, had been established in 1870 to cater for the educational needs of the fast-growing urban areas. Numbering 5,700, and containing 2.6 million pupils, they were administered by *ad hoc* public authorities, the locally elected school boards. These were, of course, secular bodies, but all their schools provided non-denominational religious teaching, with an emphasis on biblical instruction. This was particularly to the taste of English and Welsh nonconformists – Methodists, Baptists and Congregationalists – who came to regard the board schools as their especial preserve.

Reluctant though Salisbury's government had been to admit it, the status quo of 1870 could not be much longer maintained. Educational provision was lagging behind that of other countries. The voluntary schools in particular were starved of funds, for they depended heavily on subsidies drawn from national taxation. And any increase in these subsidies was now limited by the competing demands of the armed forces as a result of the south African war. Attempts by school boards to extend their educational facilities ran into legal obstacles. The *Cockerton* judgment of 1901 declared them to be acting *ultra vires* in endeavouring to assume responsibility for secondary as well as elementary education, and this finally necessitated a major overhaul of the whole schooling system. In its Bill, introduced in March 1902, the government proposed to establish a new educational authority. The county councils, hitherto only concerned with technical education, would now assume responsibility for all schools outside the independent sector, whether voluntary or board, elementary or secondary. This would make for much greater standardisation and efficiency, and the one-time voluntary schools, in particular, would be able to benefit from the Midas touch of local government. Rate-aid would prove a much more flexible and abundant financial resource than subsidies out of national taxation. These proposals seemed likely to command widespread support in all political parties. The Irish approved of them as they benefited Catholic schools, and many Liberals at first welcomed an apparently progressive measure which promised to improve educational standards and resources. The main challenge to the Bill would come from religious nonconformity. The great majority of voluntary schools belonged to its old rival, the Church of England, and it was these which stood to gain most from the Bill through a massive new injection of rate-aid. Nonconformists had bitterly opposed a clause of the Act of 1870, which had allowed the voluntary schools to educate a certain number of pauper children on the rates. Now the 1902 measure proposed, in effect, considerably to expand the public endowment of the Church of England, over and above all the advantages which it already derived from its established status. Within the government, Chamberlain especially was aware of the political dangers, for many of his Liberal Unionist supporters were of nonconformist background. He insisted that reform should be optional rather than compulsory in nature, and that county councils should only take over responsibility from school boards where this met with local approval.

The Education Bill, however, was transformed at the moment when Salisbury relinquished the premiership and Chamberlain was incapacitated. The Hobhouse amendment, carried on a free vote by 271:102, rendered it compulsory instead of optional, thereby abolishing the school boards once and for all. Nonconformists were enraged by this development. Over wide areas of England, their children would have no alternative but to attend an Anglican school, and risk indoctrination in other religious practices, all of this at the expense of the local ratepayer. The nonconformists pointed to the iniquity, as they saw it, of conferring so much public money without corresponding public control. Only one-third of the managers of non-provided schools, as the former voluntary schools would now be called, would be chosen by the local authority. Nonconformist teachers would have little chance of promotion under such a system. Unionist claims, as voiced for instance by Lord Hugh Cecil, that the Bill maintained the old balance between Anglicanism and nonconformity, no longer carried much conviction. Many Unionist MPs, dependent upon nonconformist votes, felt increasing unease, and this found expression in the Kenyon–Slaney amendment which was carried later in the autumn by 211:41. This directed that, in the non-provided schools, religious instruction had to be under the control of the school managers and in accordance with the original trust-deeds. The amendment was designed to remove control of religious teaching from the hands of Anglican clergy, in an effort to lessen the anxieties both of nonconformists and of the more evangelically inclined wing of the Church of England, increasingly worried by ritualistic tendencies in the ordained ministry. It appealed to the robust Erastianism of many Unionist backbenchers, one of whom hoped it would put an end to what he called the incessant beating of the ecclesiastical drum. But it affronted Catholics and high-Church Anglicans, who regarded it as an unwarranted reflection on the integrity of the clergy, and thereby it helped to reopen an old wound inside the Conservative party and add to the growing tensions within the ranks of the government's supporters.

The 1902 Education Act has proved one of the more enduring achievements of the Edwardian era. Its basic structure remains with us to this day. But, at the time, it was highly controversial and unpopular. Many voters resented the increased rate burden imposed upon them through efforts to improve educational provision. But the main grudge was borne by the nonconformists, some of whose leaders began a campaign of passive resistance against the Bill, involving the non-payment of rates. Legal proceedings ensued which in some cases were to drag on for years. In Wales, Lloyd George took command of a movement designed, not so much openly to defy the law, but rather to defeat its purposes by other means. Most Welsh county councils were firmly under Liberal control, and could be used to 'administer to death' the former voluntary schools now placed in their charge, for instance by insisting on the strictest possible standards regarding buildings and maintenance. The struggle over the educational issue further enhanced Lloyd George's status as a leading national politician. It also injected the Liberal party as a whole with a new-found sense of unity and purpose, while it tended to have the reverse effect on Unionists. Chamberlain lamented to Devonshire in September 1902 that 'our best friends are leaving us by the scores and hundreds and they will not come back'.[1] Balfour's cabinet, with its complement of cronies, offered Chamberlain less deference and a less secure role, it seemed, than had Salisbury's. The Education Act added to Chamberlain's restlessness and desire to dedicate himself to grand imperial questions. The war having been won in south Africa, he now determined to see Britain win the peace, and for this reason decided to undertake a tour of that country which promised to be the political event of the ensuing winter.

Chamberlain's visit to south Africa occupied the months of January and February 1903. Landing at Durban, his itinerary took in the battlegrounds of Ladysmith and Kimberley as well as the leading centres of Dutch and English settlement, Pretoria, Johannesburg, Bloemfontein, Port Elizabeth, Graaf Reinet and Cape Town. It was a speaking tour to rival the tariff reform campaign of later in the year, and in a sense it represented the high point of Chamberlain's career as an imperial statesman. Almost uniquely in British history, he combined the attributes of cabinet minister and proconsul. Once the *bête noire* of half southern Africa, he now emerged as the great imperial mediator, the exponent of reconciliation and of equal partnership between the two white races. Chamberlain took an interest in compensation claims and the work of the repatriation commissioners. He promised further largesse and an early return to free institutions in the conquered republics. He successfully urged magnanimity towards the former rebels of the Cape; and he managed to bind up the wounds of war to the extent of getting the three mutually antagonistic groups of Boers (bitter-enders, hands-uppers, and national scouts) to join together in presenting addresses to him. Chamberlain left south Africa with his sense of imperial mission reinforced, but conscious also of how much remained to be done. As he had put it in a speech at Kimberley, 'the motherland, which in a time of trial had nobly sustained its claim to the headship of the British race, could not much longer sustain the burden alone, and therefore called her children from the four corners of the world to help to maintain what in the past she had maintained by her own efforts'.[2]

The motherland, however, appeared to have other pre-occupations (Doc. 3). Chamberlain arrived home to find that the cabinet had more or less abandoned the scheme of imperial preference on which it had provisionally agreed in November 1902. There were a number of reasons for this volte-face, which Chamberlain interpreted as a slap in the face. A key role was played by Ritchie, the chancellor of the exchequer. Like others in Balfour's government, Ritchie was widely considered to have been promoted beyond his capacities. He could not speak with the same authority on matters of finance as had his predecessor, Hicks Beach, and he was therefore all the more reliant on his civil service advisers, among them Sir Edward Hamilton, staunch defender of Gladstonian economic principles and free-trade orthodoxy. Ritchie aspired, like any other incoming finance minister, to present a popular tax-cutting budget. The end of hostilities in south Africa allowed scope for such a measure, and Ritchie hoped to win back the Unionists' middle-class support in the constituencies by reducing the rate of income tax by four pence in the pound. At the same time, it was thought politically unwise not to offer something also to the large class of less well-off voters who did not pay income tax. And so Ritchie determined to remove the one-shilling corn import duty, in order to cheapen the cost of living for all consumers. This of course delighted the treasury mandarins like Hamilton, who had over the past year regarded the duty as a Trojan horse within the free-trade fiscal system. But it also found favour with a majority of the cabinet, who were anxious to restore the government's sagging popularity, and whose morale had been affected by a continuing run of disastrous by-election results. One of these was at Woolwich in March 1903, where a Unionist majority of 2,805 was transformed spectacularly into a majority of 3,229 for a Labour candidate standing with Liberal support. This was one of the young Labour party's early electoral triumphs, which helped to establish it as a significant force in British politics. In the same period, the Liberals wrested two seats from the Unionists in a mainly rural area, again on a large turnover of votes. At Newmarket, a Liberal majority of 507 replaced a Unionist majority of 1,077; and, at Rye, a Unionist majority of 2,489 was overturned in favour of a Liberal majority of 534.

Ministers therefore welcomed the removal of the corn import duty, which was thought to have been a key factor in the recent by-election upsets. Balfour's own attitude was particularly significant. He had always set great store by his political relationship with Chamberlain, and might therefore have been expected to have backed his colonial secretary in any confrontation with the chancellor of the exchequer. But Balfour knew that finance had been one of the Conservatives' weak points over past decades. It had almost broken up Salisbury's government in late 1886, and had arguably contributed to its defeat at the polls in 1892. Balfour had only recently lost the services of Hicks Beach, as chancellor of the exchequer, and had no desire to rock the financial boat by getting rid of another one so soon. Besides, he had doubts of his own about the corn import duty, which he considered a peculiarly blunt instrument so far as the protection of agriculture was concerned. In his view, it penalised the increasing number of livestock farmers who imported cheap corn as fodder for their animals, and indeed made them 'the only class in the community who are required to pay a tax on the raw material of their manufacture'. Nor, he believed, did the duty serve the wider political purposes that were claimed for it. 'You cannot', he declared, 'slide either into protection, or into a fiscal union with the colonies, as it were by accident, and through the medium of a tax never designed to carry out these objects.' More than likely, the government would be defeated at the next general election; but the defeat, he contended, would be far greater 'had we simply retained the shilling duty, which the farmers would soon have discovered did them harm rather than good, and to which the urban population would have attributed every rise in food, for which short harvests in America and Canada would be responsible'.[3]

The budget therefore, introduced on 23 April 1903, turned out to be one of the most defiantly free-trade statements for fifty years. It was the first of a series of spectacular u-turns that were to mark Conservative economic policy in the course of the twentieth century. The corn import duty, which had been declared a new and permanent addition to the fiscal system but twelve months previously, was now unceremoniously discarded. Unionist back-benchers were faced with the embarrassing prospect of repudiating speeches made over the preceding year. For some this was too much to ask, and thirty-two of them voted against the second reading of the budget in June 1903, in what was to mark the start of the disintegration of the Unionist coalition which had ruled since 1895. To Chamberlain, the budget represented a betrayal of his hopes of using economic measures to promote greater imperial solidarity; and the question must naturally arise as to why he did not seize this moment as the one at which to threaten resignation. After his triumphant tour of south Africa, he was in a particularly strong position. And, had he forced a decision, one way or the other, at this stage, much of the confusion in Unionist politics over succeeding years might well have been avoided. But his south African exertions had left Chamberlain temporarily exhausted; and in any case he was not confident of winning a showdown even with Ritchie. Since the Leamington affair of 1895, Chamberlain had been conscious of how far he represented the junior wing of the Unionist coalition. And, in early 1903, he found himself out of sympathy with several other noted figures in the cabinet – with Brodrick over army reform, with Wyndham over the Irish land purchase scheme which reminded Chamberlain of Gladstone's fatal design of 1886, and, not least, with the prime minister himself over educational policy. Anyway, Chamberlain was not naturally the resigning type. He had clung like a limpet to Gladstone's second government, despire considerable reservations and resentments, and he had even remained for some time in Gladstone's third, home rule, administration. His instinct was usually to work inside the citadel, and if necessary to undermine it from within.

Nonetheless, the situation was one calculated to make Chamberlain retire, wounded in spirit, like Achilles to his tent, or at least to Birmingham. There, in mid-May 1903, he delivered the most celebrated speech of his career, a *tour d'horizon* in his own inimitable style. In typical Chamberlain manner, he touched freely on a range of imperial concerns, and especially on the need to safeguard and develop, by means of preferential economic policies, the empire's vast potential, and to seize on what seemed to him a uniquely favourable opportunity to draw it closer together (Doc. 4). There was not much evidence of homework, or of a detailed mastery of his case, but much of earnestness and intent. This was characteristic of the Chamberlain who had been a propagandist over the years for ambitious, if somewhat nebulous, schemes of social reform, and who more recently, in 1898, had called for an effective revolution in British foreign policy, involving the ill-considered idea of a German alliance. Superficially, this latest effort on Chamberlain's part merely seemed to build on remarks that he had made exactly a year before, when he had spoken of the need to discard, if necessary, old shibboleths and economic pedantry in the interests of closer imperial union. But, for particular reasons, the Birmingham speech of 1903 came to represent a watershed in British political history to rank with the Hawarden Kite and Gladstone's conversion to home rule. Partly this was a matter of timing and circumstance. Chamberlain's latest initiative came at a moment when the Unionist majority in parliament was in manifest disarray over economic policy, and many of its members were looking for a stronger lead. But of equal significance were two parliamentary interventions on Chamberlain's part, which followed swiftly in the wake of his Birmingham address, and which abruptly raised the stakes, thereby establishing a momentum which would prove very difficult to control.

On 22 May, responding to sarcastic observations by Lloyd George, Chamberlain denied that the cause of old age pensions, which he had advocated for so long, was now moribund, but declared that it was dependent on an overhaul of Britain's fiscal system. On 28 May, he went further still, and spoke of his ideas on preference and pensions in terms of redistributive social justice. Calculating that, in aggregate, the working classes would have to pay three-quarters of any new taxes on consumption, Chamberlain declared it 'a matter of common justice that the working classes are entitled to every penny of the three fourths', and added that he 'would give them without hesitation the other one fourth as well', it being 'fair and right that the richer class should contribute in return for the indirect advantages which they gain from the great prosperity and contentment of the country'.[4] In other words, the rich would be taxed to pay for the pensions of the poor. Here, once again, was the doctrine of ransom of 1885, once the trademark of Radical Joe, as Chamberlain had formerly been called, but now propounded by a member of a largely Conservative cabinet.

This took the terms of debate well beyond the tone of general enquiry sounded in mid-May at Birmingham, which had remained broadly within the guidelines of Balfour's administration. Chamberlain now proposed not only a change in Britain's economic relations with the empire. He also appeared to commit the government to a sweeping review of the country's system of welfare and social policy. Various reasons of course had propelled him to grasp the initiative in this fashion. Personal pique and frustration with his comparative isolation and ineffectiveness in cabinet combined with growing apprehension on his part as to the future prospects of the Unionist coalition. In addition, he was anxious to take advantage of what he regarded as an exceptional opportunity to reinforce the links of empire and thereby safeguard Britain's status and security in the world. In launching his initiative entirely on his own responsibility,

Chamberlain of course stretched the theory of cabinet solidarity to the limit – and beyond – but his behaviour was substantially of a piece with earlier proceedings. For instance, through much of 1885 and 1886, he had contrived to be both a supporter and an opponent of Irish home rule in one form or another. One commentator spoke of Chamberlain's capacity to believe that things could both be and not be at the same time. He was certainly the foremost exponent of the art of politically having one's cake and eating it.

The Chamberlain programme tapped deep, even primitive, feelings across a range of Unionist opinion. Protective tariffs appeared to many in the Tory party a return to its best traditions, to the days before it had been forced to borrow many of its opponents' clothes. Such sentiments remained strong, particularly in the countryside, the Conservative heartland, where free trade was generally blamed for serious economic decline since the 1870s, for the flight of population from the land and for the undermining of the bonds of society and of a traditional way of life. Protection for agriculture also seemed advisable on wider grounds of national self-interest. It was a means of ensuring self-sufficiency in food at a time of recurrent international tension; and, like the coal export duty of 1901, it seemed a way of safeguarding a priceless national asset. Even Hicks Beach, as chancellor of the exchequer, had spoken of the need to broaden the basis of taxation; and, to many Conservatives representing suburban constituencies, protective tariffs offered a means of shifting the fiscal burden somewhat from the income tax paying middle classes. But protectionism had also a populist dimension, an appeal to Tory democrat traditions, to which the recent wrangling over the budget had given additional significance. The corn import duty, it was argued, had safeguarded jobs, not only in agriculture, but also in related industries like milling. The benefits of its repeal, amounting anyway to only £2½ millions, would be felt not by the consumer but by the middleman; and the working classes would have stood to derive much greater advantage, instead, from a reduction in the tea duty. Protective tariffs, by widening the taxable base, would also permit an increase in public expenditure for social purposes, still a cause with which the Unionists were rather more identified than were the Liberals. The recent war was held to have demonstrated the masses' willingness to make sacrifices, financial and otherwise, in a patriotic cause.

Chamberlain's ideas, however, provoked also a powerful negative reaction among significant sections of Unionist opinion. Partly this had to do with the controversial reputation and personality of their proponent. Chamberlain's passage from the left to the right of the political spectrum had left a trail of resentment across both sides of the House of Commons. Many traditional-minded Tories still regarded Chamberlain, who had for example never renounced his belief in Church disestablishment, as a radical cuckoo in their nest. Others were mindful of the way in which Chamberlain's ascent in Unionist politics had blighted the career prospects of long-established Conservatives. Perhaps it was no coincidence that prominent among Chamberlain's opponents were Lord Hugh Cecil, a leading high-Church spokesman, and Winston Churchill, conscious of the fact that his father's political demise could in part be blamed on Chamberlain. In addition, both were young and ambitious men, whose chances of advancement were hindered by the continuance of the Conservative coalition with the Liberal Unionists, of whom Chamberlain was the outstanding embodiment. But the attitude of the Unionist free traders, as such men soon came to be called, did not depend on issues of personality alone. Large principles appeared at stake in the conflict between protection and free trade, involving the very nature of British political life. To men like Churchill and Cecil, that Britain had since the Chartist era enjoyed stability and social peace seemed largely owing to free trade. The removal of tariffs, they believed, had helped to eliminate corruption from public life and to break the political power of vested economic interests. Paradoxically, the ending of agricultural protection had served to perpetuate the influence of traditional landed families like the Churchills and Cecils, by enabling them to engage in politics without the imputation of financial self-interest. Indeed, the Unionist free traders could be described as the Tory 'wets' of their day. Often blue-blooded, they believed in maintaining the economic consensus and status quo of recent decades, and in a society still based in some measure on spiritual values and on more traditional concepts of paternalism and deference; and they looked askance at what they regarded as Chamberlain's crude appeal to mercenary instincts.

As Churchill so well expressed it:

> The old Conservative party, with its religious convictions and
> constitutional principles, will disappear, and a new party will arise
> like perhaps the Republican party of the United States of America –
> rich, materialist and secular – whose opinions will turn on tariffs,
> and who will cause the lobbies to be crowded with the touts of
> protected industries.[5]

The Unionist free traders considered protection as liable to
encourage governmental extravagance, corruption, popular dis-
content and social division. They pointed to the United States as
an example of a country where high tariffs and trusts were
endangering the democratic process, and also to Europe, where
the high protective duties in force since the early 1890s had not
only failed to stem the rise of socialism but had generally had the
reverse effect.

Balfour's position, as his government and its supporters
became engulfed in fiscal controversy, was crucial yet enigmatic.
Two fundamental considerations seem to have influenced his
thinking. In the first place, he did not believe in the kind of
infallibility often claimed on behalf of the free-trade system.
Throughout his life, Balfour remained sceptical about many
articles of received wisdom, his brand of conservatism relying
more on pragmatism than on ideology. Balfour considered that
free trade had probably served Britain well at a particular stage in
its development, but was by no means necessarily suited to
twentieth-century conditions. He noted that the rest of the world
had not adhered to the Cobdenite gospel which it had for a time
embraced in the mid-nineteenth century, and that Britain was the
only major commercial power that continued to play by the rules
of the free-trade system. Whereas in terms of domestic social
policy, Balfour could point out that the Conservative party at
least had long since abandoned any strict adherence to the principles of *laissez-faire*. At the same time, however, Balfour was
deeply concerned to maintain the Unionist coalition, and not to
see it suffer the kind of schism that had befallen other parties in
government in 1846 and 1886. He had no desire to repeat the
mistake of Peel and of Gladstone, whom he regarded as having
sprung a dramatic change of policy on their supporters without
sufficient warning. Nor did he wish to reopen the old sectional

divide in the Conservative party between the interests of town and country. As he put it, 'the memory of the old corn laws . . . has produced in this country associations with a food tax which make it absolutely impossible to retain such a tax except as an essential element in a new fiscal policy which has the country itself behind it'.[6] The best course, Balfour believed, was to hasten slowly, to allow time for tempers to cool and ideas to mature, even if this meant permitting cabinet ministers for the time being to air different economic opinions. There was, after all, a precedent for this in the long-running controversy, earlier in Tory party history, over Catholic emancipation. To this end, Balfour instituted what he called a fiscal inquiry, in the summer of 1903, into the workings of Britain's commercial system. He hoped that this would allow him to retain public confidence while preparing the ground for a significant change in economic policy.

One other consideration influenced Balfour's concern to avoid an early showdown among his ministers. He was anxious to keep his government together at least until the completion of the main parliamentary business of the 1903 session. In this year, the main item on the agenda was the Irish Land Purchase Bill, an ambitious enough project even on the part of one of the more energetic reforming governments of recent times. One prominent Liberal described it as involving 'an immense social revolution' and the 'collapse of the system on which this country has governed Ireland since the act of union'. Certainly it aimed at a more or less final settlement of the land question, described as 'at the bottom of all the political agitations, and of the greater part of the crime, in Ireland for the last hundred years'.[7] Since first entering government, Balfour had strongly favoured the policy of killing home rule with kindness, which had provided Ireland with development grants, elected county councils, and extensive credit facilities to enable Irish peasants to buy their holdings from their landlords. The land purchase measure of 1903 appeared as the culmination of much of Balfour's life's work up to that date. It represented a quintessentially conservative policy of creating a peasant proprietorship in Ireland, of turning the Irish tenantry from the ways of revolution into supporters of the status quo. The first Tory land purchase act in 1885 had advanced £5 millions for the purpose, but the Act of 1903 would go a very great deal further by providing loan facilities for up to £150 millions, with repayment to be spread over sixty-eight years. This now seemed a much safer proceeding in the wake of the Irish Local Government Act of 1898, which had made Irish ratepayers responsible for default on the part of any of their number. In addition, the 1903 Act made a direct gift to Ireland of £12 millions, to be paid for by the British taxpayer, in order to bridge the gap between the price at which Irish landlords were prepared to sell and at which Irish tenants were prepared to buy. Something of the scale of this may be gauged from the fact that old age pensions, when first introduced in 1908, would only cost £6 millions. But this did not greatly worry Balfour's government, for, up to this point of time, it was the Conservatives rather than the Liberals who on the whole accepted the need for higher public spending.

The Irish Land Purchase Act of 1903 represented in its way a political and legislative triumph. Certain criticisms were indeed made. Some Unionists claimed that it mortgaged the future, advancing a great deal of money with insufficient security for repayment. The British state, it was said, would become one vast absentee landlord, or the 'national gombeen man of Ireland'. Some Liberals, on the other hand, thought the terms offered to the landlords far too generous, and a few could not resist the temptation to make party points about the government's adoption of one of Gladstone's ideas of 1886. Irish Nationalists objected that the Bill left the landless labourers in Ireland entirely out of account. But at the end of the day none of these criticisms amounted to much, and in the House of Commons only twenty MPs, mostly left-wing Liberals, opposed the bill on its third reading. The House of Lords passed the measure with a few amendments reserving landlord rights over sport and minerals. Balfour had performed an almost unparalleled political trick. He had succeeded in bringing together in support of his policy all sides of opinion in Ireland – landlord and tenant, Orange and Green – and he had achieved virtually unprecedented cross-party support in the House of Commons for a wide-ranging social reform. The 1903 Act was arguably the most enduring of his legislative accomplishments. It fastened upon Ireland a social structure which has remained substantially in place down to the present day. Balfour also hoped and believed that it would be enough to divert the Irish from home rule. Perhaps, had his government been granted a much longer stay in office, he might have been proved right.

None of this, however, cut much ice with the British electorate in 1903, whose attention was largely elsewhere. This was made clear by a number of by-elections held during the summer. The best-known of these was at Barnard Castle, where the recently formed Labour party, in the person of Arthur Henderson, scored another win, this time against a protectionist Liberal. Barnard Castle itself was not a loss for the government, but it did at this juncture forfeit two Scottish seats, St Andrews Burghs and Argyllshire, the latter on a turnover of over 2,000 votes. One factor here may well have been the newly issued report of the Royal Commission on the War, under Lord Elgin's chairmanship, which had blamed the disasters of 1899 and early 1900 on the Unionist government's complacency and lack of preparedness for a conflict in south Africa. The report focused attention on what was to remain the Balfour administration's most conspicuous failing, its inability to effect a thorough-going reform of Britain's military institutions. Indeed, 1903 was to prove a bad year for the government so far as army matters were concerned, having already witnessed a scandal in the Grenadier Guards, a backbench revolt against Brodrick's reorganisation proposals, and a costly setback in Somaliland in the course of a campaign against Islamic fundamentalist rebels commanded by the so-called Mad Mullah. But it is at least as likely that the Balfour government's low standing in the country in mid-1903 had to do with the appearance it gave of being at sixes and sevens over economic policy, which circumstances had combined to make the leading issue of the day.

This was the background to the affair of the September resignations, which so startled opinion as the summer drew to a close. As so often, the catalyst was provided by Chamberlain, who now finally signified his intention to be quit of ministerial office. Since May 1903 he had come to embrace his new protectionist faith with the zeal of a convert, and he had grown increasingly frustrated at his inability to move his colleagues in the direction of his ideas. Chamberlain sensed that Balfour was indeed sympathetic to protection, but that, with his cautious instincts, he would for the time being shy away from the full Chamberlainite programme of imperial preference along with the taxes on food that alone would make it work. Chamberlain felt himself, from his time as colonial

secretary, to be even more committed to preference than to protection. His hands seemed tied so long as he remained in a
do-nothing government, while the political running was being
made by the Liberals in speeches up and down the country.
Chamberlain longed to be able to carry the battle to his opponents
on the public platform and to rescue the Unionist alliance from
drift and uncertainty. He still resented his cabinet defeat earlier in
the year, and no doubt he reflected that his political influence had
rarely stood higher than during his period out of office between
1886 and 1895. The colonial secretaryship, in its own right,
offered him few new fields to conquer; and he also calculated that
relinquishing office would give him the appearance of disinterestedness. On 9 September 1903, and with words that would
subsequently have an ironic ring, Chamberlain wrote to Balfour
that 'with absolute loyalty to your government and its general
policy, and with no fear of embarrassing it in any way, I can best
promote the cause I have at heart from outside'. Balfour accepted
the resignation with a glowing tribute to Chamberlain's achievement in bringing home 'to the citizens of the empire the con-
sciousness of imperial obligation and the interdependence
between the various fragments into which the empire is geo-
graphically divided', and he also bestowed a blessing on
Chamberlain's long-term programme, declaring it to be his conviction also 'that this interdependence should find expression in
our commercial relations as well as in our political and military
relations'.[8] Balfour revealed Chamberlain's resignation privately
to Devonshire, who, though a stalwart free trader, was also a
respected elder statesman whom Balfour was anxious to retain in
the cabinet as a sop to moderate opinion. But, with what many
came to regard as an excess of adroitness, Balfour did not immediately inform three other ministers of Chamberlain's impending
departure. These were Ritchie, Lord George Hamilton, and Lord
Balfour of Burleigh, of all of whom Balfour was now anxious to be
rid. To him, they appeared doctrinaire free traders who were
likely to stand in the way of his own preferred compromise
solution to the fiscal difficulty, involving not so much thorough-
going protection and imperial preference but rather retaliatory
tariffs, limited in application against those countries which
discriminated against British exports. The three ministers in
question, however, from documents circulated by Balfour,

believed themselves to be faced with adoption of the full Chamberlain package. Accordingly they resigned, and were bitterly dismayed to find their resignations announced along with that of Chamberlain's own. In one sense, the unedifying business soon backfired on Balfour. In a speech at Sheffield, early in October, he elaborated his own halfway-house economic formula, involving commerical retaliation but without taxation of imported food; and Devonshire, feeling twinges of conscience at his apparent desertion of his free-trade colleagues, seized on the opportunity to depart. His was the fifth ministerial resignation within a few weeks.

This was to prove the most notorious cabinet reshuffle of the century, with the possible exception of that of 1962. On the face of it, Balfour, by considerable sleight of hand, had achieved most of his objectives. He had at last imposed authority on his own cabinet, which had been in considerable disarray over economic policy for half a year, and he was now able to define the government's line as being one of fiscal retaliation, of introducing tariffs selectively to punish excessive protectionism on the part of other countries, this being the substance of the speech which he delivered at Sheffield in October 1903. Balfour had also won back some of the initiative from Chamberlain, while at the same time preserving a close working relationship with that particular politician, in a way that had guided much of his strategy for a decade and more. Chamberlain had left the cabinet more or less with the blessing of Balfour, who had wished his departing colleague Godspeed in the country's conversion to new economic ideas; but at the same time Balfour had been careful not to commit himself to the full Chamberlainite programme of food taxes and imperial preference. Here he had agreed only to await the movement of public opinion; and Chamberlain would find it difficult to pressurise him any further, as for instance by threatening to overthrow his administration, without risking accusations of disloyalty against the Unionist alliance. In any case, Balfour had half taken the Chamberlain family hostage, by promoting the eldest son, Austen, to the chancellorship of the exchequer, one of the senior posts in the government. Joseph Chamberlain would naturally be loath to blight his son's promising ministerial career.

Balfour, notwithstanding, had gained all these advantages at considerable political cost. The resignation of five more or less prominent ministers left his cabinet seriously depleted. The loss of Chamberlain and Devonshire was especially felt, for they were among the last of the giants who had sustained the Unionist cause over almost two decades. Balfour had some difficulty recruiting new talent for what was starting to appear to many as a sinking ship. The appointments that he did make inspired little confidence. That of Lyttelton, best know as a cricketer, to the colonial secretaryship, provoked virtual derision. The transfer of Brodrick from the war office to the secretaryship of state for India seemed, as with Lansdowne three years earlier, a case of rewarding a man who had failed in one department with promotion to another. More even than Bonar Law's 1922–23 administration, to which the phrase is usually applied, Balfour's governemnt after late 1903 was one of the 'second eleven', and no doubt this partly explains its lacklustre performance in these years. Still more serious, however, than the matter of the cabinet changes was the manner in which they had been accomplished. The underhand way in which Balfour had contrived to manoeuvre three trusty ministers out of their jobs left many observers with a nasty taste in the mouth. Balfour had built much of his political career on his reputation as an incisive parliamentary speaker and as a clearsighted opponent of home rule and unnecessary constitutional change. Now he seemed to be turning his back on the principles that had helped to make him what he was. His unedifying treatment of his colleagues seemed to violate the spirit of cabinet government, itself one of the mainstays of the constitution. And, over the next couple of years, Balfour's standing as a parliamentarian also suffered a decline, largely owing to his inability or unwillingness to give any clear indication to the House of Commons as to what his government actually proposed to do about economic policy, the leading issue of the day.

Chamberlain's departure from the cabinet marked the effective start of his tariff reform campaign. Beginning at Glasgow, in October 1903, Chamberlain revealed, or purported to reveal, the basis of his plan. He demanded a general tariff on foreign imports, qualified by a system of preference in favour of colonial produce, and by commerical treaties with other countries which agreed to trade with Britain on a basis of reciprocity. For the sake of the greater imperial economic unity, which he evidently had so much at heart, Chamberlain proposed to levy import duties on food entering Britain from countries outside the empire. In return for the privileged position which this would give colonial foodstuffs in the British domestic market, the colonies would be asked to forego any further development of their own manufacturing potential so as not themselves to compete with the products of Britain's industries. Chamberlain thus aspired to transform the British empire into a closely knit, rationalised and self-sufficient economic concern, based on a kind of global division of labour. This was the grand theme which he propounded in a succession of major speeches through the autumn of 1903, at leading provincial centres such as Newcastle-upon-Tyne, Liverpool, Birmingham, Cardiff and Leeds. It was at Birmingham in November 1903 that he first used the demagogic device of holding up two loaves of bread to symbolise the greater prosperity which he believed would accrue from the adoption of his ideas.

Chamberlain strove to awaken the British people to their imperial destiny. But his tariff reform campaign represented also the last of his great domestic reforming crusades. Indeed, in language and intention, it was as radical as those which he had undertaken previously in the 1870s and 1880s. With characteristic bravado he sought a legitimacy for his new ideas in the great reforming traditions and movements of the nineteenth century. At Liverpool, in October 1903, he even went so far as to claim that Gladstone and Cobden had been covert protectionists in their dealings with France in 1861; and in the same speech he further insisted that trades unionism had originated in opposition to untrammelled free trade (Doc. 5). At Birmingham, in the following month, Chamberlain enlisted the Chartists also beneath his banner. Apparently Chartism had been in essence a protectionist movement, conceived in opposition to the free-trade dogma of the Manchester School. This interesting, not to say reckless, reading of history, was to land Chamberlain in trouble from some quarters. But its significance is clear. For Chamberlain, tariff reform was a means of realising all his old radical dreams of wide-ranging social improvement. Great play was made in his speeches with the material benefits, and long-deferred reforms, which would result from adoption of a new fiscal policy. Mention has already been made of old age pensions, which Chamberlain had tied to imperial preference almost from the first; but in his

Glasgow speech he went a stage further in declaring that tariffs would make it possible to realise the long-promised radical objective of the so-called free breakfast table. Cuts in duties on sugar, tea and coffee, Chamberlain insisted, would offset the envisaged new taxes on imported bread and meat, and mean that the average worker or consumer would be if anything better-off than before. As his campaign progressed, Chamberlain made wider and wider claims, and promised more and more to a variety of social groups. In August 1904, at Welbeck, it was the turn of the agricultural labourers to receive his blandishments. Tariff reform, Chamberlain assured his audience, would preserve the viability of small-scale agriculture in Britain by guarding against the mass import of cheap foreign food. It would put a smallholding, or at least an allotment, within the range of every agricultural labourer, and thereby prevent rural depopulation and the exodus of an unemployed proletariat to the cities. Here was the old 'unauthorised programme' of 1885, with its promise of three acres and a cow, revived in slightly different form. In December 1904 Chamberlain took his message to the east end of London, presenting tariff reform as the counterpart of anti-aliens legislation, a means of protecting Englishmen's jobs against swamping by either foreign manufactures or foreign labour.[9]

No doubt the radicalism of the tariff reform campaign was a key element in its failure. Chamberlain challenged the settled convictions, and economic and social practice, of the previous half century and more. It was like a politician of the 1990s proposing to do away with the welfare state created fifty years or so earlier in the 1940s. Free trade was one of the great Victorian verities, standing for progress, modernism and orthodoxy. It was an integral part of the long-established consensus of nineteenth-century Britain, associated with unprecedented social harmony and with the virtual elimination of corruption from public life. Chamberlain's ideas upset too many assumptions, and represented too great a leap in the dark. His undoubted demagogic talents had always been most effectively employed in defence of the status quo, as they had been on the whole since 1886. He was much less convincing as an exponent of change, even though he promised the earth, literally, it seemed, in the case of the agricultural labourer. The average elector was not particularly impressed by someone who appeared to come bearing too many gifts. Indeed, the average elector had seen it all before; and, ironically, no one could have pointed that out better than Chamberlain himself. For no one had proved more effective than he in demolishing Gladstone's attempt to build a coalition of interests in support of his central tenet of home rule, and no one had more ruthlessly exposed the spurious and self-contradictory nature of the Newcastle programme of 1891. Now Chamberlain, with his promise of largesse to all and sundry, whether in the form of land, old age pensions, or the free breakfast table, was falling into much the same kind of trap. 'And thus the whirligig of time brings in his revenges.'

Chamberlain's arguments might have carried greater conviction had he first propounded them at a time of manifest economic crisis. But his insistence that the nation's industrial life was now in perilous decline simply did not square with the everyday realities experienced by the average British citizen. To many people the country had rarely seemed more prosperous, as indeed was borne out by the official returns published in the *Economist*.[10] These showed the value of British and Irish exports to have been £174 millions in 1902, pretty much the same as they had been in 1901, 1899, and in a previous boom year, 1890, and considerably more than they had been throughout the years from 1891 to 1898. Only the exceptional year, 1900, with its £197 millions worth of exports, surpassed all other performances to date. Chamberlain's message of gloom and doom contradicted not only the received wisdom of the day but also most people's apprehension of their immediate circumstances. Furthermore, with his looseness with facts and figures, and with his often self-contradictory arguments, he left himself open to damaging rejoinders from the more able among his antagonists, in particular Asquith, who excelled as Chamberlain's *bête noire* on the campaign circuit of 1903–04. For instance at Glasgow, in the speech which effectively launched the tariff reform campaign, Chamberlain had laid great stress on the fact that since 1872 Britain's trade with foreign countries had fallen off heavily, whereas its manufacturing exports to the colonies had increased by £40 millions in value. To many, indeed, this seemed like an argument for leaving things as they were. But, as so often at this time, it was Asquith who supplied the weightiest rebuttal, with a speech shortly afterwards, at Cinderford, which demonstrated among other things that nations do not live by exports alone. The year 1872, Asquith pointed out, one of spiralling price increases, was in any case a dubious landmark to use; but, quite apart from that, there were plenty of other indications of the great increase in national prosperity in the ensuing thirty years. Between 1872 and 1902, Asquith noted, real wages had risen, housing had greatly improved, deposits in savings banks had increased by two and a half times, the amount assessed to income tax had doubled, and so had the interest earned by Britain on its foreign investments.

Chamberlain's speeches nonetheless set the terms of political debate as 1903 drew to a close. At the bar of public opinion, their impact was first tested in a series of by-elections held just before Christmas and early in the following year. The first of these, which took place in December 1903 in three relatively safe Unionist seats – Dulwich, Lewisham and Ludlow – returned an ambiguous verdict. Although the Unionists retained all three seats, still with respectable majorities, at the same time the Liberals made considerable inroads into the Unionist vote. (At Dulwich, the young Liberal hopeful, Charles Masterman, did well to cut the Unionist vote to well below that of 1892, especially bearing in mind his disastrous by-election record in the years to come.) A better test, it was thought, of the popularity of tariff reform would be provided by contests in seats which the Liberals were defending, not attacking. But the results of by-elections held early in 1904 did nothing for the prospects of protectionism. Unionist candidates failed to gain either industrial Gateshead or rural Mid-Devon, and indeed in the latter seat the Liberal majority doubled. At the same time the Unionists actually lost seats at Norwich, Ayr, and, most significantly of all, at Mid-Hertfordshire, in one of Toryism's south-eastern strongholds. After this, a good deal of the momentum seemed to go out of Chamberlain's crusade. Unionist candidates, who had willingly endorsed his ideas in the by-elections at the turn of the year, now tended to distance themselves from him. At subsequent contests, when threatened with assistance from tariff reform canvassers, such candidates offered them, as one Liberal politician humourously put it, 'sixpence to play in the next street'.[11]

'It is hard to say', a leading journalist would later remark, 'whether Mr. Balfour's cabinet has done more harm to Mr. Chamberlain or Mr. Chamberlain to Mr. Balfour's cabinet.'[12]

Between 1903 and 1906 a two-way process would indeed be in evidence. As has been seen, tariff reform was not a popular cause when it was first launched upon the British public. At the same time, it was dragged down by its associations with an increasingly unpopular and discredited government. Here lay the anomaly of Chamberlain's situation in the wake of his resignation in September 1903. He had left the government in order, from a position of greater freedom and disinterestedness, to urge his views upon the country; but, to measure the impact of his views, among other things, he had to look for standard-bearers among the Unionist candidates who came forward to fight each individual by-election, and who were also necessarily identified with Balfour's administration and its declining fortunes. Chamberlain's posture of independence would have made much more sense had the Unionists been in opposition, when, as their most prominent and popular personality, he might have expected to benefit from any turn in the political tide. This had been Gladstone's experience after he had resigned the Liberal leadership in 1875 only to be restored in triumph five years later. But circumstances were rather different in 1903 and 1904, with the Unionists hardly likely in by-elections to improve on the often record majorities which they had obtained in 1900. Chamberlain now found himself hard pressed to persuade the country that there was any movement of opinion in his favour.

A comparison between Chamberlain and Gladstone is suggestive in several ways. In examining Chamberlain's tariff reform campaign, one has the sense of his still being haunted by the ghost of the Grand Old Man who had thwarted his one-time ambitions in the Liberal party. Chamberlain seemed fatefully driven to emulate the methods of the statesman with whom he had for so long been locked in combat. The comparison should be made not so much with the Gladstone of the Bulgarian agitation or the Midlothian campaigns as with the Gladstone of the home rule crusade of 1886 and thereafter. Like Chamberlain in 1903, Gladstone had challenged the received wisdom of the preceding two or three generations. He had provoked a wide-ranging debate, which had required the country to think seriously about its national identity and place in the world for virtually the first time since the end of the Napoleonic wars. Again, like Chamberlain subsequently, Gladstone had tried to convert the country almost single-handed, barnstorming his way round the major provincial centres of population. (Interestingly neither man devoted much effort to London.) Finally, of course, each failed to realise his grand vision in his own lifetime, though Gladstone did succeed to the extent of carrying a home rule measure through the House of Commons, and thereby establishing a significant precedent for the future. Here, however, the similarities begin to fade, and it is the differences which become more instructive. Whatever Chamberlain's talents as a parliamentary debater, he was not in the same class as Gladstone as a platform speaker out of doors. He lacked Gladstone's emotional range, his richly evocative vocabulary, his ability to inspire an audience with a sense of moral outrage or passionate commitment. Sometimes, usually in the perorations of his speeches, Chamberlain tugged at the heartstrings of his listeners, as for instance at Glasgow in October 1903, when he declared that 'our children are calling to us', and that 'with them rests, as with us, the maintenance of the traditions of which we are proud – the continuance of the glorious history of our past . . . which we have received as an inheritance, due to the courage, the tenacity and the self-sacrifice of our ancestors through many generations'. But, all too often, Chamberlain diluted the visionary element in his speeches with crude appeals to self-interest, a technique at which, it must be admitted, · he excelled rather better. For instance, in a number of his speeches in late 1903 and early 1904, he showed himself concerned, not so much to advance the cause of 'our children' across the seas, but rather to confine their future development within an imperial straitjacket, so that they would not emerge as rivals to the mother country in the way that the United States so notoriously had done. Chamberlain was in many ways not the most ideal propagandist in his own cause. His record, over the years, was much longer on promises than on actual performance. Whatever one might say of Gladstone and his ideas, especially in later life, there was no denying the fact that in the course of his long career he had successfully put together and carried through parliament a succession of measures very large in scope. Chamberlain had been bringing forward wide-ranging reform programmes at regular intervals since first becoming a national figure, but, after over a dozen years in cabinet, one would be hard put to cite a significant legislative achievement for which he had been primarily responsible (Doc. 6).

Gladstone in later years was called an old man in a hurry, and this description was also coming to fit Chamberlain as he approached his seventieth year. Though Chamberlain, it should be noted, was by no means Gladstone's equal in terms of physical stamina. His south African trip of early 1903 had taken a good deal out of him, and the exertions of the tariff reform campaign of October 1903 to January 1904 were sufficient to require him to take a long holiday in France from February until April. This caused him to miss the opening months of the parliamentary session of 1904, in which the fate of the Unionist alliance rested in the balance. Chamberlain indeed was to make few significant parliamentary interventions following his resignation in September 1903. His energies were reserved for campaigning in the country, and his considerable debating talents were largely lost to the forces of Unionism which had drawn so much upon them since 1886.

The opening of a new parliamentary session, in February 1904, served to alter the political perspective. For the first time in years, a government found itself faced with the more or less constant danger of defeat and overthrow in the House of Commons. Chamberlain's inability to dictate the political agenda, especially as he was now no longer a minister, was painfully exposed. Other subjects, particularly those associated with the dubious legacy of the late war, now claimed their own full share of public attention. The return of parliament gave the Liberals their first opportunity to debate the report of the Elgin commission, issued in the previous summer, and naturally they made good use of the occasion. This document presented a sorry tale of neglect and incompetence in many fields. One MP thought it 'a hideous plagiarism of the Crimea report', showing that, after half a century, Britain had learnt nothing as to how to prepare for a major war.[13] To name but a few revelations, troops in south Africa had been issued with the wrong ammunition and with wrongly sighted rifles. The labyrinthine structure of the war office made planning and coordination difficult. For instance, vital intelligence information had not found its way into the hands of the secretary of state. No adequate strategic plans had been prepared for the eventuality of war against both the Transvaal and the Orange Free State. As one Liberal backbencher put it, 'if the people only realised that, owing to the conduct of the present government, between 20,000 and 30,000 British homes had been rendered desolate, it would go very hard with the government when they appealed to the country'. True, Balfour's cabinet had begun to address the problem of military administration at the superior level. In late 1903, it had established a vital new coordinating body, the committee of imperial defence, consisting of the prime minister, defence chiefs, lord president, and heads of the intelligence departments. The Esher committee on war office reform, reporting in the winter of 1903–04, brought about the abolition of the archaic post of commander-in-chief and the eventual creation of a general staff. What the public really demanded of the government, however, was an overhaul of the existing armed forces sufficient, though without involving either conscription or inordinate expense, to enable Britain to defend itself against possible invasion whilst at the same time meeting a great imperial emergency like that in south Africa. The public was not impressed by the constant shifts in military policy, and least of all by Balfour's attempts, even as late as November 1903, to blame recent wartime failures on the Liberal governments of 1892–95.

The south African war had left a legacy of increased expenditure which as yet showed little sign of abating. It was not just the army that demanded funding on a larger scale. The navy also wanted its share of the cake, and more. Naval expenditure increased from 17.6 millions in 1895 to 42.1 millions in 1905. Scared by its sense of international isolation in the recent war, the country seemed ready to aim for a three-and-a-half power standard, equal to the naval capacity of three or four potential foes at any one time. Austen Chamberlain, as chancellor of the exchequer, had the unenviable task of finding the necessary funds. His first budget, in 1904, raised income tax by 1d and the duty on tea by 2d. Opinion rated it safe, dull, and, ironically, as much a free-trade budget as any in the previous forty years. Joseph Chamberlain could hardly mount a protectionist assault on his own son's handiwork. However, though less controversial than its three predecessors, the 1904 budget was in its way significant. The Unionists appeared to have set their face against reduced expenditure, and the reduced taxation that might accompany it.

Not until 1922 would they again campaign on a programme of rigorous public economy. Probably the Chamberlains calculated that the more onerous the existing system appeared to be, the sooner might the country be converted to tariff reform and the resulting redistribution of taxation. But, in the meantime, valuable ground was, in consequence, abandoned to the Liberals. Hicks Beach lamented the loss of an opportunity to do something for one of the Unionists' natural constituencies, 'those who are above the income-tax limit and yet do not possess an income of more than £2,000 and are heavily rated as it is'.[14] The Liberals would now emerge as the party of income-tax reform and graduation, and, of more immediate consequence, as the opponents of 'the demon of extravagance'. Their identification, for the time being, with the twin cause of reduced expenditure and reduced taxation was to contribute substantially to their landslide electoral victory in 1906.

The Unionists' main legislative effort in 1904 proved as controversial as anything else which they attempted. This came in the form of the licensing act, by which the government hoped to placate the temperance lobby and at the same time safeguard the interests of the brewers who, for a generation and more, had been among the Unionists' more stalwart supporters. A recent legal case, *Sharp* v. *Wakefield*, had called in question the right of a publican to expect the more or less automatic renewal of his licence. Magistrates had of late been cutting down on the number of licences issued, in the general interests of sobriety. The government's measure now proposed to transfer responsibility for licensing from magistrates to quarter sessions, and at the same time to establish a special fund, made up of contributions from all public-house keepers, to compensate any of them whose licence was not renewed. To many nonconformists and temperance advocates, this appeared tantamount to endowing the drink trade by turning all publicans' licences into a species of property. Other groups were also offended, among them the JPs, who found their authority reduced, and who numbered in their ranks many traditionally Unionist voters. Liberals, on the other hand, attacked the legislation as of a piece with the government's general disposition to favour plutocratic and monopolistic interests. Balfour's administration had once again displayed its willingness to tackle highly sensitive political subjects; indeed, it had done so across a wider field than had any since Gladstone's first administration of 1868–74. In many ways, Balfour seemed especially concerned to reverse the legacy of this particular government, whether in terms of Irish land policy, temperance, education, or army reform. It remained to be seen whether his own government would founder as had his predecessor's: through defeat in the House of Commons, followed by a crushing rejection at the polls.

However, by far the most emotive issue to agitate the 1904 session of parliament was, to give it its commonest designation, that of Chinese slavery. Today this is an almost forgotten aspect of Edwardian history; but in its time it took on the dimensions of a political scandal of imperial mismanagement to rival anything seen since the trial of Warren Hastings. Few controversies, as it turned out, were better calculated to touch the raw nerves of a nation disillusioned by the recent war and by its unsatisfactory aftermath. Few illustrated more pointedly the dilemmas and internal contradictions of Britain's multi-faceted empire. The background to the problem lay in the shattered condition of southern Africa following on nearly three years of war. There was an urgent need to bring the economy back to life, but this task came up against a labour shortage which proved to be particularly severe in the gold mines, previously the powerhouse of southern Africa's development. In the past, the mines had depended heavily on unskilled native African labour, but for various reasons this was no longer forthcoming. Gold-mining had a notoriously bad safety record, twenty times worse, it was said, that that of British coal mines; and black workers were unlikely to be enticed from their ancestral villages by wage-levels recently reduced, by the mineowners, to one shilling a day in the interests of greater profitability. The recent war between white men had given black Africans a somewhat greater sense of status and opportunity. Many had been put in uniform and given arms to defend the British empire; and in so far as they now desired alternative employment, the railways offered much better wages than the mines. So how was the chronic labour shortage in the mines to be addressed? A number of suggestions were canvassed, but all seemed to come up against various constraints on imperial policy, not least due to the south African war itself. There was the idea of importing Indian indentured labour, as had been done in so many parts of the empire in the later nineteenth century, not least in Natal, where the Indian community was notoriously denied any semblance of civil rights. But the government of India in Calcutta, partly in response to an increasingly articulate Indian public opinion, was becoming sensitive to the treatment of its former subjects oversees. In any case, it hardly seemed wise to create a new class of imperial helots in the Transvaal so soon after a war which, nominally at least, had been undertaken to protect the rights of British citizens. Another idea was to compel black Africans to work in the mines under a system of forced labour. But this was likely to encounter vigorous protest from missionary and humanitarian organisations in Britain, and it seemed a betrayal of the more enlightened racial policies which had helped to pit Briton against Boer in southern Africa for almost a hundred years.

Chamberlain had encountered the labour shortage problem on his visit to southern Africa in early 1903. At that time he deprecated any further resort to Indian labour, ostensibly on the grounds that Indians were not sturdy enough for work in the mines, or any importation of black labourers from Nigeria or Uganda, for fear that this might expose southern Africa to new tropical diseases. He also set his face against the idea of importing Chinese so-called 'coolie' labour, an idea which was starting to attract support, not least from Milner, the British High Commissioner in south Africa. Probably Chamberlain would have stuck by this opinion as long as he remained colonial secretary. Unlike his successor, he was a politician of experience and capacity who had been prepared to overrule Milner a year earlier over the matter of suspending the constitution of Cape colony. He was aware of the prejudice in other parts of the empire against Chinese coolie labour, and he also understood something of the nonconformist conscience in Britain. After leaving office, however, Chamberlain loyally supported the government in one of his rare speeches in the 1904 parliamentary session. You could not, he argued, look to unskilled white labour to work in the gold mines, as had also been suggested, for the 'dominant race' could not safely be put alongside the black race in this way. 'If we admit equality with these inferior races', he added, 'we shall lose the power which gives us our predominance.'[15] Coming from Radical Joe, this sounds perhaps a little strange, not least as the

British empire's only chance of keeping the numbers of its white population within any kind of distance of that of its rapidly expanding rival, the United States, lay similarly in attracting a substantial immigration, especially from southern and eastern Europe.

Lyttelton, Chamberlain's successor at the colonial office, and, despite his cricketing prowess, a politician of the second eleven, was not the person to stand up to Milner and the south African mining lobby. In any case, the British government had a difficult enough path to tread, especially in the Transvaal. It had to try to rebuild the economy and to reconcile the recently warring peoples, and this required it to take account of local opinion, both Dutch and English. And, in the Transvaal at least, local opinion seemed to favour the use of Chinese coolie labour in the gold mines. This, at any rate, was the view of the Transvaal legislative council, albeit a nominated rather than elected representative body set up after the war to advise on the problems of governing the new colony. In December 1903, by 22 votes to 4, the council agreed to seek sanction for the importation of Chinese indentured labour. Interestingly the Boer representatives on the council seem to have sided with those of the mining interests, although quite a strong section of Boer opinion opposed the Chinese solution as likely further to complicate south Africa's already tangled racial situation. However, many Boer farmers were primarily concerned to keep black African labour on the land rather than let it be inveigled away to work in the mines.

Such considerations go far to explain the one-sided nature of the indentures under which the Chinese were to be hired. The coolies were forbidden from working anywhere but in the mines, or from leaving their employer except with his consent. They were not allowed to engage in trade, own land, move around without a pass, or live anywhere but in the compounds which, notoriously, were made their homes. They were bound to a maximum five-year contract, after which they would be forcibly repatriated to China. These were harsher conditions than prevailed elsewhere in the empire under the indentured labour system. Of course Chinese labour promised to be cheap, but its use amounted to an admission, and this on the part of an imperially minded government, that the world's greatest empire could not solve the problems of south Africa out of its own resources.

The matter came before parliament at Westminster early in the 1904 session, and was raised repeatedly thereafter. At the outset one Liberal MP referred to 'conditions almost of slavery' in respect of the new indentured labour system in south Africa; and the phrase 'Chinese slavery' now became current, with all its emotive associations with the struggle to suppress the slave trade in the previous century. But concern for the Chinese was not the main point at issue. What really exercised opposition speakers in the House of Commons was the theme of betrayal – betrayal of the noble cause for which the late war was supposed to have been undertaken, betrayal of the men who had died to make southern Africa, to adapt a subsequent phrase, a land fit for British heroes to live in. The issue of Chinese slavery gave the Liberals an opportunity of revenge for the khaki election of 1900. 'We recall', said Campbell-Bannerman,

> the terms of the war prospectus – it was to be a miners' war, there were to be new openings, fresh fields of labour, smiling homes for British families, as soon as a semi-barbarous civilisation and an effete form of government had made way for the higher ideals! Where is their valour and where is their rectitude that they have not a word to say for the British workman now that he is to be snuffed out by the Chinaman?[16]

Liberals now delighted to recall in particular Chamberlain's inflated rhetoric in 1900, and especially the speech in which he had called upon British miners to vote Unionist on the grounds that the war in south Africa was a miners' war, undertaken in order that justice might be done to British workers in the Transvaal. Now, apparently, 'the government proposed to substitute for them Chinese'. More than anything, the issue undermined the Unionists' claim to be the friend and protector of the British working man, a claim otherwise compatible enough with imperialism and tariff reform. Now, just at the moment when the government was purporting to safeguard British jobs at home by the introduction of aliens legislation, it was reducing the scope for employment in the empire by importing yellow labour at starvation wages. The whole policy could plausibly be explained as part of a wider assault by the Unionist government on trades unionism and what one Liberal MP called 'the solidarity of white labour', both at home and overseas. As such, it seemed of a piece with what could be termed the plutocratic trend of Unionist policies in other areas, for instance licensing legislation and, arguably also, tariff reform.

The spectre of the Uitlanders returned to haunt British politics in the matter of Chinese slavery. Five years earlier, this highly controversial community had seriously divided English loyalties. To the Unionists they appeared as lawful British subjects oppressed by a would-be foreign power; to the Liberals they appeared as cosmopolitan adventurers bent on dragging Britain into conflict for their own money-grubbing purposes. The issue of Chinese slavery strengthened the latter interpretation, and allowed opposition speakers to indulge in a degree of xenophobia of which even Joseph Chamberlain might have been proud. Anti-semitism was an additional element. Liberals sneered at the foreign-sounding names of many of the mineowners of the Rand – 'Eckstein, Bernstein, Goldstein, and all the other steins' – as one of them put it. The demand for Asiatic labour, he added, 'was the demand of financiers who were impatient, with their fingers itching to grasp the gold which was in the ground'. 'The trail of alien financiers', declared an Irish Nationalist member, 'is slimed all over the map of south Africa. They are a horde of hook-nosed, beetle-browed, and beady-eyed foreigners, who tell us that places like Canada and New Zealand ought to mind their own business.'[17] Here was further ammunition against the government, as well as evidence that its latest policy in south Africa was in contradiction with many of its professed intentions elsewhere. Balfour, as much as Chamberlain, desired to see a strengthening of the ties which held the empire together; but it was notorious that the use of Chinese indentured labour in the Transvaal was opposed by all the self-governing colonies, by Cape Colony as well as by Canada, Australia and New Zealand. All had sent men to fight and die in a war to secure the whole of south Africa for the empire and the British race, and all felt that they had a right to be consulted in the final settlement. This was a point pressed home particularly by Liberal Imperialists like Asquith, and also by dissident Conservatives such as Churchill and Seely, whose loyalty to their party was now close to breaking point.

Balfour's government, it must be admitted, rather bungled the presentation of its policy. Apart from the prime minister himself, it lacked debating talent, and its members tended to see the whole matter as a case of the British public in one of its periodical fits of morality. One compared conditions in the Chinese mining encampments to life in a British public school. Another said that they were no worse than those endured by the British private soldier. Balfour claimed that so-called Chinese slavery was in fact no worse than the system of indentured labour under which Indian workers had been exported to Guiana and the Caribbean. But his opponents pointed out that the latter were at least not confined to compounds and were allowed to undertake skilled work and to stay on in the colony after their contracts had expired. Much though the whole matter agitated members of parliament, it seems to have exercised opinion in the country even more, and it certainly helped to cost the government further by-election losses in the spring and early summer, for instance in East Dorset and Devonport. It also completed the disillusionment of several Unionist MPs, and persuaded them to cross the floor of the House of Commons. It was in the spring of 1904 that Churchill and Seely abandoned the Unionists and moved over to the opposition benches. Both had served in south Africa, and both would subsequently become Liberal cabinet ministers.

Tariff reform, however, remained the most potent cause of Unionist disintegration. Throughout the 1904 session, and that which followed, the government stood in constant risk of defeat in the House of Commons on a free-trade motion, whether moved by the opposition or by one of its own backbenchers. Whenever ill health, for example, forced Balfour to be absent from the house, his lieutenants had the greatest difficulty in presenting the government's case, not least because they had no very clear idea what it was. An example of this came early in the session, on the occasion of a Liberal amendment against tariff-reform agitation. Ministers responded with an amendment of their own, undertaking at least not to impose any new taxation upon food, but then had to withdraw this in response to protectionist pressure from their own backbenches. In general, Balfour's strategy was to express broad sympathy for protectionist ideas and aspirations, but not to do anything to put them into effect. He calculated that the tariff reformers in his own party would not vote against him and force a general election after the battering which their cause had received in the by-elections earlier in the year. At the same time, he counted on retaining the loyalty of at least a substantial proportion of Unionist free-traders, or free fooders as they tended to be called. These numbered some fifty or more MPs, often drawn from more traditional elites, such as long-established landed families or representatives of university constituencies. Were all the free fooders to act in unison, they could imperil the government's very existence, but Balfour reckoned that most of them would be reluctant to put him out of power and risk setting up Chamberlain in his place. Resentment against Radical Joe remained rife among more traditional-minded and high-Anglican Tories, not least because he continued to maintain his support for the principle of Church disestablishment. Balfour, by his tactics, contrived to divide the free fooders, and to ensure that they did not become too serious a threat to his government, though this proved to be at the cost of alienating a dozen of them sufficiently to impel them to cross the floor of the house and join the Liberal party.

Why did Balfour determine to cling on to office in this fashion, without, apparently, any very clear idea of what to do with it? By so doing, he forfeited much of the credibility and authority which his government had inherited from its predecessor. He had accomplished major legislative objectives in 1902 and 1903, but now he seemed unable to provide a lead on the most challenging issue of the day. His policy of commercial retaliation, if and when circumstances and public opinion seemed to require it, was vaguely formulated, and in any case Balfour never dared to put it into effect for fear of losing all the Unionist free traders. It was becoming difficult to know what the Unionist coalition stood for any more, and this was certainly one consideration which deterred Balfour from calling an early general election. Also, he believed that he could still accomplish worthwhile tasks in office. He could preside over useful reforms in the army's high command, and over the transformation of Britain's foreign policy, which was taking the country further and further away from the isolationism of Victorian days. Most of all, he could keep the Liberals out of power a while longer, during which time something might turn up that would embarrass them. Balfour continued to hope that Irish home rule might once again become, in the minds of the voters, the burning issue which it had been a decade or so previously, and thereby serve to halt the Liberal revival. This might well have happened had a minority Liberal government entered office in 1904 dependent on Irish Nationalist support. However, by hanging on to office until the end of the following year, Balfour brought about such an accumulation of grievances against his government as to ensure an overwhelming Liberal triumph at the polls.

Equally to the point is the question of why Chamberlain allowed the situation to continue for as long as it did. Naturally assertive and dynamic, one might have expected him to use his parliamentary strength against Balfour's government, rather than put up any longer with its continued shilly-shallying on fiscal affairs. Once the Unionists were in opposition, Chamberlain would be much better placed to win them round to his protectionist ideas, as against the free-trade doctrines of a Liberal administration. But Chamberlain was always more cautious than he appeared, and, apart from his sense of loyalty to a colleague of many years, he had little means as yet of measuring his resources for a trial of strength with Balfour. He had won over, by mid-1904, most of the Liberal Unionist party; but this was the minority element in the coalition, and still many of its leading figures such as Devonshire continued to oppose him. As to the majority element, the Conservatives, Chamberlain's support appeared to be broad rather than deep. True, by the end of the year, he had captured the national union of Conservative associations; but experience in 1886 had taught Chamberlain the unwisdom of relying on organisation only, and of under-estimating the strength of a party's loyalty to its leader. By-elections hardly encouraged Conservatives to throw in their lot entirely with Chamberlain in the belief that his ideas were about to sweep the country. The best that he could hope for was to keep up the pressure on Balfour, and, by continuing to stump the country and address enthusiastic audiences, persuade him to move in a more protectionist direction, while at the same time avoiding any open break.

Chamberlain began to distance himself from Balfour in a speech at Birmingham in May 1904. He protested against the electorate's being denied a clear choice when it was next summoned to the hustings. Elections, he declared, were won by leading and not by waiting upon opinion, by Cromwellian methods of 'thorough' (*sic*) rather than by 'trying to catch a breeze that will never come'. Once again he emphasised his radical credentials. Throughout his career, he declared, he had been working on behalf of the poorer classes in the community. Tariff reform would effect a wholesome redistribution of wealth and come to the aid of twelve millions of the population whom Chamberlain declared to be on the verge of hunger. During the second half of 1904, Chamberlain addressed a wider variety of audiences than those whom he had reached in the previous autumn. At Welbeck, in August, he spoke to a concourse of rural labourers on the virtues of agricultural protection. In October he visited Luton, and in December, Limehouse, in a rare public appearance in the great metropolis, whose ways, like the Chartists and Gladstone before him, he seemed to regard with some suspicion. Here, he once again lamented the decline of British manufacturing and the concomitant rise of the financial sector and of service industries. In the course of all this, and partly on the prompting of his son, Austen Chamberlain, Balfour did come some small way to meet him. In his Edinburgh speech of October 1904, he promised to call a colonial conference in the event of winning the next general election. Should it agree on a scheme of imperial preference, he would then call a second election to obtain a mandate for its implementation. Chamberlain had to accept this elaborate formula for the time being as an alternative to a showdown that might wreck the Unionist alliance. His supporters did, shortly afterwards, carry a protectionist resolution at the Southampton conference of the national union, but Balfour evaded the issue by devoting his subsequent speech to a sudden crisis which had blown up in Anglo-Russian relations. (This was the Dogger Bank incident, when Russian warships fired on British fishing vessels.) For half a century, the Russian threat had loomed large and had helped to undermine and topple several governments. Now it served to provide Balfour's hapless administration with a further lease of life.

Little good, it may be added, did it do him. The 1905 parliamentary session was to prove one of the most humiliating ever endured by a British government in modern times. Balfour had hoped that the Irish home rule issue would return to threaten Liberal party unity. Instead it exploded in his own face. In

February, he was forced to accept the resignation of the Irish chief secretary, Wyndham, who was believed to favour plans for administrative devolution in Ireland prepared by the under-secretary, Sir Anthony MacDonnell. The episode demonstrated the power of the Ulster Unionist lobby, which was to assume such proportions seven or eight years later. Along with the departure of Selborne to be governor-general in south Africa, it deprived Balfour of the services of almost the last of his confidants and able ministerial colleagues. Most important of all, it called in question the commitment of Balfour's government to the full preservation of the Irish union, virtually the one remaining matter of principle around which his supporters could rally. The Liberals could claim that their own plans for Ireland were merely an elaboration of those under consideration in Balfour's cabinet. MacDonnell himself, it was noted, did not resign; partly because, as a senior civil servant, he enjoyed the powerful protection of Lansdowne, dating from their years together in India. If the Unionists were no longer reliable on Ireland, what indeed were they good for? They could not even command majorities on ordinary Irish business in the House of Commons. Twice they were defeated there on the Irish estimates, the first time in February 1904 and the second in July 1905. On neither occasion did Balfour see fit to resign, though the Liberals had gratefully accepted an opportunity to quit office in similar circumstances in 1895.

Balfour's determination to cling on to power took some extreme forms. The most notorious example came in March 1905, when he led the bulk of his supporters out of the House of Commons' chamber, rather than allow their internal divisions to be exposed in a debate on Liberal free-trade resolutions. One observer considered that, as prime minister, Balfour had suffered a loss of dignity without precedent in the annals of parliament. His manoeuvres allowed the Liberals to pose, for a change, as the party of constitutionalism and parliamentary control. Truly, the wheel had come full circle since the period, a decade earlier, when Rosebery's government had tried to eke out its precarious existence without any clear leadership or mandate. During its final parliamentary session, Balfour's administration would have little to show in terms of useful legislation. Army reform continued to make only lagging progress. Liberals like Churchill lambasted the government's lack of a consistent military policy. Three war secretaries had come up with three successive plans for overhauling the land forces of the crown, and not one of them had yet been realised. The latest plan, proposed by Arnold-Forster, involved scaling down the volunteers in the interests of economy and efficiency, but this had come up against a powerful lobby of opinion that considered the performance of the volunteer units to have been one of the few encouraging aspects of the campaigns of 1899–1902. Other Liberals attacked the government from a different angle, for failing to follow up the findings of the committee on physical deficiency which had reported in 1903. This was another by-product of the recent war, called into being in response to the poor physical quality of many would-be recruits. Two years further on, however, nothing had as yet been done to tackle the relevant problems of childhood malnutrition and poor health.

Balfour's administration, nonetheless, did make two gestures in 1905 in connection with social policy, both of which to some extent broke new ground. One of these was the Aliens Act, following up the recommendations of a royal commission, which allowed the home secretary to debar or deport undesirable immigrants. A forerunner of the immigration legislation of more recent decades, it was designed to safeguard living standards and employment in inner-city areas, but it does not seem to have accomplished much more than to preserve one or two Unionist seats in the east of London in the debacle of 1906. The other piece of social legislation was the Unemployed Workmen Act, also carried in 1905. This allowed local authorities to undertake public works projects for the relief of unemployment in their areas. It marked a new step in official concern about an evident social problem, although one which as yet touched a relatively small minority of the population. Balfour would have pleased a much larger proportion of the electorate had he thrown his weight behind a Trade Disputes Bill which in 1905 passed the House of Commons on its second reading by 238:199. This was a private member's measure, which proposed to overturn recent legal decisions and restore to trades unions their former freedom from the law of conspiracy and from liability for damages. This would have guaranteed them the kind of privileged status which Disraeli had had in mind in his legislation of 1875. But Balfour declined to follow in the footsteps of his illustrious predecessor, and, denied government backing, the Trade Disputes Bill failed to make further progress in the House of Commons. This was to tell heavily against Unionist candidates in industrial constituencies at the ensuing general election, not least in Lancashire, where it contributed to costing Balfour his own seat.

The year 1905 set the scene for one of the more dramatic developments of Edwardian times, the sudden upsurge of feminist militancy. In one sense, of course, this was part of a long revolution stretching well back into Victorian times, which had already begun to change women's status and male perceptions of their role. Women had broken into formerly male preserves such as universities and the professions. They had won the vote at local government level, and they had come to participate actively in national political organisations like the primrose league. The campaign against the contagious diseases acts had represented a distinct success for Victorian feminism. But the movement for women's emancipation faltered somewhat at the turn of the century. A Bill to give women the parliamentary franchise on the same terms as men passed its second reading in the house of commons by 71 votes in 1897, but thereafter the subject was not raised again until 1904 when a similar motion was carried by a majority of 114. Clearly the times were now more propitious. Partly this had to do with Balfour's administration, and its willingness to tackle controversial subjects. One Liberal MP, supporting votes for women, declared that 'he did not think there had ever been any parliament which had attacked so many institutions and upset so many settled ideas'. But by 1904 and 1905 this was also a dying parliament, whose members, aware of the approach of a general election, were anxious to please as many members of the community as possible. Recent mass demonstrations by those out of work had helped persuade the government to pass the Unemployed Workmen Act, and one such demonstration in Manchester seems to have inspired the Pankhursts with the idea of direct action. Expectations were starting to run high. A general election, it was assumed, would bring to power a Liberal government, which would surely be more sympathetic to democratic reform than its predecessor had been. And, even if not, it would surely be susceptible to outside pressure in the way that Gladstone's second administration had been when faced with Irish agrarian agitation. The Pankhursts determined to push at what they believed to be a half-open door, and in late 1905 commenced a campaign of heckling and harassment of Liberal politicians which would, by degrees, assume ever more militant proportions.

By-elections in the course of 1905 contined to sound to knell of Balfour's administration. Seven more seats were lost, as against eight in the preceding year. The most serious single defeat, in the normally Conservative stronghold of Brighton in the spring, provoked calls from Lloyd George and Churchill for the government's immediate resignation. Not surprisingly, Balfour did not oblige. He regarded such setbacks as justification for his strategy of hanging on. Chamberlain took the opposite view. The longer the Unionists continued in office, he believed, the greater would be the smash when it eventually arrived. The party's present demoralisation was caused by drift and lack of leadership on fiscal policy. A period in opposition would revitalise it and enable it to agree on a common purpose, hopefully under the tariff-reform banner. Balfour and Chamberlain, who had parted so amicably as cabinet colleagues in September 1903, were now very much at cross-purposes. Each in his speeches seemed to contradict the other. Balfour refused to give government backing to the Trades Disputes Bill; Chamberlain insisted that the tariff reformers were the natural allies of trades unions seeking protection against exploitation and foreign competition. Balfour considered that the British empire was safe in his hands. He scored a parliamentary triumph with a speech in May 1905 reviewing Britain's defence position, and he seems to have believed that his foreign-policy successes, in particular the Anglo-French entente would in the end vindicate his government, just as the lack of such successes had helped to bring about the fall of Gladstone's first and second administrations. Chamberlain, on the other hand, held that the empire stood at a vital turning-point in its fortunes, and that it would soon begin to fall apart if it were not in the near future more effectively secured by the establishment of an imperial common market.

Chamberlain's campaigning speeches continued throughout 1905, with their heavy imperial emphasis. This was, after all, the aspect of his thinking most likely to inspire his audiences, and to appeal to their idealism and sense of history. But there was a sense in which Chamberlain, to borrow one of his son's more notorious phrases, had by now missed the bus. The popularity of empire, which had reached its apogee in the late 1890s and early 1900s, had just begun to wane. An example of the change in mood came in 1904 when parliament more or less repudiated Younghusband's expedition to Tibet, which had resulted in considerable slaughter and the imposition of a humiliating peace treaty upon the Dalai Lama. Younghusband possessed a herioc reputation and a stong mystical streak, much as Gordon had before him, but his type was no longer quite so much in fashion. MPs protested against foreign complications and the unconstitutional use of the Indian army outside the confines of the Raj, and Balfour's government abandoned its forward policy in Asia much as Gladstone had done after the second Afghan war. In southern Africa, memories of recent success in war were soured by continuing problems of readjustment. The war itself still had to be paid for, as was made clear in 1905 by Austen Chamberlain's second budget, which, though it reduced the duty on tea, maintained the level of income tax unchanged. And though Joseph Chamberlain continued to argue that the south African war had above all demonstrated the strength of imperial ties of sentiment, many British soldiers remembered with some resentment how well paid the colonial troops had been compared to themselves. Clearly the white dominions were prospering well enough as it was; and yet Chamberlain, it could be argued, was asking the people of Britain to make certain sacrifices in order that their kinsmen across the sea could prosper even more.

Chamberlain, in his speeches, did try to allow for this resentment. He spoke of the white dominions as younger nations, rapidly growing to manhood, yet still attached by sentiment to the mother country; but he warned that they might soon enough become sufficiently wealthy and populous to break away from Britain's orbit, and even emerge as rivals to her, unless their loyalty was in the meantime secured by powerful bonds of economic self-interest. Crucial to Chamberlain's case was his contention that the initiative in seeking closer imperial ties had come from the white colonies and dominions, and that it was up to Britain to respond to an opportunity that might never be repeated. Quite what this initiative actually amounted to was never made clear. Chamberlain claimed that, at the 1902 colonial conference, the assembled prime ministers had more or less unanimously offered Britain preferential trading arrangements if she were to do the same in turn for them. Canada, it is true, had lowered its protective walls in 1897 to allow favoured treatment to British imports, and had lowered them somewhat further in 1902. But, as to Australia, New Zealand, and the other white colonies, indications of support for Chamberlain's ideas were only of the vaguest kind. Liberal politicians, indeed, denied that such a sentiment existed to any real extent or purpose. Of the twenty-one parliaments in the British empire, only one, that of Manitoba, had come out in support for Chamberlain's plan of imperial economic union. Rosebery was probably Chamberlain's most effective Liberal antagonist on this score. Never very decisive in government, or in putting forward a strong line of his own, he was at his best in opposing a positive programme proposed by anybody else; and his speeches made at this time against tariff reform ranked as among the ablest and most effective of his career. Rosebery here enjoyed several advantages. He had all the glamour of a former prime minister, and his general devotion to the cause of empire could not be held in doubt. More than any other leading Liberal, more than Chamberlain himself, he knew the empire at first hand from his extensive travelling, and he could therefore speak with some confidence of what he under-stood to be Australia's lack of enthusiasm for closer economic ties with Britain. Along with other Liberals, he recalled the lessons of the American war of independence, a conflict engendered by Britain's attempts to keep her colonies within the economic straitjacket of the Navigation Acts. Far from promoting imperial unity, it could be argued that Chamberlain's grand protectionist design would only sow dissension between the colonies and their mother country, and would eventually do for the second British empire what mercantilism had done for the first. Rosebery also attacked Chamberlain along a wider front. If imperial matters really were as critical as Chamberlain suggested, what did this say for his record during eight years and more as colonial secretary? In campaigning for such a personal mandate to overhaul Britain's fiscal and economic system, was Chamberlain not making the same arrogant mistake as had Gladstone in 1874?

Chamberlain had long had it in his power to bring down Balfour's government, and in late 1905 he was instrumental in so doing. As a *tombeur de gouvernements* he was unrivalled in British politics, rather as was Clemenceau in France. Balfour's fall from office was to prove the only change of administration in a period of twenty years, indeed the only one within the scope of this book, and as such it is worth examining in some detail. Balfour's own intentions, as so often, remain obscure, but his hand was forced by a succession of events in November 1905. The first of these was a major speech by Chamberlain at Birmingham in which he took Balfour's government, with its 'timorous counsels and half-hearted convictions' even more to task than previously. After the humiliations of the 1905 session, and the constant 'running away from our political adversaries', Chamberlain sensed that to most Conservatives he would no longer appear disloyal in urging the party to be quit of office. In opposition, the Unionists could resume their freedom of manoeuvre, and find a new rallying-point and sense of unity. 'I would rather', said Chamberlain, not foreseeing the dimensions of the approaching Liberal landslide, 'be a member of a powerful minority than of an impotent majority'. This viewpoint was confirmed by a strongly protectionist resolution passed at the Conservatives' Newcastle conference, also in November, and Chamberlain followed this up later in the month with a speech at Bristol, to the Liberal Unionist Council, in which he proclaimed that in future the common economic programme of all Unionists would be one of imperial preference and commercial retaliation.

Balfour was now left with a restricted range of options. He could meet parliament and endeavour to struggle through another session, but, following Chamberlain's recent speeches, his survival in office would be even more problematic than in 1905. He could propose a reduction in Ireland's representation at Westminster as one measure that might still command widespread Unionist support. But this would provoke violent controversy and contradict his own recent efforts to keep Ireland quiet. Balfour, who had taken on a number of vested interests in the past few years, was not prepared to challenge this one also. Alternatively, he could dissolve parliament and call a general election, but his supporters had no agreed economic policy to put before the country. In a speech at Newcastle, Balfour had made a last effort to rally opinion against what he alleged to be opposition plans to increase social expenditure. To a considerable extent, this anticipated the spirit of Conservatism in the 1920s, but in 1905 Chamberlain had no use for cuts in public spending which might militate against his plans for a redistribution of taxation. As a final option, Balfour could resign office and hand the poisoned chalice over to the Liberals. On past performance, they might well fall out among themselves once faced with the difficulties of forming a government and making immediate policy decisions. This would hardly benefit them in an early general election, and it might prevent Campbell-Bannerman from forming any ministry at all, in which case Balfour could resume office with his position reinforced. The cue was provided by a speech made by Rosebery at Bodmin in late November 1905, in which he denounced any policy of giving Ireland home rule, even on the gradualist lines laid down by Campbell-Bannerman. This raised the old Irish bogey again within the Liberal party, putting a former prime minister in direct conflict with the present leader. Balfour judged it a good moment to depart. It was a very nineteenth-century manoeuvre, and the last occasion on which a prime minister surrendered the seals of office to the opposition front bench prior to a general election.

For a moment, Balfour's gambit looked like succeeding. The leading Liberal Imperialists – Asquith, Grey, and Haldane – still held Rosebery in regard, although he had often let them down. They had no very high opinion of Campbell-Bannerman, whose health was anyway suspect, and they tried to insist, as the price of their support, that he should go to the House of Lords upon becoming prime minister, leaving effective power in the hands of Asquith as leader of the House of Commons. But, once a change of government was imminent, the lure of office proved too strong, at least for Asquith, who felt that the Liberals had been in opposition long enough. Privately he agreed with Campbell-Bannerman about a step-by-step policy towards Ireland and home rule, and he rightly judged that after a few years more the political succession would be his. Accordingly Asquith agreed to serve as chancellor of the exchequer, thus ensuring the construction of an effective Liberal administration. Haldane was not yet a national figure, and Grey had done little to build on the reputation which he had established as a disinterested Liberal spokesman during the south African war. Both men were lucky to receive senior office, Haldane as war secretary and Grey as foreign secretary. Campbell-Bannerman could in a sense afford to be magnanimous, as he had placed other more sympathetic colleagues in senior positions, Reid in the lord chancellorship, Morley at the India office, Herbert Gladstone at the home office, and Lloyd George at the board of trade. He passed over for consideration as foreign secretary two senior House of Commons figures who were in some ways eminently qualified: Morley and Dilke. Morley was an experienced politician whose skills, diplomatic and otherwise, were to be well demonstrated during a critical period at the India office; but evidently Campbell-Bannerman thought him too fussy and over-sensitive to make a good foreign secretary. Dilke, once a rising star in the Liberal party, remained a leading authority on military matters and international affairs, but his career had been badly damaged by a divorce scandal in the 1880s, and in any case Campbell-Bannerman had never forgiven him for his desertion on the cordite vote in 1895.

Foreign policy lies largely beyond the scope of this survey. However, Grey's was to prove the most fateful of Campbell-Bannerman's appointments. A man of insular habits, who disliked foreign travel, he was to preside over British foreign policy during one of its most critical decades, and his decisions, whether soundly based or otherwise, were to play their part in the descent to Armageddon. Grey was the first foreign secretary since Palmerston to be a member of the House of Commons, but he was not much inclined to take the nation into his confidence. The secret military conversations with the French, which he initiated amidst the distractions of the general election campaign in early 1906, were for years known only to an inner circle of the cabinet, yet they provided a key factor in influencing Britain to go to war in 1914. Partly to reinforce the developing Anglo-French understanding, Grey was to reach an agreement also with France's ally, Russia, in 1907, designed in addition to safeguard Britain's imperial system and the European balance of power. But it could be argued that the agreement cost Grey as much as it gained for him. Until 1914, he would face constant criticism in parliament from Labour and left-wing Liberals, who would accuse him in effect of truckling to an Asiatic despotism. Grey seemed to become obsessed with defending the principal showpiece of his foreign policy, as he saw it, although the Anglo-

Russian agreement was in many ways to reduce Britain's freedom of manoeuvre, especially in the middle east, which once
again proved to be the main international storm centre. Fearing to
endanger the new-found understanding with Russia, Grey
arguably would lose an opportunity of befriending the Ottoman
empire in the wake of the liberalising Young Turk revolution, and
thereby of contributing to the stability of a region whose underlying tensions would erupt in war in 1912, 1913, and, most fatally,
in 1914. Of course, it is questionable whether any Unionist
foreign secretary would, in the circumstances, have acted
differently. But, among the Unionists, there were men with
greater expertise than Grey in the affairs of the Islamic world
which, ranging from the Balkans to Morocco, formed the principal arc of crisis in the decade before 1914. And as, in the latter
year, so much was to depend on the timing of moves and on the
precise location of pieces on the diplomatic chessboard, one
cannot help wondering how the world situation might have
looked had a different statesman been in charge of Britain's
foreign policy over the preceding ten years.

Notes

1 Jay, R., *Joseph Chamberlain: a political study* (Oxford, 1981), p. 264.
2 *The Times*, 17 February 1903.
3 Balfour to Sir Frederick Milner, 25 May 1903. BL Add. Mss 49855.
4 4 *Hansard* CXXIII, 175ff. (28 May 1903).
5 *Ibid*. 194.
6 *Ibid*. 155ff. Balfour to Sir Frederick Milner, 25 May 1903.
7 4 *Hansard* CXXI, 1414 (5 May 1903).
8 *Annual Register*, 1903, pp. 197–200.
9 C. W. Boyd, *Mr. Chamberlain's Speeches*, II (London, 1914), pp.
125–40.
10 *Economist*, 6 June 1903.
11 4 *Hansard* CXXX, 133 (18 February 1904).
12 'Toryism and tariffs', *Fortnightly Review*, March 1906.
13 4 *Hansard* CXXIX, 410 (4 February 1904).
14 4 *Hansard* CXXXIII, 589–91 (19 April 1904).
15 4 *Hansard* CXXXVIII, 801–13 (21 July 1904).
16 4 *Hansard* CXXXII, 252 (21 March 1904).
17 *Ibid*. 329.

3

New Liberalism for old, 1906–1910

A change of government signalled the start of a general election campaign, although parliament was not in fact dissolved until 8 January 1906. The campaign's pattern was soon established. Indeed it bore some ironic similarities with that of 1900. Once again, it was the opposition and not the government that was primarily on trial, although the two had of course only recently changed hands. Once again Balfour and Chamberlain were the most prominent of speakers, but for them it was now an uphill task. Balfour in particular had to struggle against the widely-held prejudice that he had tarried in office too long for any good that he had done. In a speech at Manchester in mid-December, he laboured hard to justify the timing of his recent resignation, partly on the grounds that he could no longer be confident of carrying a Redistribution of Seats Bill through the House of Commons.[1] But this raised a number of questions. Why had he not tackled redistribution much earlier, when he had still had a secure majority? If resignation was indeed his wish, why had he not taken this step before, for instance after defeat on the Irish estimates, or following the extension of the Anglo-Japanese treaty in the summer of 1905? On the other hand, if the Liberals really were as dreadful as he made out, why had he resigned at all and thus handed over the seals of office into their hands? In contrast to 1900, the Liberals did not offer Balfour an easy target in the election campaign of December 1905–January 1906. He tried to make something of their supposed lack of homogeneity, but this was belied by the fact that they had just come together effectively to form a government. Otherwise Balfour's one resource was to try to raise the bogey of home rule. But this was now hardly a subject with which to agitate the nation. Home rule was more or less ruled out of court by the existence of an unreformed House of Lords, which would surely reject it as decisively as had been done in 1893. Leading Liberals promised that a home rule measure would not be brought before the next parliament, and they had an ideal reply to Balfour in claiming that they only intended to build upon the devolving intentions of the late Unionist government which had culminated in Wyndham's resignation. Unionists had on occasion flirted with the Irish Nationalists when in power. Balfour's tactics now cost him, to a considerable extent, the support of both the Irish and anti-Irish vote in Britain, in sharp contrast to 1900.

Chamberlain ran a rather different campaign from Balfour's, as befitted the two men's relationship since 1903. His emphasis was still very much on fiscal reform, but here clearly he had little new to say. The arguments of 1903 and 1904, harking back to the radical Toryism of the 1840s, did service once again. There was renewed insistence on the Chartists' protectionist credentials and on the fact that free trade had been sprung upon the country by a largely middle-class electorate. After sixty years of Cobdenism, which had moreover failed to convert the rest of the world, it was time for a change.[2] Amongst the major speakers on either side, Chamberlain sounded most like a social reformer, though, as in previous years, he spoilt his own case by a muddled use of statistics, as for instance by his assertion that one million of the population were in the workhouse. Chamberlain argued that tariff reform was the only effective means of combatting unemployment and the social deprivation that went with it. He mocked Liberal palliatives such as the idea of public relief works, or national workshops on the French model of 1848, put forward by Morley in a speech at Walthamstow in November 1905. And he made much of Liberal admissions that all was apparently not well with the free-trade system, as for instance in a speech of Campbell-Bannerman's in 1903, which suggested that one-third of the population was living in hunger. But the Liberals were careful to exclude such material from their campaign speeches of December 1905 and January 1906. Denied any obvious target, Chamberlain, like Balfour, too often seemed to be tilting at windmills.

Campbell-Bannerman's government did take one policy decision in the interval between taking office and going to the polls. This was to halt immediately the importation of Chinese indentured labourers into south Africa. The Unionist response was varied. Chamberlain declared that the decision imperilled economic recovery in the region. Balfour accused the government of hypocrisy in not also repatriating all the Chinese labourers already there. But the spotlight was once again on the whole issue, which now emerged as the most emotive of the general election campaign. It was the equivalent of the pro-Boer slur of 1900. No other matter generated so much rowdyism at public meetings, only it was now the Unionists who had to struggle to make themselves heard. Balfour, in particular, was thrown onto the defensive, especially in his own constituency of East Manchester, but he also felt obliged to devote the whole of a speech which he delivered further afield, at Leamington, to justifying his actions with regard to Chinese labour. Everywhere Unionist candidates complained of the scurrilous nature of Liberal campaign literature on the subject, with pamphlets containing graphic depictions of Chinamen being manacled and flogged. This was Milner's fault, for in 1905 he had unwisely sanctioned such flogging against the strict terms of the Transvaal labour ordinance, and he could thus be said to have had a hand in Balfour's overthrow just as other 'prancing proconsuls' had done in the case of Beaconsfield in 1880. The issue of Chinese slavery caught fire particularly in industrial constituencies, where Unionists could more easily be accused of plutocratic sympathies and hostility towards trade unionism (Doc. 7). But Lloyd George did not neglect to exploit the question in his native Wales, warning that the return of a Unionist government would mean 'slavery in the hills' and Chinamen working mines and quarries.[3]

W. E. Gladstone, had he lived, could happily have been a Liberal candidate in 1906. (One cannot speak with the same confidence of 1910.) The election campaign was the last great rally of nineteenth-century Liberalism, which was able to rediscover many of the themes dearest to its heart, prominent amongst which were public economy, free trade, and opposition to imperial over-extension (Doc. 8). There was little mention of expensive schemes of social reform which Gladstone had tended to deplore. Campbell-Bannerman set the keynote in major speeches in Glasgow, Liverpool and at the Albert Hall. Like his colleagues, he concentrated on the sins of the late Unionist government, and though he acknowledged the existence of grave social problems and unemployment, he offered little in the way of definite remedies. He repeated long-standing Liberal ideas about reforming the land laws and enabling the urban unemployed to return to work in the countryside. But mainly he urged sweeping reductions in public expenditure, and therewith taxation, in order to eliminate waste and expand the economy.[4] Popular with most classes of voter, this was roughly the same programme as Gladstone had advocated in 1880 (Doc. 9).

Polling began on 14 January 1906, and as usual stretched over a fortnight and more. As in 1895 and 1900, the earliest results set a pattern which would prove difficult to break. The first day's returns brought a dramatic gain of fifteen seats for the Liberals and five for Labour, but the most dramatic news of all was that of Balfour's defeat in Manchester after a large-scale turnover of votes. The Unionists lost heavily in Lancashire at the start, and would continue to do so as the election unfolded. The second day saw the Liberal tide reach into other unexpected areas, and in particular the great metropolis. London and its suburbs had largely resisted Liberalism since the third Reform Act of 1884–85, but now it rewarded the party with over half its seats. Over the following days, the bandwagon continued to roll. Only a few Unionist citadels held out in urban England, among them Liverpool, Sheffield, and most notably Birmingham, where Chamberlain's men were re-elected with respectable majorities. Chamberlain's son, Austen, lately chancellor of the exchequer, was also returned to Westminster, but the same could not be said for most of his cabinet colleagues. A striking feature of the results was the defeat not only of Balfour but also of those who had resigned alongside him. Brodrick, Long, Lyttelton, Gerald Balfour, Fellowes, Lord Stanley – all lost their seats in what seemed a clear repudiation of the record of Balfour's recent government.

It now remained to be seen whether the English counties and the Celtic fringe would repeat the pattern revealed in the English towns and cities. Once polling began, it was clear that the electoral rot had spread to rural areas of England which the

Unionists had long considered peculiarly their own. Unionist strongholds went down even in the south-east and in the home counties, with the Liberals, most unusually, gaining 3 county seats in Surrey, 3 in Kent, 2 in Hertfordshire, and 2 in Sussex. A feature of the Liberal success was its ubiquity. The party gained no less than 7 seats in Cheshire, but it also added considerably to its tally in rural areas where it had traditionally remained strong, such as East Anglia and the West Country. Clearly the one-time agriculturalists' creed of protection had failed to impress the countryside this time round, in the way that many Chamberlainite Unionists had hoped. Perhaps they should have known better anyway. Protection, although not imperial preference, may have been regarded with affection by land-owners and farmers, but it was not seen in the same light by the broad mass of low-paid agricultural labourers, who would be the first to suffer from any increase in the cost of living. Folk memories of the 'dear loaf' of the 1830s and 1840s remained strong in the countryside, and were regularly played upon by Liberals. The last time the threat of protection, or fair trade, had surfaced at a general election had been in 1885. That was also the first year in which the newly enfranchised agricultural labourers had been able to exercise the vote, and they had recorded a decisive verdict in favour of the Liberals across most of the counties of England.

The Liberals in 1906 also capitalised on their existing strength in Wales and Scotland, indeed making a virtually clean sweep of all the seats in the principality. North of the border, they took back many of the seats lost in 1900, including 4 in Glasgow, where Bonar Law was one of the Unionists who succumbed. The Liberals would have done better still but for Labour intervention in a number of constituencies; but Scotland was an exception in 1906 to the otherwise general co-operation between the two parties, and this even allowed the Unionists to gain one or two seats, such as Govan and North-West Lanark. Elsewhere, both Liberals and Labour party (as the LRC now began to call itself) benefited from the pact, or rather understanding, agreed to by Herbert Gladstone and Ramsay MacDonald earlier in 1903 in order to avoid the kind of three-cornered contests which worked in the Unionists' favour. Both men undertook to use their good offices to persuade their respective parties not to contest a select number of seats. As a result, Labour was given a clear run against the Unionists in 31 constituencies, of which it won 24, doing especially well in Lancashire where Liberal prospects had not been thought to be so good. By the same token, Liberals were favoured by Labour's non-intervention in many other constituencies, although this was by no means universally the case. Labour fought Liberal in no less than 25 seats, though it only managed to win 6 of these, and in the process helped to let in 7 Unionists. The Labour party's successes were supplemented by the election of some 24 Lib–Lab MPs, many of them miners, who were still numbered among the Liberal party. Most of Labour's gains came early in the election, and they forced leading Liberals slightly onto the defensive. Labour's programme, Asquith argued, in order to reassure Liberal voters, was really far less radical than Chamberlain's, and as to increased rights for trade unions, this would not be in derogation of *laissez-faire*, but would enable the best and freest bargain to be struck between capital and labour.[5]

It is instructive to compare some statistics of the 1906 general election with those of 1900. One of the more striking is the overall increase in the vote. Even the Unionist tally went up markedly, from 1.768 million in 1900 to 2.422 million in 1906, whereas that of the Liberals rose from 1.572 million to 2.751 million, and that of Labour from 62,000 to 321,000. The explanation, for the increased Unionist vote at least, lies in the much reduced number of uncontested returns. Only 13 Unionists were unopposed in 1906 (mostly in Ulster or in university constituencies) as compared to 163 in 1900. There were 27 unopposed Liberal returns in 1906, 12 of them in Wales, as against 22 in 1900. The percentage poll difference, standing at 49.4 per cent to 43.4 per cent, between Liberals and Unionists was not in fact that huge, but the disparity in seats was far greater, with the Liberals garnering 400 as against the Unionists' 157. Of these Liberal seats, 306 were in England, in striking contrast to the mere 112 and 122 which they had retained in 1895 and 1900 respectively. One last quirk of the election concerns the Irish Nationalist party, which, with only 35,000 votes or 0.7 per cent of the total, returned to Westminster 83 strong. No less than 74 of its seats were uncontested, hence its low overall poll. Rarely had its predominance in some four-fifths of Ireland's constituencies seemed more complete, for it had largely recovered the internal unity still lacking in 1900. But already there was a cloud on the horizon, albeit as yet no bigger than a man's hand. In 1905 a new party, Sinn Fein, had been formed, inspired partly by the Irish language revival, and demanding a more complete separation from Britain than that envisaged by home rule. Its time was not yet, but it would come.

What would the Liberals do with their massive new majority? Historians have tended to see the parliamentary sessions of 1906 and 1907 as something of an anti-climax after a Liberal landslide unparalleled since that of 1832, although this is a view open to dispute. The Liberals, it is argued, had at this time a great reforming opportunity which was not fully grasped, partly because the House of Lords blocked some important measures, and partly because the government itself was slow to develop the concept of a 'new Liberalism', involving wide-ranging schemes of social reform, which became its hallmark some years later. Both these propositions require to be tested, beginning with the latter. It is important to bear in mind what the country had, and had not, voted for in January–February 1906. Paradoxically, it had swung to the Liberals on essentially conservative instincts, regarding the Unionists for the time being as the party of unnecessary innovation and of grandiose and expensive schemes of social engineering both in Britain and in the empire. What the country was looking for, after the alarms and uncertainties of the previous few years, was a period of calm and stable administration, some reversal perhaps of the more obvious excesses of Balfour's regime, and above all retrenchment and reduced taxation.

How did Campbell-Bannerman's government measure up to these expectations? Asquith's first budget, introduced in April 1906, was certainly safe, and some thought it rather unenterprising. The tea duty was reduced by 1d, and the coal export duty of 1901 repealed; but income tax was left at its existing high level, and the revenue surplus devoted to the reduction of debt. Clearly further expenditure cuts would have to await Haldane's review of the armed forces. In terms of social policy, the government's main achievement in its first year was the Workmen's Compensation Act. This considerably extended the state scheme of accident insurance, and, in reversal of the previous rule under the Act of 1897, declared that all categories of workmen were included in the provisions of the new legislation, unless expressly excluded. Among those sections of the workforce still excluded, however, were clerks, policemen, domestic servants and the self-employed. The Act was a long-delayed fulfilment of one of the items in the Newcastle pro-gramme of 1891, and one which the House of Lords had blocked in 1894. Somewhat more controversial was the new Trade Disputes Act passed in 1906. This restored to trade unions the widespread immunities under the law which had been bestowed upon them in 1875, but which had been whittled away more recently by legal decisions, and most notoriously by the *Taff Vale* case of 1901. This had made unions liable for damages caused by strike action, and it supplemented other anti-trade union judgments, such as *Lyons* v. *Wilkins*, 1899, and *Quinn* v. *Leathem*, 1901, which undermined possibilities of enforcing strike action by picketing or boycotting. Balfour's refusal to support legislation reversing these legal verdicts in 1904 and 1905 was thought to have been instrumental, along with Chinese slavery, in causing him to lose his seat at the general election. Some Liberals opposed restoring to trade unions the full extent of the privileges which they had enjoyed after 1875, especially as a royal commission on trade disputes, appointed in 1903, had just concluded its delib-erations and recommended compromise formulae on such thorny trade union issues as picketing and financial liability.[6] But Campbell-Bannerman was determined to have no enemies on the left, and insisted on a full restoration of what Asquith sarcastically called the unions' 'benefit of clergy'. The House of Lords accepted this measure, which became the Trade Disputes Act of 1906, having no wish to set itself up as the enemy of industrial democracy or of the working classes.

Education proved to be the main legislative battlefield of 1906. The government could hardly avoid this, as widespread dis-content with the workings of the 1902 Act had contributed to the magnitude of its electoral victory earlier in the year. On the other hand, the whole subject was fraught with sectarian rivalry and religious controversy, and the government risked stirring up the kind of hornets' nest that had had so adverse an effect on its predecessor's fortunes. Birrell's Education Bill, as introduced in April 1906, proposed to do away for the most part with the distinction between provided, or one-time board, schools, and non-provided schools, the latter being mainly Church of England foundations, in which Anglican religious teaching had remained a significant element in the curriculum. Instead all schools within the state system would now, with a few exceptions, become provided, which would mean in effect that all denominational religious teaching would cease within school hours. This would go far to destroy the particular doctrinal and liturgical ambience of the former Church of England schools. Where parents requested it, Anglican or any other denominational instruction could still be given outside school hours, but not at public expense or by members of the teaching staff. Birrell did not propose to abolish religion in schools altogether, but instead intended that it should be of an undenominational, Bible-teaching kind, as practised in board schools under the Cowper–Temple clause of the Act of 1870. The only exception allowed to this new standard of uniformity was in areas where at least four-fifths of the parents requested extended facilities, in the form of continued non-provided status and a distinct religious atmosphere for their school. This, the controversial clause 4 of the 1906 Bill, would benefit Catholic and Jewish schools in urban areas of high immigrant density, but it would do nothing for the broad mass of Anglican schools across the English countryside.

Birrell's Bill, like all forays into educational reform, risked antagonising most of the interests involved to a greater or lesser extent. Catholics feared that clause 4 would provide insufficient safeguards for their schools, and they had a phalanx of Irish MPs to speak on their behalf at Westminster. Nonconformists, on the other hand, opposed the continued existence of distinct religious schools in any form, and this occasioned a good deal of grumbling on some of the Liberal backbenches. Most resentful of all were the Anglicans, who with some justice viewed the Bill as a covert form of disestablishment. The Church of England had, out of its own funds, built five thousand new schools since 1870, but now the distinctly Anglican character of these and many others was to be taken away and replaced by an undenominational, Bible-thumping brand of religious instruction dangerously akin to nonconformity. Anglicanism was of course strongly represented within the Unionist party, and its spokesmen determinedly resisted the measure in the House of Commons, even proposing to secularise the entire educational system as a means of getting rid of the hated Cowper–Temple religious formula. They were too few to have much impact in the lower House, but it remained to be seen what the House of Lords, which they virtually monopolised, would do. The upper House passed the Bill on its second reading, but began to unpick it in committee, and for several months the measure shuttled back and forth between Lords and Commons. In the end, differences were narrowed down to a single clause (clause 7), which imposed a disability on state school teachers giving religious instruction outside school hours. The House of Lords, influenced partly by the bishops who feared that their clergy would be burdened with the extra teaching duties, wished to remove the disability. The government refused, mindful of backbench criticism that it had already compromised enough. So, in December 1906, after months of labour, the Bill was finally lost.

Should the government have dissolved at this point, and forced an early trial of strength with the House of Lords? They would probably have won against a still demoralised opposition, but their record majority of 1906 would no doubt have been considerably reduced, for the electorate would not have been pleased to have to go through the whole business again within a year. Nor was the Education Bill an ideal *cheval de bataille*, for Labour and the Irish Nationalists had little enthusiasm for it in its own right. No doubt Balfour also bore these considerations in mind, for it was his attitude as much as anyone's which determined the Bill's fate. Had he chosen not to oppose it in the House of Commons, as in the case of the Trade Disputes Bill, the Lords would have probably acted on his cue. Instead, they allowed themselves to appear in 1906, less as a revising chamber than as a committee of the Conservative party. Balfour, of course, acted for his own particular reasons. The 1902 Act, which the 1906 Bill promised to transform, was his government's principal legislative legacy, and, in addition, he was anxious to affirm his authority by giving his followers something to cheer about. Though he had returned to the House of Commons at a by-election early in the year, he was aware that defeat at the general election had weakened his position more than Chamberlain's, and on St Valentine's day 1906, in a famous open letter, he had felt obliged more or less to accept the Chamberlainite policy on food taxation and imperial preference.

The Lords had not quite finished with the Liberal government for the year, for in December 1906 they also rejected its Plural Voting Bill. This was unlikely to provoke a constitutional crisis, as the Bill was an ill-advised attempt to deal with only one of many anomalies in a representative system which boasted no fewer than seventeen different qualifications for the franchise. Unionists were hardly likely to accept the abolition of plural voting, which was believed to work strongly in their favour, so long as the much greater wrong, to their mind, of Ireland's over-representation remained unredressed. In any case, it was not clear how a ban on plural voting could be enforced, except perhaps by the threat of severe financial penalties which seemed quite disproportionate to the offence. The Lords' rejection of the Education Bill was arguably a blessing for the Liberals. Had it been carried into law, it would have entailed additional expense and local taxation, and would doubtless have involved the government in as much controversy and bad blood as that bequeathed by the Act of 1902. Nor could the 1906 Bill be said to provide the educational system with greater resources or efficiency; it merely altered the sectarian balance within it. Passage of the Bill would have divided the government's friends, and given aid and comfort to its enemies. Its failure helped to maintain co-operation between Liberals, Labour and Irish Nationalists, and to renew their resentment against the House of Lords.

Of much greater consequence in the legislative field in 1906 was the enactment of measures restoring fully representative government in the Transvaal and the Orange River Colony. Since the end of the war, the two conquered territories had been governed as crown colonies, by the British high commissioner and nominated provincial assemblies, although Vereeniging had promised the establishment of constitutional government as soon as circumstances allowed. The Liberals now judged the time to be ripe, although Balfour accused them of perpetrating the most reckless experiment ever tried in colonial policy. In effect, their proposals made it possible for the Boers to take back control, at least in terms of internal self-government, of their two conquered former republics. This involved gambling that trust and magnanimity towards a defeated foe would prove a securer foundation for longer-term British interests in south Africa than more authoritarian methods. The Transvaal Bill addressed the problem of that country's constitutional and electroral system, which had had such a significant bearing on the outbreak of war in 1899. A bicameral legislature was now established, with effective power residing in a representative lower house of sixty-nine deputies elected by single-member constitutencies, but the Liberals refused to introduce proportional representation which would have weighted the scales more in favour of the English-speaking population. In consequence, the first elections early in 1907 gave victory to Het Volk, the Dutch or Afrikaaner party led by the former Boer commanders, Smuts and Botha, but the Liberal gamble paid off, for these men, happy in the regaining of autonomy, proved willing to accept their new-found role as the watchdogs of Britain's imperial presence in southern Africa. In 1907 also, the Orange River Colony was granted internal self-government on the same generous terms as the Transvaal; and the work of reconciliation proceeded apace so that in 1910 all four south African provinces, whether English-speaking or Dutch, were able to come together in the newly created Union of South Africa. Liberal statecraft, it seemed, had brought stability to a troubled region, and established a new dominion which would remain an integral part of Britain's global role until well after the second world war.

This was an achievement which had eluded Beaconsfield or Chamberlain, and it was on a par with that which, decades earlier, had reconciled French-speaking Canada to the British empire. Churchill's resourceful management, as colonial under-secretary, of the legislation of 1906 and 1907, laid the foundations of a ministerial career which would rapidly come to seem meteoric. He largely succeeded thereby in laying the ghosts both of the south African war and of Chinese slavery, and in only one respect could he be held to have averted his eyes from a potential element of tragedy in south Africa's situation. By refusing to reserve responsibility for native or black African rights in the hands of the imperial government, Churchill and his fellow ministers helped to make possible the long-term development of apartheid in the sub-continent. All this however lay well into the future, and in 1906 it seemed a small price to pay for racial reconciliation between Dutch and English. Altogether Campbell-Bannerman's comparatively brief premiership represented a successful period of imperial management, the last indeed in which a Liberal government would be able to conduct a world policy on the basis of stable or declining arms expenditure. In 1907 Grey, as foreign secretary, defended Britain's naval interests, in terms of the right to blockade neutral shipping in time of war, which was just then being discussed at the second Hague conference, and he also reached an accommodation with Britain's old antagonist in the form of the Anglo-Russian convention. This dealt with territorial rivalries in Asia, where the two nations had long threatened to come into collision. Persia was divided up in respect of separate British and Russian spheres of influence, and Russia agreed not to intervene unilaterally in Afghanistan on condition that Britain respected the integrity of Tibet. Some saw this as a form of appeasement before its time. Curzon thought Grey had conceded too much to an old antagonist, and left-wing MPs disliked any subservience to what many of them still regarded as an oriental tyranny. But generally the agreement strengthened Britain's hand, not least because it brought the country's foreign policy more into line with that of its new-found friend, France, for many years a close ally of Russia's.

The main achievement of 1907 on the domestic front also had an imperial dimension. This was the Territorial and Reserve Forces Bill, an accomplishment to rank with that of any parliamentary session and the largest overhaul of Britain's armed forces since the Cardwell reforms of the early 1870s. Haldane, as war secretary, was concerned to remedy the deficiencies in Britain's military system revealed by the south African war, which Balfour's administration on the whole had failed to do. He proposed to streamline the country's defence forces by merging or doing away with the hitherto distinct formations of the militia, yeomanry and volunteers, and thereby to create a uniformly well trained reserve, some 300,000 men strong, which would ensure the protection of the British isles while allowing the regular army to be fully deployed overseas in time of war. This new territorial army, as it would come to be called, would be broadly under war office supervision, but would otherwise be directly administered by county associations, consisting of civilian as well as military worthies such as lords lieutenant and representatives of local government. This proved a shrewd piece of politics in what was generally a well devised scheme of reform which would serve considerably to enhance Haldane's ministerial reputation. Civilian involvement, along with promised reductions in military expenditure, pleased left-wing Liberal opinion, whereas Tories were reassured by the role accorded to lords lieutenant. Only the Labour party opposed the Bill, seeing in it a creeping militarisation and a bolstering of outdated rural institutions. Most Liberals accepted Haldane's argument that his reforms would obviate any likely resort to military conscription, and his task in steering the measure through the House of Commons was made much easier by the absence of many of the military members who had lost their seats in 1906. Haldane thus helped to give Britain the army with which the country went to war in 1914, perhaps the best army it took into any modern conflict, although it was to prove too small for Armageddon.

The year 1907 proved a productive one in terms of legislation. No less than fifty-six Bills were carried into law, albeit most of them of a workaday nature. The budget itself deserves mention as a reforming measure, even though its significance was hardly on a par with those of 1894 and 1909. It revealed considerable savings in expenditure, which Asquith promised partly to devote to the introduction of old age pensions in the following year. More importantly, it differentiated virtually for the first time between earned and unearned income, with the latter now being made liable for a higher rate of taxation. Asquith cited an ancient and dubious precedent from the budget of 1806, but in fact his proposals departed significantly from the canons of Gladstonian finance. Critics saw the 1907 budget as a further manifestation of the class bias already revealed in the Trade Disputes Act of the previous year. Otherwise the Liberal government's main reforming impulse in 1907 was towards land legislation. Some, including the increasingly estranged Rosebery, saw this as evidence of a novel and predatory attitude towards property, but in fact it was more a question of reviving the agrarian radicalism of the unauthorised and Newcastle programmes of 1885 and 1891. Liberals had generally found it easier to be hostile to the landowner than to the industrial capitalist, and ministerial speeches during 1907 pointed to land redistribution as a panacea for many social ills, including rural depopulation and therewith urban overcrowding, bad housing, poverty and physical deterioration. It was in terms of the land that Liberalism felt its way towards a wider social policy (Doc. 10). A start was made in 1907 with Lewis Harcourt's Smallholdings and Allotments Act, which extended the powers of local authorities compulsorily to acquire land for the purpose of resettling and providing greater security for the rural lower classes.

The land programme brought the Liberals into further conflict with the House of Lords, which in 1907 rejected two pieces of agrarian legislation relating to Scotland. One of these was a Land Valuation Bill which would have paved the way for the reform of the whole system of rates and local taxation north of the border, and which would have supplied a useful precedent for similar action in England. The other proposed measure sought to extend the machinery of the 1886 Crofters' Act from the highlands to the Scottish lowlands, complete with a land commission with power to adjudicate rents and questions of security as between land-lords and tenants. Neither perhaps were particularly adept attempts at legislation. There seemed to be little demand in Scotland for an extension of the system of dual ownership which had long since been condemned in Ireland, and which was any-way out of key with the principles of the land legislation which the governemnt was even then putting through for England. Both measures were hurried through the House of Commons with restricted debate, and presented to the upper House at almost the last moment. Indeed, there was a case for saying that in 1907 the real legislative logjam lay not so much in the House of Lords but rather in the lower House, where the government was trying to push through too many complex measures at the same time and without sorting out a proper order of priority. Nonethe-less, the Lords' rejection of the Scottish Land Bills encouraged Campbell-Bannerman to undertake a campaign of speeches against the upper House in Scotland in the autumn of the year. On balance, this was probably a mistake. The prime minister had been building up to it since the failure of the Education and Plural Voting Bills, and in June 1907 he had carried a resolution in the Commons calling for a restriction on the power of the Lords to obstruct legislation within the lifetime of a single parliament. But it was not certain what this would mean in practice. Campbell-Bannerman spoke of establishing a procedure whereby disputed measures could be discussed between members of both Houses in a series of conferences stretching over two or three sessions, but it seemed likely that this would merely add to the legislative logjam, and it remained unclear how the Lords could be persuaded to relinquish their right to veto. Like his predecessor, Rosebery, in 1894, he appeared to have sounded the horn before even buckling on the sword. The case against the upper House in 1907 was not particularly strong, in a year which had seen the successful carrying into law of a great deal of legislation, including controversial agrarian measures such as the Irish Evicted Tenants Act. The most conspicuous legislative failure of the session, that of the Irish Councils Bill, which, in line with Liberal undertakings at the general election, had proposed measures of devolution stopping well short of what was understood by home rule, had been brought about not by rejection in the House of Lords but at the hands of Irish public opinion. The government had withdrawn the measure after its second reading following a hostile reception from the Irish bishops and the convention of the United Irish League. Campbell-Bannerman could therefore be held guilty of making the same mistake as the previous Liberal government in the mid-1890s, that of commencing a premature campaign against the upper House which was likely only to produce sterile controversy without much practical effect. And, as in 1894, this accompanied a severe downturn in the electoral fortunes of his administration.

The Liberals had suffered very few by-election defeats in the two years following their landslide victory in early 1906. To the Unionists they had lost Cockermouth in August of that year, and Brigg early in 1907, the first in consequence of Labour intervention, but the attrition of their majority had been much less sudden than that which would affect Lloyd George in the wake of his election landslide of 1918. However, early 1908 saw the start of a very bad run of by-election disasters for the Liberals, beginning with the loss in January of the Mid-Devon constituency which they had held ever since its creation in 1885. To some extent this was part of the rhythm of political life; the tide had turned, it may be recalled, against the previous government at a similar point in time after its electoral triumph in 1900. But it also reflected other underlying forces at work.

The year 1908 was one in which the contradictions inherent in the Liberal victory of two years earlier started to become apparent. The Liberals had won in a big way both because they seemed to stand for moderation, as against the potential extremism of key elements in the ranks of Unionism, and also because their arrival in power promised certain tangible benefits in the form of long-deferred reforms and perhaps an improvement in the quality of life. For two years after their defeat the Unionists had cut an unconvincing figure in opposition, and their stance on economic policy remained unclear. Balfour had seemed to accept the full Chamberlainite package on St Valentine's day 1906, but he had qualified his endorsement in subsequent speeches, especially following Chamberlain's stroke and progressive incapacitation for politics in the summer of that year. Indeed Balfour seemed unable to provide a very clear sense of what Conservatism stood for, barring the simple negation of Liberal measures, and as the Liberals as yet were not proposing to do anything very dreadful, this line appeared unprofitable. But the start of the campaign against the Lords enabled Unionists to argue that the destructive forces of radicalism were once again at work, additional credence being given to this view by the advances apparently being made by socialism at the same time. A great stir was created in July 1907 by Labour and socialist gains at two by-elections, in Jarrow and Colne Valley respectively. Both were, in a sense, freak results, especially that at Jarrow, where a four-cornered contest had been provoked by the intervention of an Irish nationalist candidate, and both were Liberal losses. But such developments suggested that the extreme left was advancing under cover of the Liberal majority, and this helped to provoke the return of many moderately inclined voters to the Unionist side which they had deserted in 1906.

The Liberals were also coming under fire for the opposite reason. They were failing to satisfy the expectations of a large body of those who had elected them. The clearest promises made by the Liberals, and not least by Campbell-Bannerman himself in 1906, had concerned cuts in national expenditure and thereby a reduction in the general level of taxation. This was the best means, it had been asserted, of improving living standards, ensuring prosperity, and curbing unemployment. But neither expenditure nor taxation had been reduced to anything like the extent anticipated. Though the Liberals had managed to cut naval spending annually from 36 to 31 million pounds since they had been in power, they had actually increased army expenditure from 28 to 29 million per annum. This allowed insufficient scope for the sweeping remissions in taxation of which the Liberals had seemed to hold out hope. The government had been able to effect some reductions, thanks partly to the generally prosperous state of the economy, and indeed Asquith boasted of the 23 million pounds which he had devoted to the liquidation of the national debt, but this was not something likely in itself to improve the living standards of the average voter. No doubt it was good Gladstonian practice, but it also meant that the electorate was still, even under a Liberal government, paying the bills for the south African war. In particular, the high sugar duty which had been imposed in wartime still remained largely unabated, a factor of some significance in working-class households especially in a period of gradually rising prices. Renewed doubts were now being expressed as to the ability of the free-trade system to meet all the country's financial requirements, especially in connection with one policy on which many in the country believed higher expenditure to be essential.

This was the long-deferred question of old age pensions, which had been canvassed by Chamberlain as long ago as 1891, and which was thought to have been a factor in the Unionist landslide victory of 1895. Failure to do anything about it over the succeeding ten years was, it was believed, one reason for the devastating defeat of 1906, especially in the rural constituencies, where fear of the workhouse at the end of one's working life was particularly strong. Now it seemed that the Liberals in their turn were being punished for their failure to meet similar expectations. True, Asquith in his 1907 budget had promised to introduce pensions in the following year, but hopes had been too often deferred for this now to carry much conviction, and in the meantime the sum which he claimed to have set aside was held up to ridicule by Labour and other members as entirely inadequate for the purpose. In one other significant respect, the Liberals disappointed expectations among their supporters. In 1908 the free-trade system no longer seemed able to guarantee prosperity and full employment in the way that it had done a few years earlier. No doubt the reasons were largely beyond the Liberal government's control. Like any other, it was at the mercy of the international trade cycle, which was adversely affected by the collapse of a speculative boom on the New York stock exchange in October 1907. In consequence unemployment more than doubled from 3.7 per cent in 1907 to 7.8 per cent in 1908, and it remained at the same high level throughout 1909. Here were clear danger signals for the Liberals. According to the available statistics, the last time at which unemployment had approached this level had been in the mid-1890s, when it had exercised a depressive effect on the political fortunes of the previous Liberal administration.

Accordingly, in 1908, the Liberals sought to address the causes of the sudden decline in their popularity. In his third and final budget, introduced just after he had taken over the premiership in April 1908 from the ailing Campbell-Bannerman, Asquith greatly reduced the sugar duty as a sop to families on low incomes. He also, at last, announced the implementation of old age pensions, although the details were embodied in a separate Bill introduced by Lloyd George in June. This was to prove one of the most celebrated of the reforms accomplished by Edwardian Liberalism, though at the time it was, variously, criticised by both Labour and Unionist MPs for being inflexible, piecemeal and improvident. Pensions would only become available to people over seventy, and even then to less than half of those who fell into that category, for many were disqualified by being in receipt of poor law relief or, conversely, by having too much money in the bank. As far as the latter were concerned, Lloyd George agreed to a sliding scale to make his scheme less rigid. Unionists felt that pensions should be contributory, to encourage thrift, rather than paid for out of taxation as proposed. Certainly it was not clear where the money was to come from, and it was at this point that Lloyd George aroused anxieties by observing that he would have to rob someone's hen-roost in the following year. But, whatever their reservations, few MPs dared to oppose a measure that, for all its limitations, was evidently popular, and the Bill passed on its third reading in the House of Commons by 315:10. This made it difficult for the House of Lords to do anything but agree, albeit somewhat through gritted teeth.

Much more controversial, both in parliament and in the country, was the Licensing Bill of 1908. This set out to replace the legislation of 1904. A new licensing commission was to be established in order to oversee the reduction of licences throughout the country, and all public-house leases were to terminate after fourteen years so that control by the state could be resumed. Liberals heralded the Bill as a great measure of social improvement, of a piece with their legislation on pensions and insurance, which would help to banish drunkenness and poverty, and which, moreover, would also strike a blow against the monopoly interests of the brewing companies. Balfour, on the other hand, described it as a deed of spoliation and as an outrage on public morality. Large demonstrations were held, both for and against the Bill, and a by-election at Peckham in the spring of 1908, which the Liberal lost, was turned into a popular jamboree by the drink interest, with scenes reminiscent of Mafeking night. At the end of the year, the Bill was rejected by a large majority in the House of Lords, although a number of bishops supported it in the interests of temperance.

At the same time, the government was forced to relinquish its latest attempt to solve the education controversy. Its Bill of 1908 proposed to go back somewhat to the situation before 1902, with the voluntary schools losing rate-aid, but being granted more generous state subsidies by way of compensation. To many Catholics, however, such promised subventions did not seem generous enough, and their votes were one of the factors that counted against the government in the by-elections of 1908. Anglicanism, at least in so far as it found expression in a representative church council specially summoned for the purpose, took the same view, and despairing of achieving any consensus, the government gave up. Nonconformists were bitterly disappointed, all the more so as the Liberals did succeed in 1908 in passing an Act establishing an Irish Catholic university, a highly controversial matter which had been hanging fire even longer than had old age pensions.

The Liberals did enjoy one or two other legislative successes in 1908. The Port of London Authority was established, and the Children Act extended the paternalist role of the state into a relatively novel area. More significant was the miners' Eight Hours Act, which applied to Britain's largest industrial employer the principle of statutory regulation of adult male hours of labour hitherto only acknowledged in the case of the railways. Surprisingly perhaps, the House of Lords accepted it, partly no doubt because the Unionists themselves had been prepared to impose exceptional burdens on the industry in 1901. In a wider sense, however, 1908 was a year which saw the development of new and more powerful challenges to the Liberal government. One of these was the women's suffrage movement, which took a more militant turn in 1908. Partly this was the result of a split which resulted in the establishment of the Women's Freedom League, an organisation led among others by Mrs Despard, which believed in peaceful agitation and which considered the more forceful methods, championed by the Pankhursts and the Women's Social and Political Union (WSPU), to be self-defeating.

Women had secured the local governemnt franchise from a previous Liberal administration in 1894, and most recently in 1907 they had become eligible to be county councillors, aldermen and mayors.[7] Such advances only made the continued exclusion of women from the parliamentary franchise seem all the more anomalous. Feminists believed that they had won the argument and yet were denied their rightful place through the workings of the political system. Only *force majeure* would enable them to achieve it. The Women's Freedom League counselled against too ready a resort to militancy, on the grounds that such tactics might well recoil against women themselves, and especially against those less socially well placed than the Pankhursts. There was need, Mrs Despard believed, for moving forward on a number of fronts, and by means of peaceful rather than violent agitation, for instance in the direction of securing equal legal rights for women and of doing away with the double standard that was so often used against them in divorce or criminal proceedings. But the Pankhursts and the WSPU were now freed from the influence of their more moderate sisterhood and preferred to make their own way.

The Pankhursts believed, above all, in the primacy of the political battle and the struggle to win the parliamentary franchise. They were angry and frustrated at the *non possumus* attitude of the Liberal government. No Liberal legislature, it should be said, devoted itself less to political reform than did that of 1906–10 with its mammoth parliamentary majority. Its energies were almost entirely taken up with social, financial and imperial concerns. By 1908 the WSPU sensed the government's growing vulnerability, especially at by-elections, and the organisation spent much energy in harrying Liberal candidates and in claiming credit for the reverses which they sustained. The more militant suffragists also took advantage of other movements of protest, such as the large unemployed demonstrations of the autumn of 1908, to develop new forms of direct action of their own. This was the first year in which women attempted in large numbers to rush the doors of the House of Commons, and it also saw the full use of the argument of the broken window pane. Of course, just like the now constant harassment of ministers at public meetings, such activities did not amount to much more than causes of irritation or embarrassment, but by 1909 they were threatening to turn into something more. Women were by now inviting martyrdom by having themselves sent to prison, especially when, if they went on hunger strike, they were put through the ordeal of forcible feeding. A significant section of Liberals saw this as a form of barbarity towards women, and the issue threatened to create a crisis of conscience inside the party similar to that over Irish coercion in the 1880s which had paved the way for Gladstone's conversion to home rule (Doc. 11).

Much more substantial, however, at least in the immediate term, was the challenge posed for the government by increasing public alarm over the navy. Like the phenomenon known as the *grande peur* in revolutionary France, fear of invasion was the recurrent nightmare of Victorian and Edwardian Britain, and in 1908–09 it passed through a further intense phase. Several factors seem here to have been at work. A sense of vulnerability had been bred in Britain by both technological and political developments. The launching of the first dreadnought in 1906 represented a revolution in battleship design, and although Britain had thereby grasped the lead, she had at the same time forfeited her considerable advantage in terms of numbers of pre-dreadnought classes of battleship, which were now rendered semi-obsolete.

Thanks to a rapid expansion of capacity at Krupp's, Germany would soon, it appeared, be in a position to match British naval construction, especially as in 1907 Britain's Liberal government had reduced naval expenditure in the interests of economy. In the same year, the second Hague conference failed to reconcile naval disagreements between the great powers, and in 1908 further developments pointed to an increase in Anglo-German antagonism. The kaiser's clumsy excursions into diplomacy, in particular the *Daily Telegraph* interview, aroused British anxieties, as did the revival of the eastern question, brought about by Austria-Hungary's annexation of Bosnia-Herzegovina with Germany's support. Lurid spy stories appeared in the British popular press. Against this background, Balfour and other Unionists warned that Germany might well have overtaken Britain in naval construction by 1911. Certainly the two-power standard, which his own government had maintained, was no longer operational; indeed the country would be hard put even to preserve a one-power standard in relation to its new and redoubtable rival on the other side of the North Sea (Doc. 12).

The 1909 budget – known to history as the people's budget – was born of the twin need to provide for naval rearmament and old age pensions. The latter, carried into law the previous year, still remained to be paid for, while the government had responded to the recent naval scare by presenting revised esti-mates allowing for the construction of up to eight new battleships. This was a notable u-turn on the part of a political movement which, since Gladstone's day, had generally upheld the ideas of public economy, thrift, and individual responsibility. On their side, the Unionists had accepted old age pensions, and their only qualms about naval rearmament were that it did not go far enough. And yet the budget would prove the most bitterly contested affair since the great reform act of 1832. Nothing that any Labour government would attempt in the twentieth century would be half so controversial. To understand why, it is neces-sary first to examine the budget in some of its details.

To meet the threatened deficit, it was required to find an additional sixteen million pounds, and partly to this end it imposed no less than seven new taxes. Four of these were on land or on site values, including one of 20 per cent on unearned increment, but, though they were to prove a contentious element in the budget, their net yield was to be no more than half a million pounds. A new vehicle licensing duty and a tax on petrol added a further half million, but the most remunerative of the imposts would be surtax, which along with other adjustments in income tax would bring in an extra three and a half million pounds. To a large extent however, the people's budget relied on exploiting older sources of taxation. Excise and customs on alcohol and tobacco were increased so as to realise an additional six million pounds, and the death duties, which had proved so controversial in 1894, were raised by a further three and a half million.

The budget offered a fundamental challenge to both the old Conservatism and the new. The landed aristocracy, for so long the bedrock of the Tory party, regarded the threatened increase in death duties with dismay. Many of its members had been struggling to keep their family estates together since 1894, and they feared that the latest proposals would go far to encompass the destruction of traditional rural English society. As to the new land taxes, Unionists saw them as the thin edge of a fiscal wedge which would be used to extract ever-increasing amounts in future. It was noted that they were to be accompanied by land valuation provisions, described by Churchill as 'an up-to-date domesday book' for the whole country. Other features of the budget proved equally objectionable to other powerful Unionist interests, and in particular to the tariff reformers. These had long urged a broadening of the basis of taxation, but they now faced a budget which went out of its way to make it as narrow and selective as possible. As far as direct taxation was concerned, the weight of the increases fell exclusively on the better-off – on landowners, those earning over £3,000 a year or living on unearned income, owners of motor-cars. For those earning less than £2,000 a year, the rate of income tax remained unchanged at 9d in the pound, enabling Churchill to claim that Liberal budgets had actually benefited three-quarters of the country's income taxpayers.[8] As far as indirect taxation was concerned, smokers and drinkers found themselves heavily penalised, to the advantage of almost every other kind of consumer. Unionists generally deplored what they regarded as the budget's socialistic tendencies: its seemingly confiscatory attitude towards property, its class bias and social divisiveness. They saw it as the culmination of a long line of Liberal measures which had undermined domestic investment, driven capital abroad, and contributed largely to the increased unemployment and economic recession of 1908 and 1909 (Doc. 13).

The budget also offered a direct challenge to that most well entrenched of Unionist institutions, the House of Lords. Although ostensibly a money Bill, it contained a wide range of controversial matter. It provided for compulsory land valuation, increased liquor licences, public works projects to help the unemployed along with a new development commission to oversee

113

them. The first two of these items had been rejected by the Lords when proposed as separate legislation in 1907 and 1908, and as for the development commission it seemed to many of their Lordships part of the government's socialistic tendency to hand over areas of the economy to bureaucratic and non-accountable organisations. Not surprisingly, Unionists regarded the tacking of diverse material onto the budget as a cynical manoeuvre to outflank the authority of the upper House. If the government was able to get away with it this time, they warned, it might try to use the same device to pass home rule.

Traditionally the House of Lords, whatever its veto powers over ordinary legislation, did not interfere with the annual Finance Bill. At least it had not done so for many years, and as with much else in the British constitution, it seemed that this had hardened into custom. Liberals assumed that, as with the falling into disuse of the veto power of the crown, the Lords had lost the authority to refuse supply by failing to exercise it. But precedent here was open to different interpretation. The practice of combining all the money Bills in any one year into a single budget only dated back to the 1860s. Prior to that time, the House of Lords had rejected individual money Bills, as for instance during the Napoleonic wars. And, on a celebrated occasion in 1860, it had rejected the Paper Duties Bill, only to be obliged to accept it in the following year after Gladstone had subsumed it in the budget. The constitutional implication here seemed to be that, though the Lords could not amend the annual Finance Bill, they could perhaps reject it. In 1909 the House of Lords determined to make use of its reserve power, fearful that if it did not do so it would lose all credibility as a revising chamber.

The political temperature was considerably heightened in 1909 by platform oratory. Lloyd George made a further name for himself by rabble-rousing attacks against the peerage in speeches at Limehouse and Newcastle in June and October. In practice, Lloyd George was usually much more conciliatory, and he even amended his budget in the course of the session to grant income tax relief to agricultural landowners under schedule A. But it was his demagogic utterances that were remembered, especially his equating of dukes and urban landlords in particular with the idle rich, who refused to contribute their fair quota of taxation to naval rearmament or to make land available for low-cost housing. Such

114

tactics not only provoked the House of Lords, but made it feel that it had little to lose by rejecting the budget. Evidently its position would be an issue at the next general election in any event, and it seemed better to go down fighting. Almost as notorious were Churchill's speeches in 1909, for instance at Leicester, where he too singled out ownership of land as deserving to have particular fiscal burdens placed upon it. It seemed a far cry from Gladstone's day, and that prime minister's belief in aristocracy as being synonymous with the idea of public duty. Equally significant, though in a different way, was Asquith's platform oratory, which presented a reasoned defence of the budget on essentially financial grounds.

The prime minister tackled head-on one of the leading criticisms, that fear of punitive taxation was depreciating consols and starving Britain of investment capital by driving it abroad. He demonstrated that the fall in consols had begun with the south African war, and that Britain had often exported capital in the past, usually to the country's own as much as to anyone else's advantage. It was unlikely that British capital would be attracted to any of its industrial rivals, where rates of taxation were even higher. Above all, Asquith insisted, the only alternative to the people's budget was tariff reform and the taxation of food. The Liberals had shown that the country could retain the free-trade system, and at the same time afford expensive social reforms such as old age pensions, in a way that Chamberlain and his followers had been declaring to be impossible since 1903. Here was a challenge which the bulk of the Unionist party could hardly ignore. The Liberals seemed about to bring off an almost unheard-of political triumph. They appeared to have recaptured the initiative in the country while at the same time imposing swingeing increases in taxation. Once the economy improved again and unemployment declined, thanks to the normal working of the trade cycle, tariff reform would lose much of its appeal and the Liberals would be in a position to renew their lease on power with another general election victory. The Unionists felt the situation to be slipping out of their hands in 1909. The new land taxes, along with the rhetorical assault on landlordism, had forced them onto the defensive, and they had failed to make some expected by-election gains, as at High Peak in July. Joseph Chamberlain, once himself the scourge of the upper House, now declared it to be the duty of the Lords to reject the budget and thereby refer it to the electorate. Though tariff reform was uppermost in Chamberlain's mind, opposition to the 'hen-roost policy' of the budget was, as Balfour well understood, something which could usefully unite all sections of the Unionist coalition.

The House of Lords, in compensation perhaps for the treatment which it would accord the budget, acquiesced in a range of Liberal reforms in 1909. In the imperial domain, the year saw the enactment of south African federation and also of a measure extending the representative and deliberative functions of Indian councils. At the same time the government passed a new Irish Land Act, adding further to the generous financial provisions of that of 1903, though many Unionists saw it as a capitulation to the revival of disorder and cattle-driving, especially in the western and grazing counties of Ireland in the course of 1909. More significant still were two domestic social reforms, establishing trade boards, to ensure payment of minimum wages in sweated industries, as well as labour exchanges to assist with the reallocation of labour especially in times of unemployment.

These were the product of several factors. Partly they derived from the Liberals' need to head off the challenge of the Labour party in this field, for instance as contained in the Unemployed Workmen Bill of earlier in the year. They also owed something to the reports, especially the minority report, of the poor law commission which had presented its conclusions at the start of 1909. Most of all, perhaps, they were a function of Churchill's restless energy which found expression in grandiose schemes of social reform in this, the most radical, phase in his career. From his speeches of 1908 and 1909 Churchill's ideas on domestic policy seem markedly more visionary and coherent than those of Lloyd George. He aspired to establish machinery to ensure a national minimum standard of life for the 'left-out millions' of the population. He spoke enthusiastically of European war being rendered much less likely by the new 'international solidarity of labour', and of the need to preserve the British empire, 'the burden of which could never be borne on the shoulders of the stunted millions crowded into the slums of cities'. It was the Liberal party, he asserted, which was now the custodian of these ideals, and the only force which could plausibly stand between the extremes of revolution and reaction[9] (Doc. 10).

The question of the hour, however, was that of the people's budget, where both parties in the House of Lords accused each other of promoting extremism. Unionist peers saw the budget as 'cunningly devised as a scheme for socialistic revolution', though none of them provided a very clear indication of what they understood socialism to be. Liberal peers, on the other hand, regarded their opponents as the real revolutionaries in threatening financial chaos and in departing from constitutional practice, whereby they risked 'giving a lesson which may be improved upon'.[10] However, encouraged by a Unionist by-election gain at Bermondsey in October 1909, which seemed to suggest that even working-class constituencies were not enamoured of the budget, the House of Lords voted in the following month, by 350:75, to withhold its assent until the budget had 'been submitted to the judgment of the country'. This added a democratic gloss, but in effectively rejecting the budget the Lords left themselves open to the twin charge that they were acting first and foremost in the political interests of the Unionist parties and in the economic interests of the landowning class (Doc. 13).

The Liberals therefore seemed to enter the election campaign in a favourable position. They had a powerfully demagogic theme to work upon, more so indeed than had been at the Liberal party's disposal since at least 1868, and, in Lloyd George and Churchill, leading orators who were more than capable of exploiting it. The Unionists, for once, rather lacked speaking talent. Balfour was indisposed until the later stages of the campaign, and younger firebrands like F. E. Smith and Bonar Law were not yet established national figures. In these circumstances, many peers had to be pressed into service on the public platform, but they were a dubious asset, as their appearance tended to focus attention even more strongly on the constitutional controversy. The issue of peers v. people could be used by the Liberals to subsume most other matters, and promised to be an ideal rallying cry. But its effectiveness was offset by a number of factors. One was the sheer length of the campaign. Christmas prevented the holding of the general election before January 1910, and it proved difficult to maintain at white heat a sense of outrage for nearly two months after the Lords' rejection of the budget. Moreover, the Liberals provided no details as to how exactly they proposed to end the veto power of the upper chamber. Asquith gave several hostages to fortune in his keynote speech at the Albert Hall in December, which marked the start of the campaign. Among other things, he promised to end the Lords' absolute veto and to ensure that in future all measures passed within the lifetime of a single parliament. Most Liberals assumed that he had already received from the king guarantees as to a mass creation of peers that would destroy the Unionist preponderance in the upper House. But, a few days later, the king gave Asquith to understand that he would not commit the royal prerogative on such a scale without at least the test of a second general election. This greatly discomfited the prime minister, who took nearly a year to recover his political poise. In any case, the cabinet was divided as to what kind of upper chamber it wanted to see established in the future, and this also tended to have an inhibiting influence on ministerial oratory.

Two other questions put the Liberals somewhat on the defensive. The economy had been in recession during 1908 and the first part of 1909, and though recovery now seemed to be beginning, the free-trade cause could not be pleaded with the same confident optimism as four years earlier. As a result, Unionists in general put tariff reform more at the forefront of their campaign than in any election before 1923. Tariffs promised a cure for unemployment, which had stood at a high level in 1908 and 1909, and they also re-emphasised the gross unfairness, as Unionists saw it, of the people's budget, which placed a disproportionately heavy burden, not only on agriculture, but also on the working man's beer and tobacco. Tariff reform, it was argued, would spread the fiscal load much more evenly. Leading Liberals, of course, were very happy to join battle on these terms, and Asquith and Churchill fought the election very largely on free trade, enjoying considerable success, at least in the north of England, and especially in Lancashire, where the tally of Unionist gains was kept to a minimum. Elsewhere in England, the story was rather different, with industrial constituencies in the west midlands moving back firmly into the Unionist camp.

Apart from the economy, the one major issue which proved problematic for the Liberals was that of naval rearmament. The government had considerably expanded the programme of naval construction early in 1909, but the opposition insisted that it was still not enough, and they were backed up by an influential series of alarmist articles in the *Daily Mail*, penned, ironically though it might seem, by a socialist journalist named Blatchford, who saw Germany as the prime threat to his utopian ideal of Merrie England. Indeed, the shadow of Germany loomed larger in this election than in any other before or since. Lloyd George and Churchill insisted that Germany was not a threat, and accused the Unionists of indulging in scaremongering tactics and of perverting patriotic feeling for party political purposes. But they were quite ready to make use of anti-German sentiment where it suited them. Germany, they declared, was a country of high tariffs, and consequently of high prices, where the working classes were forced to subsist on horseflesh and black bread. Certainly it had been a pioneer in the field of welfare legislation, but its pension scheme, based as it was on the contributory principle, was, it was claimed, as nothing compared to that which had been introduced by Britain's Liberal government in 1908. Protectionist Germany, declared Lloyd George at Reading, had accomplished less in twenty years than had free-trade Britain in one.[11]

Social reform was a significant issue in the January 1910 general election. For once, the Liberals could point to a solid record of achievement in this area, for most of the leading measures of the previous parliament had related to social or imperial affairs. Old age pensions were evidently popular, and Unionists were to some extent forced on to the defensive in having to explain their party's apparent lukewarmness on the issue down to 1908. Historians have often held that social reform was the objective which the Liberals ought to have pursued more wholeheartedly in the years before 1914. Certainly it loomed larger in January 1910 than in any other general election of this period, but it cannot be said that on this particular occasion it did the Liberals all that much good.

For one thing, Unionists had become adept at outbidding the Liberals on certain items of social reform. After all, it had been a Conservative, Bridgeman, who in 1909 had in vain proposed an amendment to remove the pauper disqualification which barred several hundred thousand old people from receiving pensions. Unionist candidates here made much of the government's apparent meanness, and they also attacked Lloyd George's loosely sketched ideas on invalidity and unemployment insurance. Such schemes, they declared, were as yet too vague to amount to very much, and, in any case, what was really needed was action to safeguard jobs and employment, not sops for those unfortunate enough to be unemployed. In these circumstances, tariff reform was presented as the progressive social policy of the future, one which would yield new sources of revenue to fund increased social expenditure and which would defend British jobs against foreign competition in the way that protectionist Germany evidently had done on behalf of its own thriving economy. Somewhat glibly, tariff reform was seen as a method of making the foreigner pay for Britain's social progress. The arguments advanced in its favour in January 1910 provided a foretaste of those which would be expressed much more gaudily on the subject of reparations in 1918.

The Unionists therefore were more than ready to take issue with the people's budget. Whereas the Liberals defended it as an attack on plutocracy, landed privilege and powerful vested interests, Unionists saw it as a revolutionary fiscal measure which threatened to cast a blight over the whole of the British economy. In singling out land and higher incomes generally for apparently punitive taxation, the Liberals could be said to be undermining the foundations of confidence and prosperity. In consequence, capital was fleeing the country and seeking out more secure fields of investment overseas, where it would end up aiding the development of Britain's industrial rivals. The Unionist contention was that one could not hurt land and capital without ultimately hurting labour too. Unionist spokesmen also attacked the regressive fiscal characteristics of the budget, such as the greatly enhanced duties on drink and tobacco, and they ridiculed its claims to be an instrument in defence of free trade, pointing out that it maintained taxation on such essential items of the working-class diet as sugar and tea. Behind the people's budget, the Unionists claimed to discern the lurking spectre of socialism. Most of them would have been hard pushed to define this as an ideology; but, for rhetorical purposes, it could readily be equated with high taxation, land nationalisation, and the servile state. In referring such a contentious and innovatory measure to the arbitrament of the people, the House of Lords, it could be claimed, was acting, not in abuse of its position, but in its traditional role as the watchdog of the constitution.

Faced with these arguments, the electorate in January 1910 returned an ambiguous verdict. Pollings in the cities and boroughs of England revealed a strong swing against Liberalism across much of the midlands and the south. London, however, proved something of an exception, for though the Liberals lost ground there, they did not suffer defeat on anything like the scale of 1895 and 1900. Across the industrial north of England, and notably in Lancashire, with its once strong Tory tradition, the Liberals to a considerable extent held their own. The real shock for the government came with the English county results during the last eleven days of January. This was the crucial phase of the election, for had the Liberals done as well here as in 1885 and 1923 they would have returned to power with a majority independent of Irish Nationalist support. Instead they faced a trail of disaster across much of rural southern and central England, losing, for example, all three county seats in Oxfordshire, four each in Essex, Suffolk and Wiltshire, three each in Cheshire, Kent, Nottinghamshire, Somerset and Surrey. It is interesting to consider reasons for this debacle.

To some extent, the Liberals were guilty of taking the English countryside too much for granted. Few of their leading orators campaigned there, except right at the end, when a last-minute speaking tour by Churchill arguably helped to save a batch of seats in Devon. Evidently the Liberals assumed that the agricultural voter would be motivated primarily by gratitude for old age pensions and by fear of increased food prices consequent upon protection. But the latter bogey was not as powerful in 1910 as it had been in 1906. For one thing, food had become dearer anyway, tariffs or no tariffs: the price of the quartern loaf had increased from 4½ to 6d during the Liberals' time in office. The electorate was less impressed by the government's achievements than by what seemed to be its broken promises, its failure to reform rural rates or to introduce the free breakfast table. Most of all, the Liberals under-estimated the resentment provoked by the people's budget across a wide range of English rural society. In a world in which deference was still important, Lloyd George's verbal and fiscal assaults on the aristocracy were bound to appear as an attack on the values of the countryside in general, not least as they appeared to threaten the viability of the large estates on which so much rural employment depended. The Liberals would have done well to remember the lesson of the death duties budget of 1894, which had greatly incresed taxation on land, and which had contributed to the defeat of many Liberal candidates in rural constituencies in the following year. In 1906, the Liberals had perhaps benefited from a sense that the countryside was in decline, but they had clearly done nothing to reverse the process. To rephrase a notable comment made in 1885, they now lacked a rural cow, whereas the Unionists at least now offered a policy of sorts, with their proposals to extend owner-occupation among English tenant farmers. In addition, their promise to impose a duty of two shillings per quarter on imported foreign corn seemed well calculated to protect English farming without raising the price of food too high for the agricultural wage-earner. Lastly, Irish home rule again emerged as a leading issue in the January 1910 election. Asquith had given it prominence in his Albert Hall speech in mid-December, no doubt rightly calculating that Irish votes would be needed to enable the Liberals to hang on to many urban constituencies in the north of England. But the effect was to make many voters in the English countryside feel that they now stood low on the government's agenda, and, as in 1886, their resentment found expression in a repudiation of Liberalism in a large number of English rural constituencies.

The outcome of the general election was effectively a dead heat as between Liberals and Unionists. Respectively they would have 275 and 273 MPs in the incoming parliament. The Unionists had gained no less than 127 seats from their opponents. Liberals and Labour, by contrast, had managed only 21 gains, partly by winning back seats lost at by-elections. The Liberals had lost their overall majority in England, but this was compensated for by their overwhelming ascendancy in Wales and Scotland, where Unionists only held 2 and 9 seats respectively, as against the Liberals' 24 and 57. Clearly, resentment against the House of Lords had been strongest here and in the north of England, and the issue also served the Liberals well in another sense by enabling them to contain any possible challenge on the left from Labour. With so much emphasis in the campaign on the traditional Liberal issues of free trade and the iniquity of the upper chamber, Labour had difficulty in making its own distinct voice heard. Indeed, its dependence on the Liberals was re-emphasised just prior to the election by the Osborne judgment, handed down by the House of Lords in December 1909. This challenged the Labour party's financial position by undermining its right to receive trade union subventions. Labour fought 78 seats in all, but only 27 of these were in triangular contests. It won 40 seats, mostly in England, with only 4 in Wales and 2 in Scotland. One other point of interest about the general election was the partial return to two-party politics in the south of Ireland. Independent Nationalists fought 18 seats and won 8 of them, notably in the area around Cork. Their leaders, Healy and O'Brien, had no liking for Redmond, whom moreover they considered to have sacrificed Ireland's economic interests in the matter of the people's budget. They would prove a thorn in Redmond's side over the next few years, and a factor which he could not ignore.

Notes

1 *The Times*, 11 December 1905.
2 For instance in a speech at Derby, *The Times*, 5 January 1906.
3 Speech at Pwllheli, *The Times*, 17 January 1906.
4 *The Times*, 22 December 1905 and 10 and 16 January 1906.
5 *The Times*, 23 January 1906.
6 As originally envisaged by the attorney-general, Sir Joseph Walton, trade unions would have remained liable for damages under the law of agency, and peaceful picketing would have been allowed if conducted 'in a reasonable manner' under the terms of an Act of 1859.
7 The 1907 qualification of women act was criticised by some as an early surrender to feminist militancy.
8 Speech at Edinburgh, *The Times*, 19 July 1909.
9 Speeches at Birmingham and Swansea, *The Times*, 14 January 1909 and 17 August 1908.
10 5 *Hansard* (Lords) IV 1271 (30 November 1909).
11 *The Times*, 3 January 1910.

4

Challenges to the constitution, 1910–1914

The indecisive election result left both main parties demoralised and uncertain. Especially was this true of the Liberals, who had relinquished their grand majority of 1906 with nothing much to show for it. There was no immediate prospect of forcing a showdown with the House of Lords, for this would require either the threat or reality of massive peerage creations on a scale sufficient to overwhelm the powerful Unionist majority in the upper House, and this the king had refused without at least the verdict of a second general election. True, the House of Lords had committed itself to passing the people's budget should the government retain its majority in the lower House; but even this was by no means certain, for the Irish Nationalists were strongly opposed to the proposed increases in whisky duties, and demanded immediate action to end the veto power of the House of Lords as the price of their support. Exhausted, the prime minister took himself off for a vacation in the south of France, leaving his colleagues to try to sort out what should be done before parliament convened. Among them, it was Grey who for the moment assumed pride of place, anxious, above all, that the Liberals should not appear to be dictated to by the Irish National-ists. This, he believed, had proved fatal to the party on previous occasions – for instance, the general elections of 1886 and 1895.

Clearly the problem of what to do about the powers of the House of Lords could no longer be avoided. But Grey preferred to proceed by way of reforming it rather than by simply limiting its authority. This would involve giving the upper House more of a representative character, in the place of the purely hereditary form in which it was at present cast. In a way, this would serve to enhance its status and authority, thus opening the way to achieving inter-party support, for a number of Unionists were by now sympathetic to the idea of House of Lords reform. The plan which Grey had in mind had been under discussion in Liberal circles for some time, although over-ruled by Campbell-Bannerman in 1907. It proposed that, in the case of disagreement between Lords and Commons, the upper House should delegate its powers to a select 100 of its members, and that these should then exercise their votes sitting together in a joint assembly with all the members of the lower House. Precedents existed for such a procedure in the British system of government. The House of Lords had already so delegated its judicial responsibilities, and the practice of joint assemblies was recognised in the Australian and South African constitutions. Grey was confident that this proposed scheme would put the Liberals at an advantage in any early appeal to the country on the question of the House of Lords. It would prevent them from appearing as a revolutionary party, intent on doing away with the constitutional balance of powers and establishing arbitrary rule by a single chamber; and it would also wrong-foot the Unionists, who would find it difficult to argue before the electorate against introducing the elective principle in so moderate a manner into the upper House.[1]

Other Liberals, however, were unhappy at some of the proposed scheme's implications. It was feared that it would put the House of Lords on the same level, legislatively speaking, as the Commons, and that, in practice, it would make it impossible for the Liberals to carry controversial measures into law without a majority of at least seventy in the lower House. Also the scheme, with its creation of a new body of representative peers, seemed unnecessarily complex, and not easily to be understood by the average citizen. Campbell-Bannerman had thought it reminiscent of the constitutional musings of the Abbé Sieyès. The prime objection, however, was that it would not find favour with the Irish Nationalists, who would therefore vote down the government over the budget and thereby plunge both the Liberal party and the country into the turmoil and uncertainty of a further general election only three months after the preceding one. Lloyd George was a particular exponent of this point of view, and he also proposed a compromise formula whereby the cabinet would accede to Redmond's demands for moving against the veto powers of the House of Lords, but would at the same time refuse his demands for amending the budget, thereby appearing not to give in entirely to Irish pressure. On this basis, the people's budget was reintroduced and swiftly passed through all its stages in parliament in late April 1910. At the same time, a Bill was tabled in the House of Commons proposing to restrict the veto power of the House of Lords to a maximum of two years.[2]

Abruptly the situation changed again with the sudden death of the king in early May 1910. Both main parties drew back from outright confrontation over the upper House. Neither knew how the new and inexperienced monarch, George V, would react in a constitutional crisis, especially in regard to using the prerogative power of the crown to effect a mass creation of peers. Moreover, many Unionists were anxious not to go into another general election with an unreconstructed House of Lords hung round their neck like an albatross; and, for their part, with the people's budget safely passed, Liberals were happy to explore ways of diminishing their dependence on the Irish vote at Westminster. The upshot was the constitutional conference of June–November 1910, an intriguing episode in early twentieth-century political history, which sought to discover an agreed solution between Unionists and Liberals as to the powers of the upper House. The conference considered these powers in respect of three separate categories of legislation: ordinary, financial and constitutional. It seemed possible that, in order to preserve the traditional structure of the House of Lords so far as possible, Balfour might accept the replacement of the absolute with a suspensive veto in respect of ordinary legislation. He also appeared agreeable to ending the upper House's veto over financial legislation, as long as that was strictly defined; and here Asquith was willing enough to accommodate him by giving the speaker of the House of Commons authority to prevent any recourse to tacking and to decide what was and what was not a money Bill. The main difficulty concerned constitutional legislation, and what exactly was understood by that term. No doubt it included anything relating to the monarchy and the protestant succession. But did it also cover significant political reforms, such as an extension of the franchise? More vital still, did it encompass the supremely contentious question of home rule? Once again Ireland threatened to become a stumbling block in the way of Britain's political development.

Deadlock at the constitutional conference prompted Lloyd George to come up with one of his more tantalising initiatives. This was his proposal for a grand coalition between Unionists and Liberals, whereby both parties would for the time being sink their sectarian differences and jointly tackle the very real problems facing their country at home and abroad. Among these, naval rearmament and social reform offered good prospects for agreement, taxation and devolution much less so. But Lloyd George, in his unfastidious way, believed a trade-off to be possible, with the Liberals swallowing a degree of colonial preference in return for progress towards some form of Irish home rule, perhaps in the context of devolution all round for the component parts of the United Kingdom. Lloyd George knew the latter idea to be attractive to some younger Unionists who were worried by their party's lack of movement where Ireland was concerned. The whole project is a fascinating anticipation of what was to happen a few years later, when coalition had, among others, the unintended effects of advancing the fortunes of Labour and ending the Irish union. In 1910, Lloyd George canvassed support among those whom he deemed to be fellow-spirits on both sides of the House of Commons, but he failed in the end to win over Balfour, who was, nonetheless, intrigued by the whole idea. Balfour's twin preoccupations were maintenance of Conservative party unity and of the Act of Union with Ireland, and both seemed threatened by coalition. Moreover the idea of such a political marriage of convenience had had unfortunate connotations since the notorious Fox–North alliance of the 1780s.

The failure of coalition meant also the failure of the constitutional conference. Unionists and Liberals were unable to agree on the all-important question as to how to settle differences between the two Houses of parliament regarding proposed changes in the constitution. Balfour advised bringing in a device hitherto unknown in the British system of government, that of the referendum, but Liberals shied away from this, believing it to savour too much of Jacobin and Bonapartist practice. Asquith was inherently conservative where constitutional matters were concerned, and had no desire to diminish the sovereignty of parliament. In any case, the two parties could not agree as to whether to treat home rule for Ireland essentially as a political or as a constitutional question. Lloyd George, always resourceful, suggested that the Liberals might undertake to submit the next Home Rule Bill to the arbitrament of a general election. Balfour demanded that this should be done in respect of every subsequent such Bill. In the end, it seems, the difference between the two main parties came down to this. Balfour preferred that the constitutional conference should break up over home rule, as that was the issue over which his followers were most united. For his part, Asquith could not afford to alienate the Irish Nationalists if he was to stay in power, and he also saw in the breakdown of the conference a chance to pressurise the king into granting another dissolution of parliament, with the promise of creating new peers in sufficient quantity to overawe the House of Lords in the event of a further Liberal victory. The omens seemed favourable, for just at this moment, in November 1910, the Liberal candidate won an increased majority at a by-election in Walthamstow, the second-largest constituency in the country. Prosperity seemed to be returning. Unemployment had declined to 4.7 per cent in 1910, as compared to 7.7 per cent in the previous year, and, in a giveaway budget, Lloyd George had removed the pauper disqualification for old age pensions, making an additional £500,000 available for 200,000 extra recipients.

The constitutional imbroglio of 1910 brought the monarchy closer to political controversy than at any time since the 1830s. George V reluctantly acceded to Asquith's request for constitutional guarantees, promising, in effect, to create Liberal peers in sufficient quantity to swamp the House of Lords should Asquith's government be returned to power and find itself unable to carry legislation restricting the Lord's power of veto through the upper House. Normally the British constitution functions admirably enough under the convention that the monarch only acts on the advice of his ministers, but this particular interpretation was now being stretched almost to the limit, even though precedents existed from the reigns of Anne and William IV.

With whatever democratic justification, George V was now being asked to lend his name to a party manoeuvre which would go far to undermine the peerage, one of the traditional pillars of the state. He would probably not have consented had he not been persuaded by one of his influential private secretaries, Knollys, that he had no alternative. Knollys suppressed information to the effect that Balfour was prepared to take office at the head of a minority government were the king to refuse Asquith's request for guarantees. Knollys's motive was to keep the monarch as far as possible out of party controversy, into which it would surely have been plunged had George V granted a dissolution to Balfour after refusing one to Asquith. It is interesting to conjecture what might have happened had Balfour had the chance to form a government at this juncture. He might have been able to maintain himself in power, either through a deal with the Irish Nationalists on the basis of tariff reform, or by playing the anti-home rule card at a general election. The history of the next few years would certainly have been different, with Ireland less to the fore, and with perhaps an altered emphasis in foreign policy that might have had some bearing on the circumstances which took Britain into the first world war.

The government took a risk in dissolving parliament just before Christmas in 1910. The country had arguably had its fill of electoral politics earlier in the year, and had no wish to be put through it all again on the eve of the festive season. Thirteen years later, the Consevatives were to be severely punished at the polls for dissolving after a similarly short interval and in the same season of the year. Circumstances, however, seemed to augur well for the government in late 1910. Asquith, in particular, faced the electoral contest with much greater confidence than in the preceding winter. Continuing economic recovery made the position of free trade apparently impregnable, and tariff-reform propaganda was distinctly muted in comparison with January 1910. Even more to the point, Asquith was now much more certain of his ground as far as the constitutional issue was concerned. He had obtained royal guarantees, and he now had a definite plan to put before the electorate. The Parliament Bill, based on the resolutions of the previous spring, had been introduced into the House of Lords in November. This proposed to effect a further shift of power from Lords to Commons, but not in too drastic or revolutionay a fashion. Though the Lords were to lose their absolute legislative veto, along with any remaining role in matters of finance, Liberals were at pains to stress how far these proposals stopped short of the oft-cited Unionist bogey of single-chamber government. No measure could be carried through parliament in less than two years against the determined opposition of the House of Lords, and a reduction in the maximum life of any one parliament from seven to five years made that body more accountable to the electorate. This was, for the Liberals, very favourable terrain on which to fight. They could pose, not only as the champions of people against peers, but also in their traditional guise as the custodians of ordered constitutional progress. How Gladstone would have relished fighting a general election on such a theme. Almost his last act as prime minister in 1894 had been to sound a clarion cry against the upper chamber, and he would have been in his element explaining how a necessary adjustment could be effected in the relations between the two Houses of parliament whilst at the same time remaining true to the spirit of the constitution. As it was, Asquith, with his clarity of mind and conservative instincts, more than rose to the occasion. His speeches at this juncture were as impressive as those in defence of free trade a few years ealier, and his triumph in the December 1910 election probably marked the high point of his premiership (Doc. 14).

By contrast, the Unionists found themselves in a much more invidious position. In the circumstances of late 1910, they were forced to make all the running and to try to recapture the initiative. The issues which had served them well at the beginning of the year could no longer be relied upon. The people's budget had since become law, finally accepted by the Lords with hardly a murmur in April 1910. As for the upper House, many Unionists were no longer content to fight solely in defence of the constitutional *status quo*, for they felt that associations with hereditary privilege had done them harm in northern constituencies earlier in the year. Economic recovery in the course of 1910 made the protectionist gospel far less persuasive, and Balfour was faced with the old Unionist electoral problem of balancing between the interests of town and country. Tariff reform had done the Unionists no harm in rural England in January 1910, but had arguably prevented them from making expected gains in Lancashire and the north of England which might have won them the election. Balfour therefore decided on a bold manoeuvre which he hoped might enable him to seize the centre ground. At the Albert Hall, in late November, he declared it his intention, should he regain office, to submit any proposed tariff reform scheme to the electorate, by means of a referendum. In this way he hoped, at one and the same time, to retain the loyalty of committed protectionists and also win over nervous, uncommitted voters, worried about the early imposition of food taxes.[3]

This was to prove the keynote speech of the election, with much of the ensuing party battle fastening onto it. Balfour had been encouraged to make his move, partly by the airing of the referendum issue at the recent constitutional conference, and partly by the support of younger protectionists like Bonar Law, engaged in fighting a Lancashire seat where free-trade sympathies remained strong. Whatever the tactical arguments, however, Balfour was gambling with the goodwill of other Unionists, not least Austen Chamberlain, with his strong sense of filial piety regarding his father's uncompromising protectionism. Balfour's calculations can be readily discerned. He was anxious to free his party from the incubus of special privilege which had attached to it in January 1910, for the referendum could be defended as an impeccably democratic device for settling disputes between the upper and the lower House. It would also enable Balfour to sidestep, for the time being, the thorny problem of reforming the actual composition of the House of Lords, where the Liberals had accused him of trying to perpetuate Unionist ascendancy in a different guise. Offering a referendum on tariff reform, furthermore, allowed Balfour to counter Liberal claims that it was merely a device to be used against proposed Liberal reforms. At the same time, it gave him, so he believed, an opportunity of exposing Liberal hypocrisy. At the Albert Hall, he had challenged Asquith to submit the contentious issue of Irish home rule in his turn to the verdict of a popular referendum. In addition, he questioned the sincerity of Liberal tirades against the House of Lords, given that they apparently had no intention of abolishing that institution or even of altering its composition. Rather they wished to preserve it, effectively shorn of its powers, as a gilded sham, in order to disguise what they really had in mind. This, according to Balfour, was single-chamber rule, the dictatorship of the house of commons, which, when controlled by Liberals dependent on

Labour and Irish Nationalist votes, would prove inimical to the rights of free-born Englishmen.

Balfour's referendum proposal was a daring manoeuvre, but also one which left his flanks vulnerable to attack. To begin with, it represented a sharp reversal of policy, a conspicuous volte-face. The Unionists had fought the previous general election as staunch defenders of the status quo. Now they had opted for constitutional innovation, thereby implicitly accepting much of the case made out by the Liberals in preceding years. To Churchill, it seemed the biggest rout of the political old guard since Marston Moor and Naseby. What, he demanded to know, did the Unionists now stand for?[4] Less than two weeks previously, at Nottingham in mid-November, Balfour had delivered a very different political speech, in which he had spelled out proposals for the reform of the House of Lords, and had placed protection at the forefront of the Unionists' economic and social programme.[5] Now reform of the upper chamber was placed on one side, and tariff reform itself was relegated to the Greek calends, or at least to such time as the Unionists won both a general election and an ensuing referendum. The Liberals, in government, were in the enviable position of being able to fight the election on their opponents' record and programme rather than their own. Asquith delighted in drawing attention to all the unanswered questions contained in Balfour's referendum proposal, much as the Unionists had done regarding his own Albert-Hall speech a year previously. At what stage, Asquith demanded to know, in the progress of a bill or budget through parliament, should it be offered to the electorate in the form of a referendum? Who would be entitled to vote on such an occasion? Should use be made of the parliamentary franchise, or of the local government franchise, or should the suffrage now at last be conferred on all adult males? Would women have the chance to vote in referendums? And what should be done about plural voting, the abolition of which had previously been blocked by the House of Lords?

How Asquith enjoyed returning so many balls into his opponents' court. In addition, he demanded to know how Balfour proposed to define which measures would or would not justify the calling of a referendum. The Unionists, it seemed, threatened to establish a hitherto unknown distinction in English law between one kind of parliamentary legislation and another. And this was the fundamental point of the Liberals' campaign. Compared to their own modest proposals for setting a time limit to obstruction in the House of Lords, the Unionists appeared to contemplate undermining the very bases of the British constitution. Referendums would unsettle the parliamentary timetable and cause regular disturbance in the body politic. They would promote governmental instability and force a more frequent resort to general elections. They would sap the foundations of responsible and representative government and call in question the very principle of parliamentary sovereignty. Liberal speakers hastened to identify their opponents as red revolutionaries and themselves as upholders of constitutional continuity. Asquith warned that democracy without representation very soon degenerated into either anarchy or dictatorship. Here was a further indictment: Unionist plans for plebiscites or referendums were not only newfangled but foreign, drawing their inspriation from the somewhat unedifying experiments attempted under the Jacobin republic and the Bonapartes (Doc. 14).

In these circumstances, the Unionists experienced some difficulty in carrying the battle to their opponents. They renewed their denunciation of Irish home rule, fear of which had been enhanced by the existence of a hung parliament and the threat of single-chamber government. Redmond now replaced Lloyd George as the main bogey figure in Unionist election literature, being regularly depicted as the leader of a subversive political party, financed by Irish American dollars, which could dictate its own terms to a Liberal administration dependent on Irish Nationalist votes in order to survive. Lloyd George, in particular, sought to counteract such anxieties in major speeches at Mile End and Edinburgh. As to the fear of single-chamber government, he ridiculed the idea that a Liberal House of Commons, containing millionaire coalowners within its ranks, could be said to be composed of 'wild revolutionaries picked up somewhere at the street corner'. As to the Irish themselves, the Unionists, Lloyd George declared, seemed unable to fight an election campaign without resorting to some kind of bogey. The Germans had served this turn in January 1910, the Dutch in 1900, and the Irish again in 1895. And what right had the Unionists to complain of American funding when British aristocrats were so keen to marry transatlantic heiresses? 'Many a noble house tottering to its fall', he observed, 'had had its foundations underpinned by a pile of American dollars.' This reflection on the recent marriage of the Duke of Marlborough made the Mile End speech seem offensive even by the standard of Lloyd George's previous efforts at Limehouse and Newcastle. Today it can be read largely as political knockabout in the chancellor of the exchequer's inimitable style. Lloyd George laid stress on the origins of the British aristocracy in the freebooting activities of Norman conquerors or the plunderers of the church at the time of the Reformation. Provocatively, he enquired how Australians would feel if they were asked to establish an aristocracy based on the land-grabbing activities of earlier convict settlers. They would probably reply, he suggested, that they would rather be ruled by souls than by sods. This piece of innuendo landed Lloyd George in further trouble with the Tory press, but his aggressive banter did not detract from a more serious argument.

The House of Lords, he asserted, was an institution entirely out of touch with everyday life and ordinary people. It represented a narrow caste, based on snobbery and the worship of wealth and rank without merit. It was a thoroughly unbusinesslike organisation, which had nothing to offer the aspirations of all those who had to work for their living, whether in the lower or in the middle classes. It was quite an achievement of Lloyd George's to attack the composition of the upper House so effectively when the Liberals had in fact no intention of changing it, but his assault on its anachronistic nature somehow reflected on the Unionists as a whole. Rarely had the latter seemed more a party of the past than in December 1910. Apart from the ill-digested referendum pledge, they appeared to have little to say or offer on the great questions of the day. They had more or less dodged the tariff-reform issue, and, apart from the extension of freehold ownership, the most that Balfour could be got to say about social reform was that 'the poor law is a tremendous question'. Even so naturally entertaining a speaker as F. E. Smith was reduced to talking about the Tory record of the late nineteenth century and the Workmen's Compensation Act of 1897. Gleefully Lloyd George pointed to the Unionists' uncertainties and divisions over many leading issues. What, for instance, was their attitude to providing payment for MPs, in the wake of the *Osborne* decision of late 1909? Even more to the point, what would they do about the people's budget, were they to return to power? Would they repeal the controversial land duties, and once again show favouritism to landlords and brewers? And, if so, how would they make up the resulting loss of revenue?[6]

The general election of December 1910 ranked as a qualified victory for the Liberals. That of January 1910 had been a qualified defeat, for the Liberals had then forfeited their previously immense majority. Now, despite dissolving at an unpopular time and for no very clear reason that could be vouchsafed to the electorate, the Liberals had forestalled any further swing against them and won a mandate to govern for the third time in succession. No party since the 1860s had won three or more general elections in a row. In terms of seats, the result in December 1910 more or less repeated that of the previous January. Liberals and Unionists had 271 and 273 seats respectively, although the government's position was marginally strengthened thanks to the gain of 2 seats each by Labour and the Irish Nationalists. However, over 50 seats changed hands in consequence of shifts in regional behaviour. The Unionists picked up seats in Lancashire and the west country, places where they had hoped to do rather better in the preceding January. The Liberals, on the other hand, won back several county as well as borough seats elsewhere, and they also recorded a net gain of 4 seats in London, where they had been noticeably weak before 1906. Another achievement of the Liberals was to contain the advance of Labour. Though that party had slightly increased its tally of seats, it had fought fewer constituencies, 56 against 78 in January 1910. Lack of funds, especially in consequence of the *Osborne* case, had made it difficult for it to fight two general election campaigns within a single year. In any case, it lacked a distinct voice, for the battle in December 1910 took place very much on Liberal terrain, concerning issues pre-eminently constitutional.

The short parliament of 1910 was succeeded by the long parliament of 1911–18, though only its first half will concern us here. This would prove to be one of the great reforming parliaments, not least in the sphere of political and constitutional change, and especially in the first and last years of its existence. The 1911 session was dominated by two great measures, the first being the

Parliament Bill, which proposed finally to put an end to the absolute veto of the House of Lords. This was inevitable following the December 1910 election, which had returned the Liberals to power secure in the possession of the royal guarantees, although the existence of these was not made fully public until July 1911. The Liberals believed that they had framed a moderate and statesmanlike bill for dealing with the upper House. Its preamble, which of course did not carry the force of law, spoke of the need to effect a more revitalising transformation of both the powers and the personnel of the House of Lords in the fullness of time. But, as a first step, the Bill proposed to do away with the upper House's veto entirely in respect of finance, and to make it suspensory rather than absolute in regard to other categories of legislation, with an effective power of delay lasting up to two years. The Bill also proposed to repeal the Septennial Act of 1716, and make the maximum life of any parliament five years. This, it was thought, would head off accusations about establishing single-chamber rule, along with demands for resort to referendums, by making the House of Commons more accountable to the electorate.

Even without knowledge of the royal guarantees, the House of Lords was not in a good position to resist the proposed change in the constitution. As Bagehot had once written, 'the ultimate authority in the English constitution is a newly-elected house of commons'. The verdict at the hustings had been in favour of the Parliament Bill, introduced just prior to the dissolution, and against the new-fangled device of the referendum, as canvassed by the Unionists. In the upper House, Lansdowne strove to avoid the final reckoning by belatedly introducing his own scheme of House of Lords reform. This proposed to turn it into a composite body, made up of four categories of representative peer, some chosen by the crown, some by the House of Commons, some by the rest of the peerage, and some sitting ex officio by virtue of their ministerial positions. It was hardly a well judged scheme, for it abandoned traditional Tory principle, and conceded much of the government's case against the existing House of Lords, without reaping any tangible benefit in return. It promised too little in the way of democratisation of the upper House to win much popular support in the country at large. Even if the House of Lords had been able to upset the government at a late stage in the passage of the Parliament Bill, the Unionists would still have been placed in an invidious position. They could hardly take office and risk incurring the odium of having to dissolve parliament for the third time within eighteen months. And by-elections during the first half of 1911 gave little indication of a movement of opinion in their favour, with the Liberals easily retaining seats at Barnstaple, Bethnal Green, and Middleton.

Knowledge, revealed in July 1911, that the government was after all in possession of royal guarantees, provoked a major crisis within the Unionist party. Balfour, Lansdowne, and much of the old guard, now counselled acceptance of the Parliament Bill, on the grounds that it still left the Unionists in a fairly favourable position. They would be able to delay home rule, and other measures obnoxious to them such as Welsh disestablishment and the Plural Voting bill, for at least two years, during which time anything could happen. The alternative was the creation of some five hundred upstart Liberal peers which would destroy the conservative character of the upper House for the foreseeable future. Asquith had held off from any such mass creation prior to the crucial vote in the House of Lords, for he desired to do as little obvious violence as possible either to the royal conscience or to the country's institutions. Also he trusted that the threat would be sufficient to enable him to get his way. But a sizeable proportion of Unionists, nicknamed diehards or ditchers, wished to continue the struggle to the bitter end and force ministers to carry out a mass creation of peers. Such an action, they believed, would reveal the government in its true revolutionary colours, and, moreover, by making the existing House of Lords appear ridiculous, it would force the issue of the upper House reform to the top of the political agenda (Doc. 15). Unlike Balfour and his immediate supporters, few of the diehards had previously held high office, and they were deeply suspicious of the cosy atmosphere of frontbench collusion which had seemed to permeate the constitutional conference discussions of the preceding year. If Balfour, as they believed, was now prepared to compromise over the House of Lords, might he not soon enough do the same over the Irish Act of Union. As will be seen, the Parliament Bill of 1911 was to cast a distinct shadow over the home rule controversy of succeeding years.

Eventually, however, the government got its way without

having to resort to a mass peerage creation. Enough Unionist peers abstained, and thirty-seven even voted with the government, thus earning themselves the privilege of being called rats by their diehard colleagues. Along with the Liberal peers, and a number of temporising higher clergy, this made for a small but sufficient majority of 131:114, and the Parliament Bill duly became law. In one sense, it represented a triumph for a long-established Liberal policy, for Bright and then Gladstone had both sounded the clarion cry against the House of Lords. In another sense, it proved a Pyrrhic victory, as subsequent events were to make clear, and it might have been better for the Liberals had they been able to carry out their threat to dilute the peerage and remake the House of Lords more in their own image. In the short run, however, the Parliament Bill, and the demoralisation which it caused in the Unionist ranks, helped the Liberals to carry through the last of their major social reforms in the period before the first world war, the National Insurance Act of 1911. This was a very large undertaking, ambitiously dealing with the wide field of health as well as unemployment provision, and, like other Liberal welfare measures of these years, it was based not so much on one particular ideology as on principles and practices borrowed from a variety of sources.

As finally enacted, it combined both liberal and illiberal traditions. That part of the act which concerned health was much the more wide-ranging, though it stopped well short of being comprehensive. Free access to a doctor, along with sickness and disablement cover in the event of loss of earnings, became available for workers in full-time employment, but their wives and dependants were much less well provided for. However, the Act did introduce maternity allowances, and it also established free hospital treatment in special sanatoriums for the victims of tuberculosis. Evidently expensive, the whole scheme was paid for, partly out of taxation, and partly out of contributions compulsorily levied on both employers and employees. This was the point of Lloyd George's boast that he was giving the average worker 9d for 4d. Overall the state would contribute two-ninths to the insurance fund, and employers and employees three-ninths and four-ninths respectively, although this would not obviate considerable popular resentment against what was seen as an enforced docking of wages. Despite its compulsory nature, the Act made little use of the machinery of the state except in so far as it established an insurance commission to oversee its workings. Basically it co-opted and made use of intermediary organisations: friendly societies and trades unions as well as large industrial insurance companies such as the Prudential. Deposit insurance through the post office became available for those who could not otherwise find an appropriate body to take them on, perhaps because they were too old. Most categories of worker were included in the scheme, comprising even domestic servants. Three million working women, it was said, were brought within the Act's provisions, although one million were excluded, and this, along with the introduction of the maternity allowance, enabled Asquith to claim that his government, despite controversy over the franchise, had done as much as any other to advance the interests of women.

The second part of the 1911 Act, concerning unemployment insurance, was more restricted, yet in its own way equally significant. Some two and a half million workers, mainly in construction industries, were to be covered by a scheme, to which employees and employers would each contribute 2½d a week with the state adding a further 1d. Essentially it bore the imprint of Churchill, in what was arguably the most radical phase of his career. Churchill broke new ground, dispensing even with the Webbs' concern to make unemployment relief dependent in some measure on the good character of the recipient. His scheme led the rest of the world, including Germany, and was to be considerably extended in 1916 and 1920. Along with labour exchanges, it has been described as the only major social reform of the new Liberalism to survive to the present day without basic modifications.[7]

After protracted debates, the National Insurance Bill eventually passed its third reading in the House of Commons by 324:21 in December 1911. The opposition, such as it was, comprised a very mixed bag. It included right-wing Conservatives like Gretton and Page Croft, independent-minded Irish MPs like Healy and O'Brien, and prominent socialists like Snowden and Lansbury. The bulk of the Unionist party had no wish to be accused of unfriendliness to social reform, and the size of the Commons' majority in favour of the Bill made it easier for the House of Lords to acquiesce in its passing. In any case, their

Lordships seemed to have learnt something from recent experience. Lansdowne argued that national insurance should be treated as financial legislation, a debatable proposition and not one that he had been anxious to apply to the people's budget. No doubt he also felt, in contrast to two years earlier, that it was better for the electorate to feel the effects of major financial measures before passing judgement on them. This calculation, if such it was, proved shrewd. During the next year and more, the Liberals were to go through one of their deepest troughs of unpopularity, thanks in large part to working-class resentment at bearing what appeared a disproportionately large share of the costs of the new social policy. Starting with Oldham and South Somerset in November 1911, the Liberals suffered a run of severe by-election losses which continued for much of the following year. Partly this was due to the intervention of Labour candidates in several contests – as for instance in that which cost the Liberals Gladstone's old seat of Midlothian in September 1912 – itself due to the Labour party's unease about national insurance and its desire to be seen to flex its muscles at a time of prevalent industrial unrest. But the Unionists also picked up support in their own right, thanks to widespread popular animosity against the new and regressive national taxation levied by the insurance act. Many working-class voters resented paying flat-rate contributions, indeed a poll tax, as they saw it, on behalf of the deadbeats of society, and some were even persuaded that the money was intended to defray MPs' salaries or supplement Liberal party funds. As a social experiment, national insurance proved no more popular than had the Education Act of 1902. It would take the first world war, and a much wider degree of national compulsion, to make free medical treatment acceptable as an integral part of British life.

Like national insurance, the other great reforming measure of 1911, the Parliament Act, proved a double-edged sword for the Liberals. Many of their troubles over the next few years were in some way attributable to it. Each one of its provisions, intended though they were to enhance the authority of the elected chamber, contained a particular inconvenience. Even the preamble, which portrayed the Parliament Act as an interim measure preparatory to a comprehensive reform of the composition of the upper chamber, enabled the Unionists to argue that no measure as significant as home rule should even be attempted while the constitution was still partly in suspense. The much more rigid definition of financial Bills would upset Lloyd George's effort in 1914 to bring in a budget as ambitious in scope as that of 1909, and the two-year suspensive veto would give the House of Lords a potential stranglehold on government legislation during the first half at least of what would now be quinquennial parliaments. The delaying power of the upper chamber had received, as it were, an institutionalised recognition. The effect was to be seen in early 1913, when, by crushing majorities, the House of Lords rejected both the Irish Home Rule and Welsh Disestablishment Bills after their first parliamentary circuit, and it repeated the treatment after a second such circuit later in the same year. Under the new dispensation of 1911, any measure on which Lords and Commons disagreed had to pass through the parliamentary mill in three successive sessions before becoming law.

The Parliament Act, and its attendant struggles, brought also an added virulence and recrimination to British party politics. The House of Commons was more disorderly in 1911 and 1912 than for many years past, and an alteration was marked in another way by a change in the Unionist party leadership. Balfour resigned his position in November 1911 as a direct consequence of the debacle in Unionist political fortunes over the previous twelve months. Between 1906 and 1910, it could be claimed, his dexterous management had brought his party back from the depths of electoral disaster to something like parity with the Liberals. But the recovery had not been sustained in the second general election of 1910, and in 1911 the party had suffered humiliation over the Parliament Act. Both these defeats could plausibly be blamed on Balfour's over-subtlety and compromising of basic Unionist principles. Bonar Law, his replacement, represented a different breed of Unionist statesmanship: middle-class, provincial, not university educated, and without frontbench experience. Truculent and unaccommodating, Bonar Law was determined to mark himself out as distinctly as possible from his predecessor. Home rule was one subject where, to preserve their remaining credibility, the Unionists could afford no hint of compromise, and where, moreover, they must show no quarter to their adversaries. Like many

141

in his party, Bonar Law believed that the government had
obtained the Parliament Act by essentially unconstitutional
means, and that therefore almost any means could justifiably be
used against it. The Liberals, as he saw it, were kept in power by a
corrupt bargain with Irish nationalism, but their hearts were not
really in an outright battle for home rule, and they would give
way if things were made sufficiently hot for them (Doc. 16).

The Liberals, not surprisingly, had rather different expectations of the third Home Rule Bill when it was introduced in
parliament in April 1912. In contrast to 1886 and 1893, when
home rule had almost seemed a counsel of despair, they now
considered the case for it to have been sufficiently established.
Devolution had become an accepted principle of imperial policy,
and the Liberals were confident that they could apply to Ireland
the prescription which appeared to have been so successful in
south Africa. A majority of British constituencies, unlike in 1886
and 1893, now seemed to favour Irish home rule, and recent
social reforms, such as pensions and national insurance, had, it
was thought, given Ireland too large a financial stake in the
maintenance of the Act of Union for her to want to push home
rule to the point of complete separation. Not that the government
totally under-estimated the problems before it. Home rule,
though broadly supported by the great majority of Liberals, was
liable to provoke resentment should it appear that Ireland was
benefiting more than seemed fair from any reorganisation of the
United Kingdom. The financial arrangements presented particular difficulties, more indeed than in 1886 and 1893. Thanks to
Liberal welfare reforms, Ireland was faced with spiralling social
expenditure, and now found itself asking, paradoxically, for both
greater autonomy and increased financial subventions at one and
the same time. The government suffered its only defeat over
home rule in the House of Commons on a question of finance, in
November 1912, when Liberal MPs deserted in the belief that
Ireland was being treated over-generously. At the same time,
again in response to Liberal backbench pressure, and much to the
chagrin of Redmond and his followers, Ireland was refused any
right to vary customs duties under home rule. Imposing this
concession on Redmond made it more difficult for the government to ask further sacrifices of him over Ulster later on. In any
case, without Ulster's inclusion in a home rule Ireland – and the

province was understood to contribute four-fifths of the country's income tax revenue – the complex financial arrangements would fall to pieces (Doc. 17).

Ulster of course was the rock which would ultimately sink home rule, although this did not become immediately apparent. The Liberals have here received much criticism for their want of statesmanship, some of it well founded and some of it less so. Ulster, the most northerly of Ireland's four ancient provinces, contained also the greatest concentration of its Protestant population, although, in fact, Protestants were in a clear majority in only four of Ulster's nine counties. Indeed half the province's representation at Westminster was made up of Nationalist MPs. This, and the long tradition of Ulster Liberalism, which had endured for much of the nineteenth century, made the government reluctant to award the province special status, especially as it had not threatened to be too much of a problem in either 1886 or 1893. On the other hand, and this might perhaps have alerted the Liberals, Ulster had been throughout history readier to resist established authority than any other Irish province. It had been in the vanguard of opposition to the Stuart kings, to the eighteenth-century Dublin parliament, and even to the Act of Union, although it had been swiftly reconciled to the latter, not least thanks to the industrialisation and prosperity that had overtaken the north-eastern corner of Ireland. The first and second Home Rule Bills had not stirred Ulster unduly, perhaps because they seemed unlikely to pass, but the same could hardly be said of the third Home Rule Bill on its introduction in 1912. In any case, by then the Ulster lobby had greatly increased its standing within the ranks of Unionism. In 1905, it had held Balfour's government to ransom, and forced the resignation of the Irish chief secretary. And in 1911, Bonar Law's replacement of Balfour had brought to the Unionist leadership a Scottish–Irish Presbyterian with close family ties to Ulster.

In retrospect, it can be said that the Liberals should have conceded something to Ulster at the outset, while they still clearly held the initiative. This would have spared them the humiliation of having to climb down later, and it would also have rendered them less dependent on the House of Lords, whose two-year delaying power enabled it to sabotage any subsequent attempt to amend the Home Rule Bill. Lloyd George and Churchill, at least, seem to have taken this view in cabinet in 1912. Lloyd George's background gave him an understanding of the power of Celtic nonconformity, while Churchill, whose own father certainly had not under-estimated Ulster's feelings, had faced violent demonstrations on a visit to the province in early 1912. Asquith assessed the situation rather differently. His instinct was not to meet troubles half way. The phrase, 'wait and see', which, along with the mental attitudes which it implied, was to become such a count against Asquith's wartime leadership, had become associated with him in parliamentary debate in 1910. Masterly inactivity, however, had served Asquith well on various occasions. In 1911, it had enabled him to see off opposition to the Parliament Bill, for Unionist nerve had collapsed before the prospect of *résistance à l'outrance*.

No doubt, Asquith expected Ulster's opposition to home rule to crumble in much the same way. After all, Liberal governments in the past, not least in Gladstone's day, had coped well enough with both the threat and reality of widespread disorder in Ireland. However, Asquith's government had to a considerable extent tied its own hands in this matter, for it had dispensed with much of the coercive legislation which had served law and order in Ireland well over previous generations. The Peace Preservation Act, for instance, had been allowed to lapse in 1907, and with it had gone the power to seize arms or to prevent their importation. Nor was Birrell, in charge at Dublin castle, the very model of an effective Irish chief secretary. As a cabinet minister, his record of legislative achievement was, to say the least, uneven, and his name was particularly associated with the failure of the Education and Irish Councils Bills of 1906 and 1907. It is tempting to speculate what the outcome of the home rule struggle might have been had Asquith, early on in the proceedings, replaced Birrell with Lloyd George. No more than in 1916 could it have been seen as a demotion. Lloyd George's skills as a conciliator were unrivalled, and in 1921 they were to prove instrumental in securing the nearest thing possible in Ireland to a final settlement.[8]

As much as any other prime minister, Asquith enjoyed the perquisites of office and wished to continue doing so. He knew that his government would be brought down were the Irish Nationalists to desert his side and vote with the opposition.

Asking Redmond to accept partition would, he feared, cause this to happen, especially as the Irish leader was under pressure from rival nationalist groups, such as O'Brien's movement and Sinn Fein, not to agree to any compromise. But it was unlikely that things would in fact have turned out in this way. Once he stopped supporting the government, Redmond had really nowhere else to go. Whatever he might have done in 1910, he could hardly in 1912 use his party to place a stridently anti-home rule government in power. At most he could have abstained, and that would have left Asquith still in office with Liberal and Labour support. Partition was, in fact, proposed in June 1912, in an amendment to the Home Rule Bill standing in the name of a Liberal backbencher, Agar-Robartes. This would have excluded the four strongly Protestant counties of north-east Ireland – Antrim, Down, Londonderry and Armagh – from the Bill's operation. Unionists supported it, as did a number of Liberal backbenchers of markedly nonconformist or federalist leanings, and the government's majority fell to sixty-nine. This was not, however, enough to make Asquith change his mind, and the chance of some kind of Irish settlement on the basis of partition, nearly a decade before it actually came about, was lost. Nationalists were encouraged to continue believing in the imminent possibility of a united home rule Ireland, making the disillusionment and bitterness all the greater when this proved unattainable (Doc. 18).

Ulster's intransigence became much more marked in the summer of 1912. It found particular expression in the drawing up of a solemn league and covenant, pledging its signatories to do all in their power to prevent the establishment of a home rule parliament, and to refuse any recognition of its authority. This was signed by 471,000 Ulster men and women in September 1912. Some historians have seen it as a useful safety valve, in that it diverted Ulster's energies from inter-communal violence at a time of rising tension. But it was backed up by the threat of armed resistance to home rule, especially after the formation of the 100,000-strong Ulster volunteer force in January 1913. The Ulster movement indeed was a powerful compound of the old and new. It built upon atavistic sentiment, and the fear that victory for home rule would reverse the battle of the Boyne and hand over Ulster's Protestants into the power of their ancient enemies. But it also reflected pride in the thriving prosperity of Belfast and its hinterland which might be adversely affected by political sea change. In its way, it was an expression of regional nationalism, which was to have such an effect on twentieth-century Europe, and which was even then starting to tear the Balkans asunder. It had also a further dimension, in the form of the uncompromising support promised by the Unionist leader, Bonar Law, who, in a speech at Blenheim in July 1912 declared that he could imagine no lengths of resistance to which Ulster might go which he would not be prepared to support. Language like this had not been held about Ireland by a responsible British statesman since the seventeenth century, and it is unlikely that Balfour or the other leadership contenders in 1911, Chamberlain and Long, would have gone so far. Bonar Law's strength of feeling derived partly from his Ulster connections, and partly from the conviction, shared by many Unionists, that the Liberals had done violence to the constitution in 1911, and that almost any methods could justifiably be used against them. Bonar Law was also keen to give a lead to a still somewhat disunited party, and he counted on being able to force the government to concede a general election on home rule, which, if 1886 and 1895 were anything to go by, and given the current trend in by-elections, the Unionists could be expected to win (Doc. 16).

This was, to say the least, a very high-risk strategy. It relied on activating constitutional forces which had long lain dormant. If the Liberals were to be forced to call a general election against their will, the reserve power of the crown might well have to be brought into play. George V must be persuaded, by the threat of civil war in Ireland, that his duty lay either in vetoing the Home Rule Bill or in dismissing his ministers and dissolving parliament. Neither procedure had been resorted to in living memory, the power of the crown having last been so employed in 1708 and 1834–35 respectively. Alternatively, the Unionists could use the House of Lords to obstruct the Army Annual Bill and thus deprive the government of control over the forces of law and order. For a party calling itself Conservative to fall back on such methods has an ironic ring, and there were also other difficult questions to be answered. If a general election were to be held, and the Liberals won, would Bonar Law continue to support the possibility of Ulster's armed resistance? And what would his attitude be if the government was after all to offer Ulster exclusion from the application of the Home Rule Bill? In other words, was Bonar Law's main obligation to the Protestant majority in Ulster, or to the thinly spread but influential Unionist minority in the rest of Ireland, including political grandees like Lansdowne, who feared partition as a sell-out of their particular interests? The radical stance adopted by Bonar Law in opposition to home rule had helped to change the terms of the debate. In asserting that Ulster's Protestants were a distinct community with a right of self-determination, Bonar Law, and those most closely associated with him like F. E. Smith, by implication conceded the case of the Catholics of the rest of Ireland. This was not a conclusion that Balfour would willingly have come to, and it underlines the significance of the change in Unionist leadership which had occurred in 1911.

However, in the battle of wills that pitted government against opposition over Ireland during 1912 and 1913, it seemed likely that the Liberals might weaken first. The cabinet contained, as has been seen, some restless spirits on the subject of home rule. Churchill was one of those who hankered after a federalist solution, in which Ireland's particular problems might be subsumed in a general scheme of devolution for the whole of the British isles, with even England being divided up in a new version of the Anglo-Saxon heptarchy. Propounded by Churchill on his own initiative at Dundee in Septempter 1912, this scheme had no actual sequel, but it provided a first indication of a wavering of resolution among ministers. More significant, a year later, was an intervention by Loreburn, until recently lord chancellor, suggesting an inter-party conference to seek out a compromise solution. Loreburn had been close to Campbell-Bannerman and to the Gladstonian tradition, and thus might have been expected to take a different line. But he was clearly impressed by the military showing of the Ulster volunteers, and he remembered how coercion and the effort to defeat the land league in the early 1880s had nearly broken the heart of the Liberal party and led it to concede to Parnell most of his demands. Loreburn's initiative paved the way for secret exploratory talks between Asquith and Bonar Law during October–December 1913. Both men indicated a willingness to make concessions, without committing themselves to anything more specific. Asquith, for the first time, seemed to contemplate partition, based now on the exclusion of six Ulster counties in which the bulk of the Protestant population was concentrated. Bonar Law, for his part, now seemed willing to throw over the interests of the southern Irish Unionists, as long as he could obtain security for Ulster. Both men, as responsible party leaders, were reluctant to become the prisoners of their extremists. At the same time, both had taken up other positions too recently to feel able to abandon them easily.

Asquith revealed the government's change of thinking early in March 1914. Each Ulster county was to be given the option of remaining outside a home-rule Ireland for six years, at the end of which time it would be automatically included unless parliament should otherwise determine. This was a subtle formula suggested by Lloyd George. He calculated that Ulster would hardly take up arms against a contingency only possible in six years time, and that rejection of the offer would make the Unionists seem undemocratic, for at least two general elections would fall due within the six-year period. Asquith had won Redmond's very grudging acceptance, partly by representing to him the dangers of royal intervention and an enforced dissolution of parliament that would undo all the home-rule effort of the previous two years. But Carson, speaking for Ulster, rejected the offer out of hand. 'We do not', he declared, 'want sentence of death with a stay of execution for six years' (Doc. 19). He knew that Ulster would brook no compromise on exclusion, but his intransigence now threatened to distance him from Bonar Law, who understood that 'it was really the certainty of British support which made the strength of the Ulster position'. Asquith seemed about to open a breach in the Unionist ranks of the kind which he had exploited so successfully in 1911. But at this point, the events of the Curragh 'mutiny' supervened. This, the most celebrated episode in the whole crisis, was provoked by plans, apparently hatched by Seely and Churchill, for a military and naval show of force inside and off the coast of Ulster. Interestingly the two men, respectively war secretary and first lord of the admiralty, were both former Unionists. Their concern was to prevent any arms seizures by the Ulster volunteers, and to forestall any attempt by Carson to establish a provisional government in Ulster. They may also have hoped to provoke acts of defiance against the military which would have cost Ulster the support of British public opinion. But, if this was the plan, it soon misfired. Fifty-eight cavalry officers, stationed at the Curragh outside Dublin, preferred to face dismissal rather than move against Ulster, and, in order not to lose their services Seely provided a written reassurance that the army would not be used to impose home rule upon the province. This was repudiated by Asquith, once he heard about it, and Seely had to resign. But by then the damage had been done. Down to this point of time, the government had seemed able to rely on the army in the event of any final showdown with Ulster, but now this instrument had broken in its hand. In Ulster, however, the episode had further strengthened the forces of resistance to home rule, which, in April 1914, were able to reinforce their position still more by carrying out a spectacular gun-running operation at Larne.

The Curragh incident engendered much bitter mutual recrimination in the House of Commons. But, in other respects, it encouraged the movement towards an agreed political solution. The government's credibility had been damaged, but not fatally. Asquith's authority was, if anything, enhanced, for he had not been party to the original manoeuvres, and his assumption of the war secretaryship steadied Liberal nerves. He still had some cards to play. As a last resort, he could threaten to blockade Ulster by sea and starve it into surrender. But, more to the point was the fact that in May 1914 the Home Rule Bill at last completed all its parliamentary stages, requiring only the royal assent to become law. The House of Lords could delay it no longer, and the government had avoided having to call a premature general election. Asquith repeated his offer to Ulster, whereby counties could individually opt out of home rule for six years, and this was incorporated in an amending bill which was introduced in the House of Lords in June. For their part, Bonar Law and Carson, having failed to force a dissolution of parliament, had no wish to be associated, if they could avoid it, with sectarian bloodshed and armed resistance to authority. But they intended to obtain much better terms on Ulster's behalf, and they used their position in the House of Lords to amend the Amending Bill itself, so as to exclude all nine Ulster counties, and for an indefinite period. This was the situation on the eve of the first world war in July 1914, when the speaker of the House of Commons, at royal instigation, presided over the Buckingham palace conference in an endeavour to bring all parties in the dispute together. Here Liberals and Irish Nationalists made a further concession, in agreeing to the more or less indefinite exclusion of part of Ulster. But the conference broke down over the precise delimitation of this area, with the main stumbling-block being the county of Tyrone, where the Protestant and Catholic populations were evenly balanced and inextricably intermixed.

This episode is often seen as the nadir of pre-war Liberalism. The government, it has been said, had got itself into a situation in Ireland in which the likeliest outcome was civil conflict, an eventuality that was only averted for the time being by the outbreak of European war. But was this really the case? An alternative interpretation is that Asquith had brought all parties within measurable distance of agreement, narrowing down the area in dispute between Redmond and Carson to the muddy byways of Fermanagh and Tyrone. Only a few months previously, Nationalists had declared that it would be an act of blasphemy to partition Ireland, and to exclude, from the territory to be given home rule, 'the country of Hugh O'Neill and Owen Roe, the country where St. Patrick lies buried, the country where his great cathedral was founded, the hills where he laboured as a slave' (Doc. 18). For their part, many Unionists had hoped that the Ulster movement would be sufficient entirely to frustrate the prospect of Irish home rule. Now the third Home Rule Bill was on the point of becoming law, a fact which had served to concentrate the minds of politicians wonderfully. Perhaps there was something to be said for Asquith's 'wait and see' strategy after all. At any rate, thanks partly to the prime minister's exploitation of the mood of wartime consensus, the Home Rule Bill duly received the royal assent in September 1914, and was placed on the statute book. Its operation was suspended for the duration of the war, by the end of which circumstances had so changed that it was never put into force. Nonetheless, its enactment represented a significant milestone in Anglo-Irish relations. For better or for worse, it marked a new point of departure in the history of the Irish question (Doc. 19).

The first world war removed home rule for the time being from the arena of practical politics. No one can safely predict, least of all in Ireland, what might have happened had it not broken out when it did. But one or two things can be stated with confidence.

There would almost certainly have been a general election before home rule was finally implemented. The king might well have insisted on this as a condition for giving the Bill the royal assent, at least in peacetime. Alternatively, the life of the parliament elected in December 1910 might anyway have come to the end of its term. A point not often noted is that, under the Bill's provisions, a year could elapse between the royal assent and the assembling of a home rule parliament. An intervening general election would have had a vital bearing on the situation. Should the Liberals have won, the Unionists would have found it impossible to continue on the path of undying opposition to home rule in any form, without the risk of appearing as an anti-constitutional party, a latter-day version of the Jacobites. Should the Unionists have won, on the other hand, which many thought more likely, they would hardly have been in a position to repeal the Home Rule Act without risking, throughout the greater part of Ireland, the kind of widespread disorder and defiance of the law which Ulster had promised in the event of being required to submit to home rule from Dublin. As a counterpart to the Ulster volunteers, a similar but rival force of Irish volunteers had been formed in November 1913 in the Nationalist areas of Ireland, and the long struggle over the third Home Rule Bill had aroused passions and expectations which, had Europe remained at peace, would have been with difficulty contained. Ironically, Bonar Law, had he become prime minister in late 1914 or 1915, might well have had to set his seal on a home rule settlement, much as his Unionist colleagues would have to do in 1920 and 1921.

Ireland apart, perhaps the main question mark over Asquith's peacetime premiership concerns his handling of women's suffrage. This still carries echoes to this day. The image of the suffragette militant or martyr provides a disturbing commentary on the Indian summer of the years before the outbreak of the first world war. For once, a Liberal government was found wanting in the extension of democracy, in endorsing progress towards emancipation and equality. Several counts can indeed be made against Asquith himself, a man who all too obviously enjoyed the company of young women while resolutely denying them the vote. In particular he could be accused of failing to grasp a great historic opportunity. Liberal governments had aided the advance of women in the past, for instance towards the franchise and responsibilities in respect of the poor law and local government, and Asquith himself boasted how much his own administration had done to safeguard women's interests in industrial employment.

Votes for women was a subject which commanded a broad consensus in the House of Commons, supported in varying degrees by all political parties. Private members' Bills to enfranchise women regularly passed on second reading by large majorities, indeed in successive years from 1908 to 1911. That of 1910, standing in the name of a Labour MP, Shackleton, would have placed over a million women on the parliamentary electoral register. Its second reading was carried by 299 votes to 189, the majority including 161 Liberals, 31 Labour, 20 Irish Nationalists, and 87 Unionists. (The minority comprised 60 Liberals, 2 Labour, 14 Nationalists, and 113 Unionists.) It only remained for the government to allow parliamentary time and facilities to enable such a Conciliation Bill, so-called as it enjoyed support in all parties, to pass into law. But here Asquith's conservative, 'wait and see' attitude, which had served him well in combating tariff reform and referendums, now arguably let him down; and he used his position to block progress towards women's suffrage, ostensibly on the grounds that there was no electoral mandate for it and that it would impair the bases of chivalry and understanding between the sexes.

However, Asquith was not the only barrier to female suffrage. His cabinet was divided on the issue, with some significant figures, such as the colonial secretary, Lewis Harcourt, in opposition to it. More significantly, Asquith's government depended upon a coalition of interests in the House of Commons, all with differing priorities. The Irish Nationalists, after 1910, were vital to his government's survival, and prior to 1912 they had broadly supported proposals for female enfranchisement. But in that year they shifted their position, and helped to defeat the conciliation bill by 222 votes to 208, thereby inflicting the first serious parliamentary setback on women's suffrage for some considerable time. Foremost in Irish Nationalist calculations was the fear that attempting to carry votes for women would consume too much parliamentary time, and thereby threaten the progress of the Home Rule Bill, which was just being launched in its career. Many Liberal MPs also had an ambiguous attitude towards women's suffrage. A majority of them supported it in principle, but they set greater store by the attainment of full manhood suffrage. This still had some considerable way to go, for, due to continuing property qualifications, less than 60 per cent of all adult males possessed the vote between 1884 and 1918. Many Liberals indeed saw women's suffrage as a potential threat to their party's interests, for if women were in fact to receive votes on the same terms as men, under existing arrangements this would only benefit a minority, composed mainly of independent and probably unmarried householders. Apart, as some Liberals piously claimed, from undermining the institution of marriage, the effect would be to enfranchise a propertied class of, in all likelihood, staunchly Conservative voters.

Asquith sought a way round the problem, in his own as well as his party's best interests. His proposed solution was to introduce a large-scale measure, the Franchise and Redistribution Bill of 1912, the main purpose of which was to add a further two or two-and-a-half million to the seven or eight million men already on the parliamentary electoral register. Male lodgers and sons still living at home with their parents would be the principal beneficiaries, and, in addition, plural voting was to be abolished, thereby removing half a million mainly Unionist voters from the register. But Asquith also promised to give precedence to the consideration of any female suffrage amendments, and to allow Liberals to exercise a free choice on this issue. In this way he hoped to keep the political damage to a minimum. However, this ambitious scheme, which among other things might have enfranchised up to ten and a half million women at a stroke, fell foul of the government's crowded legislative timetable. Unionists bitterly attacked the idea of forcing through another major and controversial measure under the procedure of the Parliament Act of 1911. Bonar Law described it as a revolutionary manoeuvre, worthy of the worst excesses of the Long Parliament; and, although his main objection was to manhood suffrage and the abolition of plural voting, he saw a chance to spring a mine under the government. In early 1913, in response to his intervention, the speaker ruled that any female suffrage amendment would so transform the Franchise and Redistribution Bill as to necessitate its withdrawal and re-intoduction as a different measure. The government's strategy had backfired. With other controversial measures facing further parliamentary circuits, it had no opportunity to press a major franchise Bill through 1913 and 1914. The last real chance of enacting women's suffrage before the first world war had gone.

These events helped to make 1913 notorious in terms of militant outrages. Suffragette militancy, following something of a truce in the election year, 1910, had been developing a new intensity. March 1912 had witnessed a concerted outbreak of window smashing in the west end of London, and in July of the same year a new dimension had been opened with an arson attack on the home of the colonial secretary. During 1913 arson and bomb attacks, on both public and private property, became much more the order of the day, beginning with Lloyd George's residence at Walton-on-the-Heath. The Pankhursts, in particular, regarded the speaker's ruling and Asquith's broken pledges as acts of masculine conspiracy and betrayal, which merited retribution. Militancy on this scale, however, remained the tactic of a minority in the feminist movement, and specifically that of the Women's Social and Political Union. A larger organisation, the National Union of Women's Suffrage Societies, considered violent actions to be harmful to the cause, and stressed the need not only to acquire the vote but also to work to improve women's economic and social position in general. All in all, militancy proved both the inspiration and the bane of feminism before 1914. On the one hand, it had put women's suffrage squarely on the political agenda, and provided the movement with valued martyrs, especially those who had been subjected to forcible feeding, who had attracted wider public sympathy. On the other, it had helped to split the ranks of feminism, and had generated a powerful male backlash, enabling women to be more easily stereotyped as irresponsible and unbalanced. Ominously, the backlash even reached the House of Commons. The defeat of the Conciliation, or Parliamentary Franchise (Women) Bill in March 1912 was due not only to Irish Nationalist defections but also to resentment against the window-smashing tactics employed earlier in the same month. Churchill was among those who now changed his opinions about women's suffrage and was one of nine cabinet ministers to vote against the Bill. Nor did the cause fare any better in the following year when a Liberal back-bencher, Dickinson, introduced his Representation of the People

(Women) Bill. This would have given the vote to six or seven million women by extending the householder franchise to wives and not just to widows and spinsters, but it failed by 221 votes to 269. Unionists disliked its sweeping nature and voted proportionally by 5 to 1 against it; but, influenced by the rising level of suffragette outrages, many Liberals also opposed the Bill as a surrender to violence and intimidation (Doc. 11).

The years immediately before the first world war witnessed an unusual degree of antagonism between the sexes. Christabel Pankhurst seemed a particular proponent of sex war, partly because of her determined onslaught on the double standard which governed men's and women's sexual conduct. To some extent her efforts did bear fruit: for instance, in the passing of the Criminal Law Amendment Act in 1912, which made procuring a more serious offence. More counter-productive was her allegation, published in *The Great Scourge*, that three-quarters of all men were suffering from venereal disease, and that only female suffrage could cure the world of male immorality. Her slogan, 'votes for women, chastity for men', had a certain force but probably did not endear her to the bulk of the male population. Men tended to respond by declaring themselves to be 'controlled and worried enough by women at the present time' and warning against allowing harpies like the Pankhursts loose inside the House of Commons.[9] The hardening of male attitudes was revealed by the Prisoners (Temporary Discharge) or 'Cat and Mouse' Act of 1913, whereby imprisoned suffragettes on hunger strike could be released and then rearrested at executive discretion. Some saw this as a betrayal of Liberal values, rather like the Official Secrets and Mental Deficiency Acts of 1911 and 1913; but the measure was carried by a large majority, not least because the home secretary insisted that the only alternative was to extend the controversial practice of forcible feeding.

The question of women's suffrage had reached an impasse by 1914. The government was unable to do much to curb the actions of the militants, but, at the same time, the suffragettes had lost a good deal of goodwill and support in the House of Commons. The only franchise measure still before parliament was the Plural Voting Bill, which had first been introduced in 1913, and which only applied to male voters. Under the terms of the Parliament Act, this would have become law in 1915, aiding the Liberals in any subsequent general election, had peace endured. Unexpectedly, however, war was to change the whole terms of debate. It led to the formation of a coalition government, and thereby took franchise questions for the time being largely out of party politics. It speeded up the giving of all men the vote, thereby removing a main argument against extending the privilege to women. It diverted the energies of the militants into other directions, so that they ceased to prejudice their cause. And, given the contribution of women workers to the war effort, it became difficult to argue as had often been done before 1914, that the female sex should be denied any role in vital national decisions or the management of a great empire.

Ireland had proved the bane of Liberal governments for half a century. Often enough it had helped to tumble the Liberals out of office, though rarely had it prevented the party returning to power on a subsequent swing of the pendulum. Historians, however, have identified a much more substantial long-term threat to the Liberals on the eve of the first world war, in the form of the emergent Labour party. At the start of the period covered by this book, this had appeared as a cloud no bigger than a man's hand. The Labour Representation Committee, as the party was originally called, was formed early in 1900, and won two seats at the ensuing general election. Intended, first and foremost, to protect trades union interests, it benefited in particular from controversial legal decisions such as *Quinn* v. *Leathem* and *Taff Vale*.

In 1906, the Labour party, as it now came to be called, scored its most signal success before the first world war when it first entered parliament in force and secured favourable trade disputes legislation. In the 1910 general elections, its progress was much less marked. It remained, to a considerable extent, dependent on the Liberals and their particular political agenda. But a glance at the electoral figures for 1910 reveals how vital for the Liberals were the implications for their future relationship with Labour. Though, in both January and December, the Liberals won practically the same number of seats as the Unionists, they did so with markedly fewer votes. In January, they garnered 2.86 million votes in all, as against the Unionists' 3.1 million. In December, on a lower poll generally, the proportion was 2.29:2.42 million.[10] In the two general elections,

Labour won 505,000 and 371,000 votes respectively. Clearly the Labour party had come to stay, and clearly also it had the power to do considerable damage to the Liberals, though in any initial trial of stength it was likely to come off worse. This was revealed by the by-elections of the years 1911–14, when, due to losses and defections, Labour's parliamentary representation was reduced from 42 seats to 36. Thus two midlands mining seats, Hanley and Chesterfield, were surrendered to the Liberals, and a third, North-East Derbyshire, was lost to the Unionists on a three-way vote. Nonetheless, Labour's poll in the by-elections of this period did increase overall, but it was still far from being a truly national party. Its electoral strength remained disproportionately based in the north of England, especially in cotton textiles and mining areas. As yet, it hardly penetrated the south, London, rural England, and the Celtic fringe.

How much of a challenge did the Labour party represent in other terms? How effectively did it rate as a parliamentary force in these years, and with how distinctive an identity? The party leadership had been placed on a rotating basis, and in the years immediately before 1914 MacDonald acted as chairman and Henderson as secretary. Within its ranks, the Labour party contained some effective parliamentarians and prominent political figures of the next generation, such as Snowdon, Thomas and Lansbury. But its internal discipline was poor, and attendance in the House of Commons tended to be uneven. It was divided on key matters like national insurance and women's suffrage, the latter costing it a parliamentary seat which it could ill afford to lose after Lansbury had resigned as MP for Bow and Bromley in order to test opinion locally on the issue at a by-election. Individual Labour spokesmen intervened effectively in the House of Commons on certain issues, especially where they were able to act in concert with left-wing Liberals or occasionally even with Unionists. Thus the government found itself harried over the spiralling costs of the naval arms race with Germany, over support for French political and economic ambitions in Morocco, and over acquiescence in Russia's interference with the independence and integrity of Persia. But Labour never put the government in any real danger, and its 40 or so MPs never came near to emulating the success of the 39 Irish Nationalists who had contrived to overthrow a numerically rather stronger Liberal administration in 1885. Probably the Labour party had no great interest in doing so. Perhaps its best chance of shaking the government to its foundations came in November–December 1911, following the major war scare over Morocco. In a wide-ranging debate, concern was expressed from all quarters of the House about ministers' handling of foreign policy. Labour MPs, along with Irish Nationalists and left-wing Liberals, opposed what was seen as needless provocation of Germany and unquestioning support of French concession-hunting and colonial ambitions. Tory spokesmen worried that the British empire, which contained so many Muslims, was risking a confrontation with the Islamic world in general. But Labour did not press the matter to a division, and the opportunity was lost of a dramtic upset such as that which had been dealt Palmerston in the China debate of 1857. In truth, Labour was too closely tied to the Liberals on leading issues like free trade and home rule. Defeat of the government would put too much at risk, not least the seats of Labour MPs who would have a hard time defending themselves at a general election in which Liberals could more easily assume the patriotic mantle.

The years immediately preceding the outbreak of the first world war were, as is well known, ones of intense labour activity on a wider front. They witnessed a dramtic surge in industrial militancy which one historian has characterised as an unprecedented national upheaval. The available statistics tell their own story. Between 1901 and 1910, the number of days lost through strikes averaged only five million a year, but in 1910 and 1911 the figure doubled, and in 1912 alone it amounted to no less than thirty-six million. In this latter case, a considerable proportion, perhaps thirty million days lost, was caused by a month-long stoppage in the coal industry. Other major strikes in this period involved the railways in 1911 and transport generally in both 1911 and 1912. Troubles in one industry tended to have a knock-on effect in others, as workers strove to match wage increases that seemed to be achieved elsewhere. A powerful stimulus was given to trades union combination, as employees in the same sector came together for their own protection. It was at this time that the national union of railwaymen was formed out of three railway unions.

To some extent, the whole country appeared caught up in a frenzy of protest and direct action, augmented perhaps in 1911 by the abnormally hot summer of that year. There was even a schoolchildren's strike in 1911, ostensibly against harsh discipline. But, whatever the various factors, one fundamental cause underlay the massive wave of industrial disaffection. This was the fall in real wages, brought about by the build-up in international inflationary pressures since 1896. Prior to that date, for a period of nearly a quarter of a century characterised by economic historians as the great depression, prices had remained relatively low. But, in the final years of the nineteenth century, the world economy had entered a period of boom which, with one or two interruptions, would maintain an increasing momentum until the outbreak of the first world war. Whereas food prices, for instance, had remained largely stable during the long period of late nineteenth-century agricultural glut, now the world's rapidly expanding economies competed for increasingly scarce natural resources. In these circumstances, wages had a strong tendency to lag behind prices, a situation which in Britain at least was all the harder to bear, given the militancy of other sections of the population, such as suffragettes, as well as the ostentation and conspicuous consumption that had become characteristic of the wealthier classes in Edwardian society. British trades unionists also felt particularly able to flex their muscles in the years before 1914, when unprecedented prosperity had so reduced unemployment as to make the use of blackleg labour against strikers most unlikely.

How far did this upsurge in industrial militancy constitute an indictment of Liberalism in general? Was it indeed part of what one writer, in a memorable phrase, has termed the strange death of Liberal England? To some extent the governments of Campbell-Bannerman and Asquith could be blamed for the onset of industrial disorder. The Trade Disputes Act of 1906 had freed trades unions from previous constraints relating to strikes and picketing. By intervening increasingly in industrial disputes, beginning with Lloyd George's arbitration in the railway strike of 1907, ministers had in a sense encouraged the trades unions to exert pressure on the government through direct action, and in 1912 they had been forced to pass a Minimum Wages Act in order to bring to an end a major stoppage in the coal industry. Conservatives of course continually harped on the Liberal government's financial and economic record, which they claimed lay at the root of the country's industrial malaise. Heavy direct taxation, it was said, especially since 1909, had provoked a flight of capital abroad, and thereby starved the country of funds, not only for necessary social investment such as housing, but also for the modernisation and re-equipment of Britain's manufacturing base. In consequence, British industry remained under-capitalised and labour intensive, its declining competitiveness responsible for the low profit margins which compelled employers to resist demands for increased wages. Tariff reform, Conservatives insisted, would raise rates of pay all round by securing British goods against unfair foreign competition. It would help to pay for such costly social programmes as pensions and national insurance, which at present diverted resources from the overall wages fund.

The link between social reform and industrial militancy is indeed an interesting one, for it may seem paradoxical that a government which had been responsible for such wide-ranging welfare legislation should at the same time be faced with virtually unprecedented popular protest. But in fact social reform was part of the very problem which it was designed to solve. It addressed the difficulties of the more vulnerable members of society, the aged, sick, and unemployed, but often enough at the expense of workers in full-time employment and in the prime of life. These found themselves called upon to pay for welfare legislation either out of their own pockets, as in the case of national insurance, or in terms of their traditional working practices. It was perhaps no coincidence that the troubles in the coal industry, which were such a major element in the industrial unrest before the first world war, should have begun in the south Wales coalfield with a dispute over a reorganisation of shifts resulting from the imposition of the Miners' Eight Hour Act of 1908. Social reform all too often ran counter to the libertarian traditions of the British working class, to its rooted dislike of interference by the state. For decades past, the state had regulated the railways in respect of fares and hours of labour. The railway companies had responded by exercising a maximum restraint over wages, and in consequence the industry had one of the worst records in labour relations in recent years, and it provided the setting for two major judicial confrontations which gave rise to the *Taff Vale* and *Osborne* decisions (Doc. 20).

Industrial unrest undoubtedly posed problems for Asquith's government, but ones which it was in general able to surmount, and indeed without recourse to the kind of emergency powers legislation enacted by the post-war coalition and applied by the first Labour government of 1924. But in all it hardly added up to a fundamental challenge to the ethos of Liberalism, any more than did the industrial troubles of 1919 for the principles and practice of coalition or the 1926 general strike for Conservatism. As has been noted, industrial militancy was to a considerable extent the product of prosperity, of the last great boom in the world economy under the conditions of the international gold standard, which was to founder in the first world war, and Liberals therefore had some justification in viewing the record of these years as a further endorsement of Britain's free-trade system. Indeed, industrial militancy offered as much of a challenge to the emergent Labour party as it did to Liberalism. It was an indication that Labour members in the House of Commons were losing touch with their supporters in the country, that they had concentrated too much of their effort on foreign and colonial affairs, and had done nothing to help mitigate a 12 to 15 per cent erosion of working-class living standards. MacDonald attacked the recourse to direct action by trades unions as a derogation from democratic principles. If one interest group could impose its will upon the majority in the community by *force majeure*, so could another, perhaps with reactionary tendencies, such as Ulster Unionism. His reward was to be attacked by grassroots sections of his party for enjoying too cosy a parliamentary relationship with leading Liberals. The breach thus opened up with his supporters would deepen considerably during the war, and not be repaired until the early 1920s.

Lloyd George at least, among ministers, tried to see lessons for Liberalism in the prevailing industrial unrest. He regarded it as furnishing ammunition for a renewed Liberal offensive, one that would reassert the party's radical and reforming spirit to a greater extent than anything seen since the days of the people's budget. Like other radicals before him, Lloyd George diagnosed the problems of industrial Britain in terms of land. The decay of agriculture had, in his view, forced many labourers to migrate to the larger towns and cities, where their numbers contributed to overcrowding and urban deprivation, the very problems which, along with an excess of casual employment, had contributed so substantially to industrial militancy.

The solution, he believed, lay in the reinvigoration of English rural life. This was to be achieved by providing much-needed security for what he regarded as the two downtrodden classes of the English countryside, the tenant farmers and agricultural labourers. The former would be favoured with much greater security of tenure along with abolition of the game laws. The latter would gain access to better housing and to minimum wages. In the Miners' Minimum Wages Act of 1912, Lloyd George saw a valuable precedent for what he hoped to achieve in the countryside at large. He aspired to impart a new radical impulsion to the government, which he feared it might be in some danger of losing following the resignation of two former stalwarts of Campbell-Bannerman, Loreburn and Pentland, in 1912. Churchill by now seemed to have gravitated to the non-radical side of the cabinet after his translation from the home office to the admiralty in October 1911. Lloyd George spent much of his time on public platforms in 1912 defending the virtues of national insurance, on whose supposed unpopularity the Unionists were making every attempt to play. His instinct was to carry the battle to his opponents, and he noted that, at the North-West Norfolk by-election in May 1912, the Liberal candidate, emphasising rural issues, was able to see off a strong challenge from the Unionist candidate fighting on national insurance. Similarly, at Holmfirth in June the Liberals held on despite hefty competition from both Conservatives and Labour in a mining constituency. True, over the next few months, the government went through one of its more unfortunate patches, losing by-elections at Crewe, North-West Manchester, and even Gladstone's old seat of Midlothian. But the lesson seemed clear. If the Liberals were to recover their popularity in time for the next general election, they would need a good rallying-cry, and Lloyd George believed that this could be provided by the land campaign to which he now proposed to devote increasing attention (Doc. 20).

One other key influence on the last phase of Liberal politics before the first world war deserves consideration. This was the Welsh church disestablishment measure, debates on which occupied much of the time of parliament between 1912 and 1914. Like

Irish home rule, Welsh disestablishment failed to get past the House of Lords on its first two parliamentary circuits but eventually under the terms of the Parliament Act it reached the statute book in 1914. Like home rule, its operation was suspended for the duration of the war, but unlike home rule it was put into effect, albeit with some amendment of its financial provisions, in 1919, by which time much of the heat had gone out of the whole controversy. In a sense, therefore, it was the final significant reform of Britain's last Liberal government. Historians have tended to overlook it, as peripheral matter involving affairs in a provincial backwater, but this is to neglect its real significance. The Bill, which was eventually to become law, removed the political status of the Anglican establishment in Wales, as represented among other things by the right of its bishops to sit in the House of Lords. More significantly still, it disendowed the Anglican church in Wales to the extent of making Welsh county councils responsible for administering tithes and charitable trusts. Liberals justified this as returning such funds into the hands of the majority of the Welsh population, for whose benefit they had arguably been intended, at least before the widespread development of nonconformity had turned Anglicanism into a minority denomination in the principality. Unionists, on the other hand, regarded the whole transaction as a deed of sacrilege and spoliation, as a blow against religion in general, and in particular against a thriving religious community which, given the divisions among nonconformists, still remained the largest single denomination in Wales.

The debates on Welsh disestablishment raised some of the touchiest issues in politics, concerning morality, money and the principle of nationality. The proposed sequestration of Welsh church property generated far more passion than the nationalisation measures of the Attlee government. Historians have tended to view disestablishment as a somewhat nineteenth-century issue, as representative of the old Liberalism rather than the new, but Lloyd George at least defended it as making possible the application of charitable endowments for useful secular purposes such as museums and cottage hospitals. The whole question also helped to revive in Lloyd George the hatred of landlordism which had loomed so large at the time of the people's budget and which would inform much of his land campaign rhetoric of the last year or two before the first world war. In speeches to parliament, Lloyd George attacked the attitude of Unionist politicians whose families, he claimed, had plundered church lands at the time of the Reformation but who now defended religious property in Wales as sacrosanct. In speeches outside parliament in mid-1912 Lloyd George sought to widen his attack against the landowning classes in general. At Swansea he declared that though Britain possessed a constitutional monarchy the country had also ten thousand little tsars. At Woodford he called for the final dismantling of feudalism throughout the countryside.

Lloyd George's colleagues appeared to have been won round to his ideas by the end of 1912. At Ladybank, in October 1912, Asquith defended the land campaign as providing a middle way between the extremes of land nationalisation and the wholesale extension of private ownership. But thereafter the whole question seemed to hang fire for the best part of a year. Information as to the problems of rural life was being steadily accumulated by a Liberal land inquiry committee, established in mid-1912, but the political pressures to do anything about them were in the immediate term diminished. After losing a batch of by-elections in the late summer of 1912, the government enjoyed a good electoral run right through to the end of the following year, apart from the loss of Newmarket in May 1913. During this period the Liberals actually gained a seat from Labour at Chesterfield, whereas the Unionists lost seats at Londonderry and Kendal to a Nationalist and to an Independent respectively.

Political attention was also in large measure diverted elsewhere, by a protracted crisis in the Balkans which produced two savage local conflicts that for a time seemed likely to give rise to a major international confrontation. Lloyd George himself was for much of this same period preoccupied by a scandal which threatened his whole political career. This was the Marconi affair, which raised serious questions about his probity, veracity and political judgment, as well as those of less senior figures in the government. Lloyd George had bought shares in the American Marconi company at a time when its sister organisation, the English Marconi company, was in receipt of lucrative government contracts. Even more to the point, in a statement of October 1912, he misled the House of Commons as to the extent of his involvement. Public interest was thoroughly aroused once it was also revealed in the spring of 1913 that the Liberal chief whip had invested party funds in the American company. In June 1913, Lloyd George was perhaps lucky to survive a censure debate on the whole affair, thanks partly to an intervention by Asquith, who assured the House that he had, inadvertently, encouraged the chancellor of the exchequer to make his statement of the previous October.[11]

The land campaign was finally unleashed in October 1913. Lloyd George delivered two major speeches in characteristic vein at Bedford and Swindon. They contained passion, argument, invective, along with a due measure of both religion and vulgarity. Lloyd George set forth ambitious schemes of cottage-building and minimum wages to benefit the agricultural labourers. The interests of farmers were to be met by rent controls and by the abolition of the game laws. Only the landlord class had little to hope for in the new utopia. The whole rural programme, it was proposed, was to be overseen by a new ministry of land and natural resources. Several cabinet ministers, however, had doubts about Lloyd George's latest enterprise, and indeed his land campaign was to carry suggestive parallels with the tariff reform crusade of ten years previously. Like Chamberlain, Lloyd George was trying to appeal to competing interests within the community, and like Chamberlain also he was often careless with his information and statistics. And there was a parallel also with the land campaign conducted by Chamberlain when still a Liberal in 1885.

That was the year when the Liberals had been said to lack an 'urban cow'. They had possessed a programme with which to sweep the countryside, but not the towns and cities. The situation seemed similar in 1913–14. The Liberals did well in early 1914 in the largely rural constituency of Wycombe, but between November 1913 and May 1914 they lost a succession of urban by-elections – at Reading, South Lanarkshire, Bethnal Green, Leith and Ipswich. Lloyd George tried hard to remedy the position with speeches at Glasgow, Middlesbrough and Holloway, promising boons to the urban electorate in the shape of slum clearance rating reform and leasehold enfranchisement. But, certainly in the initial stages, the rural bias of the land campaign was evident enough. The rural report of the Liberals' land inquiry had been published in October 1913, coinciding with the launch of the campaign, for Lloyd George was anxious to avoid the mistake of getting too far ahead of public opinion as had happened with national insurance. The urban report had to wait until April 1914; and in the meantime Lloyd George had offended many urban voters by suggesting that rural housing could be paid for out of national insurance contributions levied principally in the towns.

Finance, as with so much in politics, was the key to the whole issue. More even than home rule or franchise reform, it was likely to decide the government's fate. In one sense the Liberals had a considerable opportunity before them. The years immediately prior to the outbreak of war in 1914 were ones of exceptional prosperity. Lloyd George was able in his 1912 and 1913 budgets to meet the continuing cost of social programmes without any increase in taxation. Radical and Labour members, particularly Snowden, urged the government to seize its opportunity and safeguard working-class support by cutting the remaining taxation on essentials such as tea and sugar. Lloyd George was certainly tempted by this argument. In a provocative interview, published in the *Daily Chronicle* in January 1914, Lloyd George argued that only the cost of naval rearmament prevented the Liberals realising their long-term objective of the free breakfast table. That cost was now threatening to rise appreciably once more, for Churchill, as first lord of the admiralty, was pressing for a £10 million increase in the 1914 naval estimates to a total of £54 million. Churchill was sensitive to Unionist criticisms that the navy was not as numerically supreme as ten years previously, and he was eager to convert the battleships from coal to oil. Lloyd George, on the other hand, believed that Anglo-German tension generally was now on the wane, thanks partly to the failure of the Balkan crises to lead to more general conflict. But in reality Lloyd George was pulled two ways. He wanted to retain his influence on the left of the Liberal party and to fund valuable reforms, but at the same time he supported the government's blue-water strategy and had remained suspicious of German intentions since the Moroccan crisis in 1911. He regarded Churchill as his friend, and indeed also as his rival, and had no wish to see him assume a monopoly of patriotism in the Liberal party. As so often, therefore, it was Lloyd George who found a compromise. He prevented the government from breaking up by persuading his colleagues to agree on slightly reduced naval estimates of £51.5 million (Doc. 12).

No doubt Lloyd George also had earlier experience in mind. In 1909 he had had to find money both for social welfare and naval rearmament, and he had saved the government's fortunes by a famous budget. In 1914 he aspired to do something similar. Direct taxation would of course need to be increased, but Lloyd George hoped to sweeten the pill politically by substantial hand-outs, including generous grants-in-aid from the treasury to local authorities for social welfare purposes, and also a new national valuation scheme to enable undeveloped land to be rated more punitively than farmland or buildings. The budget was cast in ambitious terms, and intended as the first major reform of local government finance since the time of Elizabeth I. Lloyd George calculated on securing the support of both tenant farmers and agricultural labourers by means of rating reform and minimum wages. He hoped to avoid a repetition of the January 1910 election, when the Liberals found themselves penalised by appearing to have too little to offer to the countryside. But if these were his calculations, they went badly wrong. In June 1914 two blows befell the budget. The speaker of the House of Commons disallowed discussion of national valuation, on which rating reform was to have been based, as being not, strictly speaking, a budgetary matter – at least not under the terms of the 1911 Parliament Act, a measure which Liberals were now finding to be not entirely to their advantage. And a revolt of Liberal backbenchers forced Lloyd George to reduce his proposed income-tax increase by 1d, and with it to scrap the whole scheme of grants-in-aid for the forthcoming year. Economy, it seemed, was still a watchword among many Liberals. Lloyd George here suffered one of the worst reverses of his parliamentary career, and possibly his reputation would not have recovered but for the outbreak of the first world war.[12]

Even so, the land campaign cannot be written off too easily. Lloyd George had the knack of recovering readily from misfortune, and he might well have found a way to implement his programme in 1915 had peace endured. The urban aspect received a boost when Asquith at last agreed to the principle of an urban minimum wage in June 1914. As to the countryside, the Wycombe by-election suggested that the Liberals might well regain a good number of the rural seats lost in January 1910. Certainly Unionists were worried by the implications. They feared Lloyd George's demagogic appeal, and were divided over how to respond to his proposals. The most they could agree on was a land purchase scheme for tenant farmers, which would have meant little to the agricultural labourer. Bonar Law pessimistically averred that the Liberals, like the Whigs after 1832, might remain in power for forty years by exploiting class antagonisms. Even his younger supporters were not immune to Lloyd George's blandishments, as was proved in late 1913 when the chancellor won a debate on his land proposals at the Oxford union.[13]

Who indeed would have won a general election such as would have fallen due in late 1914 or 1915? This question has haunted the imagination of historians who have made the election-that-never-was among the more fiercely contested of modern times. Even less confidently than usual can bets be staked on its outcome. So much would have depended on the twists and turns in the Irish situation and on which party would have been blamed by the electorate for any large eruption of violence. A good deal would also have hinged upon the attitude of the Labour party and on its willingness to renew with the Liberals the electoral arrangements which had proved so mutually beneficial in 1906 and 1910. Increased funding, in consequence of the 1913 Trade Disputes Act, had encouraged a mood of independence on the part of Labour. Quite apart from this, it appeared that by 1914 Asquith's administration was in any case running out of steam. Ironically, in significant ways it now resembled Balfour's beleaguered administration of some years earlier. Like the Unionists before them, the Liberals had now been in power for nearly a decade and were suffering electoral unpopularity. They were similarly associated with high taxation and expenditure, and with a cavalier and high-handed attitude towards the constitution. The National Insurance Act of 1911 had upset key interests in the country as had the Education Act of 1902. In some respects indeed the Liberals were even less well placed than had been their Unionist predecessors, for they had been singed by scandal in the Marconi affair and were accused of making a politically corrupt bargain with the Irish in order to maintain themselves in power.

However in retrospect Asquith's government should not be written off too easily. His party was far less divided than the Unionists had been between 1903 and 1905, nor had it suffered anything like the same degree of ministerial wastage. Indeed Asquith could, if anything, be criticised for not reshuffling his cabinet more vigorously and relegating less satisfactory colleagues such as Burns and Birrell. In addition, the Liberals still disposed of some considerable assets, not least the prime minister himself. Asquith was far from being the played-out figure who would eventually lose his seat in 1918. He still dominated the cabinet and had been able to impose his authority on difficult situations such as Marconi and the Curragh. He was an old political hand, who had seen off the master dialectician, Balfour, in the December 1910 election and who relished the chance of taking on the relatively untried Bonar Law at the next such opportunity. It is unclear how the Unionist leader would have fared in such a contest. He had rallied much of his party behind him by his uncompromising attitude on contentious questions such as Ulster, and he had endeavoured to build up a reputation for honesty and plain speaking in contrast to his predecessor Balfour's penchant for over-subtlety and disingenuousness.

But such a reputation could only with difficulty survive the wear and tear of political life. In late 1912, after the Unionists' failure to make an expected by-election gain at Bolton, Bonar Law more or less discarded food taxation from his immediate programme. In any general election, Asquith would have had a field-day exposing Unionist divisions and inconsistencies on the issue of tariff reform. In early 1912 Bonar Law had also contradicted himself over his willingness to repeal the National Insurance Act should he gain power. All told, his party had few positive policies on offer with which they could expect to sweep the country. Though worried about the electoral appeal of Lloyd George's land campaign, the Unionists had not been able to come up with a coherent and satisfactory alternative. Reform of parliament, involving a restoration of authority to the upper chamber, was not likely to win them many votes, nor was military conscription for which some Unionists were nonetheless enthusiastic. Tariff reform, however defined, would hardly make the party appear a plausible advocate of low inflation and reduced taxation. The best that the Unionists could hope for was that a general election would signal a change in the popular mood, probably born of a weariness of the upheavals and incessant legislative activity which had marked the Liberals' long years in power. Something similar had happened forty years earlier, when Disraeli had toppled Gladstone's initial, and most energetically reforming, government and won for the Conservatives their first electoral triumph in a generation.

All this is speculation. The coming of Armageddon in July–August 1914 was to transform the political landscape and, as we now know, sound the knell of Liberalism as a force in government. This was not an outcome that could be easily predicted at the time. Britain's entry into the first world war was, in a sense, the Asquith administration's finest as well as its worst hour. Remarkably, the prime minister carried with him a more or less united cabinet, as well as party, parliament and country. Speeches by Grey and Asquith in the House of Commons on 3 and 6 August 1914 sought to justify the war on clearly stated Liberal principles. It had to be undertaken, so they claimed, in order to safeguard international law, the concert of Europe, the rights of small nations, French civilisation, and Britain's good name and self-respect which were so vital for the future welfare of the world. All told, Britain stood to lose more by remaining at peace than by entering into hostilities. Its navy, on which the Liberals had lavished so much attention, would render it inviolable in any circumstances. Gladstone himself, Grey was careful to point out, had justified the possibility of war in 1870 in order to defend Belgian neutrality and to prevent the 'unmeasured aggrandisement' of any foreign power. Certainly the wheel had come full circle since the occasion in 1864 when a Liberal cabinet had decided against going to war with Prussia and Austria over Denmark, and Palmerston had defended the decision partly on the grounds that war might impair the country's unexampled prosperity of recent years.

The Liberal government bore a measure of responsibility for the outbreak of war in 1914, though precisely how much has remained a matter of debate, like most of the other circumstances of that year. Grey and other leading ministers were criticised at the time, and have been rather more so since, on several counts. They were accused of excessive secrecy and of not taking the country properly into their confidence. They lacked, it was said, any kind of coherent policy regarding the Mediterranean and the crumbling Ottoman empire, whose problems would play such a crucial role in the coming of the first world war. They had failed properly to develop Britain's military, as opposed to its naval, capacities, so that the country was in less of a position to make its foreign policy effective. Grey had won something of a reputation as the peacemaker of Europe after he had helped to settle the first Balkan conflict of 1912–13, but in the crisis of July–August 1914 he was unable to do much more than react to events as they unfolded. Certain of his decisions as foreign secretary had, of course, been crucial, notably his initiation of military conversations with France in 1906 and their extension to the naval sphere in 1912. Thanks to this, Britain, as one cabinet minister put it, had all the obligations of an alliance without its advantages. Years previously, Gladstone had warned that England 'should not foreclose and narrow her own liberty of choice by declarations made to other powers in their real or supposed interests of which they would claim to be at least joint interpreters'. In 1914 Britain had finally to decide whether or not it would stand by France, a friend if not quite an ally, in that country's supreme hour of need, knowing that, if it did not do so, Britain would be left demeaned and isolated in the world whoever won the war. The evasions and ambiguities of pre-war diplomacy had at last run their course.[14]

That said, it is unlikely that matters would have turned out very differently had a Unionist rather than a Liberal government been in power. Some of the emphases in foreign policy would have been changed, but at the end of the day Britain would surely have ended up going to war in order to preserve France and Belgium and prevent German domination of the continent and arguably the rest of the world. The pre-war naval arms race with Germany would have been even more intense had the Unionists been in office. However, in 1914 the vital decision was made by a Liberal administration which thereby helped to dig its own grave. Ironically the first world war advanced Liberal objectives in some important ways. It brought about universal manhood suffrage and an extension of unemployment insurance as well as the introduction of controls on liquor. In other parts of the empire – for instance, Canada and Australia – Liberalism continued to prosper as a force in government. But in Britain it went all too rapidly into decline, due to wartime failures of leadership, internal divisions, and the transformed prospects of the Labour party. But that is another story.

Notes

1 J. Jaconelli, 'The parliament bill of 1910–1911', *Parliamentary History*, 1991.

2 R. Fanning, 'The Irish policies of Asquith's government and the cabinet crisis of 1910', *Essay Presented to R. Dudley Edwards* (Dublin, 1979).

3 *The Times*, 30 November 1910.

4 Speeches at Lambeth and Sheffield, *The Times*, 29 November and 1 December 1910.

5 *The Times*, 18 November 1910.

6 Speeches at Mile End and Edinburgh, *The Times*, 22 and 28 November 1910.

7 B. B. Gilbert, 'Winston Churchill *vs.* the Webbs: the origins of British unemployment insurance', *American Historical Review*, 1966.

8 There is a good defence of Birrell in P. Jalland, 'A Liberal chief secretary and the Irish question: Augustine Birrell, 1907–1914', *Historical Journal*, 1976.

9 5 *Hansard* LII 1735ff. (5 May 1913).

10 Seventy-two Unionist and 35 Liberal seats were left uncontested in December 1910, as compared to 19 and 1 earlier in the year.

11 B. B. Gilbert, 'David Lloyd George and the Great Marconi Scandal', *Historical Research*, 1989.

12 B. B. Gilbert, 'David Lloyd George: The Reform of British Landholding and the Budget of 1914', *Historical Journal*, 1978.

13 Among other places, the land campaign is dealt with in J. Loades ed., *The Life and Times of David Lloyd George* (Bangor, 1991), and A. J. P. Taylor ed., *Lloyd George: twelve essays* (London, 1971).

14 C. Nicolson, 'Edwardian England and the coming of the First World War', in A. O'Day ed., *The Edwardian Age: conflict and stability 1900–1914* (London, 1979).

Selected documents

Document 1

The personality of Joseph Chamberlain, leader of only the fourth largest party in the House of Commons, dominated the 1900 election as have few politicians in any campaign before or since. His apparent branding of the Liberals as traitors to their country is one of the most celebrated of election smears. In fact, his oratory, as the following extract, typical of his speeches during the campaign, makes clear, was a shade more subtle. Chamberlain professed to believe that the mass of ordinary Liberals were patriotic, but that they were betrayed by their parliamentary representatives who, divided amongst themselves, sailed under false colours and in reality put party before country.

From a speech by Joseph Chamberlain at Tunstall, as reported in *The Times*, 28 September 1900.

> He believed to a large extent that the Liberals throughout the country were with the government in this issue but that they were misled by their representatives in the house of commons . . . In recent times a party had grown up who were described as Little Englanders, and the position today was that two thirds of the Liberal members in the house of commons were against the war, against annexation, and only one third called themselves Imperialists, and they, as he had already pointed out, had never given them a hand in the heavy burden that the government had had to bear until the Boers had actually invaded Her Majesty's territory, and they then saw the feeling of the country and dared not oppose it. It was a marvellous and a curious thing that they were all Imperialists now (laughter and 'hear, hear'). Imperialists grew up

around them now like mushrooms in a single night . . .

They had to say whether they would leave the settlement to the party which believed in the war from first to last, or to the party which above all other questions had resolved if possible to defeat their political opponents. On that last matter only was there agreement among them . . . The electors should not fail to heed what was said by the mayor of Mafeking, who, speaking the other day, said that every seat lost to the government was a seat gained by the Boers ('hear, hear').

Document 2

The Liberals' view of the dirty tricks which, they claimed, had been employed against them in the 1900 election campaign, is revealed in the following extract. It dates from 1906, when the Liberals felt obliged to defend themselves in their turn against accusations of indulging in unscrupulous propaganda about Chinese slavery.

Parliamentary Debates, fourth series, CLII 652 (23 February 1906).

(Mr. Mond) He asked the honourable and learned member for the City whether he approved of the posters at the previous election. In his constituency there was a big poster displaying the Commander-in-Chief, Lord Roberts, in full uniform on a horse with a drawn sword, and directing the electorate to vote for the Tory candidate. There was a similar picture of Lord Kitchener of Khartoum. He would ask the honourable and learned gentleman opposite whether that was fair electioneering – whether there was any right to drag the names of our great generals and army into electioneering?

Document 3

Although not a politician as such, Rudyard Kipling contributed forcefully in his writings to the polemics of his day. He greatly admired Joseph Chamberlain and defended Ulster's right of resistance to home rule. His evocative poem, quoted from here, reveals the radical element at the heart of the imperialist message. Kipling, like Chamberlain, hoped that the south African war might promote reconciliation and strengthen the wider British world, but at the same time he feared that the home country would not be able to live up to its imperial destiny.

Selected documents

From Rudyard Kipling's poem 'Chant-Pagan (English irregular, discharged)'.

Me that 'ave been what I've been –
Me that 'ave gone where I've gone –
Me that 'ave seen what I've seen –
'Ow can I ever take on
With awful old England again,
An' 'ouses both sides of the street,
An' 'edges two sides of the lane,
And the parson an' gentry between,
An' touching my 'at when we meet –
Me that 'ave been what I've been? . . .

Me that 'ave watched 'arf a world
'Eave up all shiny with dew,
Kopje on kop to the sun,
An' as soon as the mist lets 'em through
Our 'elios winkin' like fun –
Three sides of a ninety-mile square,
Over valleys as big as a shire –
Are ye there? Are ye there? Are ye there?
An' then the blind drum of our fire . . .
An' I'm rollin' is lawns for the Squire

I will arise an' get 'ence –
I will trek South and make sure
If it's only my fancy or not
That the sunshine of England is pale,
And the breezes of England are stale,
An' there's somethin' gone small with the lot.
For I know of a sun an' a wind,
An' some plains and a mountain be'ind,
An' some graves by a barb-wire fence,
An' a Dutchman I've fought 'oo might give
Me a job were I ever inclined
To look in an' offsaddle an' live
Where there's neither a road nor a tree –
But only my Maker an' me,
And I think it will kill me or cure, –
So I think I will go there an' see . . .

175

Document 4

Although the south African war ended in 1902, Joseph Chamberlain, as one observer put it, continued to make the political weather for some years afterwards. His Birmingham address of May 1903, here quoted at some length, remains one of the landmark speeches of the twentieth century. It signalled a new era in British politics, and sketched forth many of the themes of the tariff reform campaign which properly began a few months later. Note particularly the stress on the recent lessons of war, and the dangers of neglecting an unparalleled opportunity.

From a speech in West Birmingham, 15 May 1903 (C. W. Boyd, *Mr. Chamberlain's Speeches* II, London, 1914).

> It is two months now since I returned from a voyage which will always be one of the most memorable incidents of my life . . . my whole mind was turned to the problems connected with the birth of a new nation in South Africa, and, above all, to the question of how it was possible to reconcile the two strong races who were bound to live there . . . It is to the Empire, with all that that means, that I look to produce that union in South Africa which we all desire to achieve . . .
>
> I did not require to go to South Africa in order to be convinced that the pervading spirit of Imperialism has obtained deep hold on the minds and hearts of our children beyond the seas. It has had a hard life of it. This feeling of imperial patriotism . . . was discouraged by our apparent acceptance of the doctrines of the Little Englanders, of the provincial spirit which taught us to consider ourselves alone, and to regard with indifference all that concerned those, however loyal they might be, who left these shores in order to go to our colonies abroad. But it was never extinguished. The embers were still alight, and when, in the late war, this old country of ours showed that it was still possessed by the spirit of our ancestors, that it was still prepared to count no sacrifice that was necessary in order to maintain the honour and the interests of the Empire that was committed to its charge, then you found such a response from your brethren, your children across the seas, as had never been known before, astonishing the world by an undeniable proof of affection and regard. I have said that that was a new chapter, the beginning of a new era. Is it to end there? Are we to sink back to the old policy of selfish isolation which went very far to try, and even to sap, the loyalty of our colonial brethren? . . .

Just let us consider what that Empire is. I am not now going tonight to speak of those hundreds of millions of our Indian and native fellow-subjects . . . I consider only our relations to our own kinsfolk, to that white British population that constitutes the majority in the great self-governing colonies of the Empire. Here, in the United Kingdom, there are some forty millions of us. Outside, there are more than ten millions . . . Now how long do you suppose that this proportion of the population is going to endure? . . . Do you wish that, if these ten millions become forty millions, they will still be closely, intimately, affectionately united to you? Now is the time when you can exert influence . . . The question of trade and commerce is one of the greatest importance. Unless that is satisfactorily settled, I, for one, do not believe in a continued union of the Empire . . . And first among those means is the offer of preferential tariffs. Now that is a matter which, at the present moment, is of the greatest possible importance to every one of you. It depends upon how we treat this policy of the colonies – not a policy inaugurated by us, but a policy which comes to us from our children abroad . . .

The ministers of Canada, when they were over here last year, made me a further definite offer. They said: 'We are prepared to reconsider our tariff with a view to seeing whether we cannot give you further reductions, especially in regard to those goods in which you come into competition with foreigners, and we will do this if you will meet us by giving us a drawback on the small tax of 1s. per quarter which you have put upon corn.' I need not say that, if I could treat matters of this kind solely in regard to my position as secretary of state for the colonies, I should have said, 'That is an offer which we might ask our people to accept.' But, speaking of the government as a whole, I am obliged to say that it is contrary to the established fiscal policy of this country; that we hold ourselves bound to keep open market for all the world, even if they close their markets to us; and that we are therefore not in a position to offer any preference or favour whatever, even to our own children . . .

Well, ladies and gentlemen, you see the point. You want an empire. Do you think it better to cultivate the trade with your own people, or to let that go in order that you may keep the trade of those who are your competitors and rivals?

Document 5

Chamberlain's tariff reform crusade, which was launched in full in late 1903, combined radical and imperial themes. The newness of the colonies fascinated Chamberlain, and he saw them as having something to teach a country perhaps too set in its ways like Britain. 'The vast majoirity of working men in all the colonies are protectionists', he claimed in a speech at Glasgow, for they had rid themselves of 'a good number of old-world prejudices and superstitions'. Many of Chamberlain's speeches, as in the example quoted below, appealed to class feelings and antagonisms, as he had done all his life. He even claimed an affinity with Chartism – indeed his campaign seemed to concentrate on one-time Chartist strongholds – though his particular reading of history was to land him in further controversy.
From a speech at Liverpool, 27 October 1903 (C. W. Boyd, *Mr. Chamberlain's Speeches* II, London, 1914).

> It is rather an interesting thing, which seems to me to have escaped altogether the attention of my opponents, who probably have not read the history of the Anti-Corn Law movement, that when Free Trade was carried, the working classes were neither represented or consulted. I do not say that that makes Free Trade good or bad, but it is a fact that the movement was a manufacturers' and middle-class movement . . . the leaders of the Free Trade movement believed that the big loaf meant lower wages. The radicals of those days were represented by the Chartists. The Chartists were entirely opposed to the free trade movement. They said that they alone had the right to speak for the unrepresented classes, that free trade was a red herring drawn across the path of electoral reform . . .
>
> I want you to bear in mind that it is absolutely impossible to reconcile free trade with trade unionism . . . Free trade says you are to buy in the cheapest market. Free trade says you are not to interfere with the freedom of independent men, not to prescribe to an employer what he shall or shall not do, but to leave him free to bargain as he likes with his workpeople, and, on the other hand, you are not to make combinations which tend in the slightest degree to destroy the liberty of the workman to sell his labour just as low or just as high as he pleases. Those are the doctrines of free trade; and all these doctrines we have put aside now for twenty years in our endeavour to benefit the conditions of the working men and to raise the standard of living.

Document 6

Joseph Chamberlain's tumultuous career effectively ended in July 1906 when a stroke left him disabled and unfit for active politics. A few days earlier, he had celebrated his seventieth birthday, an event which prompted the following shrewd assessment. *Economist*, 14 July 1906.

The unfortunate feature of Mr. Chamberlain's career, at any rate since he entered parliament, is that he has advocated rather than promoted schemes. The future historian will see in him a distinct lack of constructive statesmanship. He boasts of his many unauthorised programmes, but they have been parts of great departments of reform which either still await achievement or have eventually been carried out in quite other shapes by other hands. In 1892 he took up old age pensions with enthusiasm, but we still await a workable scheme, and such schemes as are before the public are the work of others. Later he took up the 'imperial idea', but the most substantial results are a steamship line and the south African war. Meanwhile, so far as his activity is concerned, social reform has had to wait. From the time of his entrance into public life he has been always in extremes – carried away by one idea at a time, but never working any of them out into a practical shape. His speeches, indeed, indicate that he is incapable of grasping details or accurately reproducing them. Almost every one of the great addresses which he delivered in the capacity of a missionary of tariff reform contains some grotesque mistakes – whether it was a misrepresentation of Adam Smith, or a misunderstanding of the industrial conditions of the district, or one of the usual assertions of the capacity of tariff reform to achieve opposite results at the same time. Almost every one of the constituencies in which these speeches were delivered, and certainly every home of a distressed industry, rejected the Chamberlainite candidate . . . it is significant that Mr. Chamberlain gets no further with his propaganda. One speech is substantially the same as the last. Secure regular work at good wages; treat the foreigner as he treats you; bind the empire together – these principles are reiterated in slightly different phrasing, but there is no attempt either to meet the criticism of more learned economists, or even to avail himself of the material which he has just praised so highly, collected by his own tariff reform commission. There are learned arguments by scientific, if rather erratic, economists in favour of Mr. Chamberlain's plans. Mr. Chamberlain seems never to have heard of them.

Document 7

Balfour's experiences in the 1906 general election were most unhappy. He was in the unenviable position of a leader of the opposition forced to spend his time defending his own record in government. As the following extract shows, all too often he succeeded only in touching the electorate's raw nerve, and in demonstrating his lack of sympathy with the aspirations of organised labour.

From Balfour's speech in East Manchester, *The Times*, 10 January 1906.

> He understood that they wanted to hear about Chinese labour; and there was no subject upon which the misrepresentations of their opponents had been more persistent or more contemptible. He understood the critics of his government to say that they had practically introduced slavery into south Africa. (Voices – they live in compounds and so it is slavery . . . they were imported because they took less than the black men). He was attempting to deal for the moment with the case of British Guiana and not for the moment with south Africa. He asked why British Guiana should not be discussed. (A voice, 'Because we are not going to vote on British Guiana, but on Chinese labour and south Africa'; another voice, 'Explain why they are there' and 'Because they can be got for 32s. a month and kaffirs are dearer', and disorder) . . . It was impossible to say that Chinese labour in south Africa was slavery and coolie labour in British Guiana was freedom (A voice, 'Two blacks don't make a white', and cheers) . . . Chinese labour, which they had allowed to be imported at the request of the white population of the Transvaal (Voices, 'Mineowners and millionaires' . . . 'There are no compounds in British Guiana; you allow Chinamen to go as slaves at the request of the mineowners') . . . The whole charge of slavery was a mere election dodge ('Why did not you stop it?').

Document 8

The speeches of the 1906 election campaign, which produced one of the landslides of the twentieth century, repay examination. One made by the young Winston Churchill is worth quoting at length, not because he was as yet a very senior figure on the Liberal side, but because it offered evidence of the talent which would make him the most powerful orator of his generation. Moreover it provides an excellent example of the main thrust of the Liberal message in 1906, which stressed the late government's iniquities and the virtues of traditional Liberalism, but offered little in the way of practical social improvement. Unlike Churchill's subsequent efforts, it is a speech of which W. E. Gladstone himself might have been proud.

From a speech by W. S. Churchill at Deptford, *The Times*, 20 December 1905.

Mr. Churchill . . . accused the late government of administrative incompetence of the grossest kind. It was proved by their maladministration of the army, which, although they had repeatedly reformed it from top to bottom, was according to Lord Roberts no better than when they began, while it cost £10 million a year more than it did eight or nine years ago . . . it was proved by wasteful and ridiculous expeditions like that of hunting the mad Mullah round Somaliland, and wicked and sanguinary invasions such as the expedition to Tibet; it was proved by their flagrant neglect of every social problem, and by the neglect to carry out their own pledges in respect of old age pensions and the like. The second charge he brought against the late government was that of profligate finance; they had found in the spending of money an easy solution of every difficulty, and every department had bathed its hand in the golden stream. Many had come to them; none had gone empty away except the poor. The effect was felt by all classes in the country; it was felt by the masses of the people through the taxation of tea, sugar and coal; it was felt also in the diminution of credit due to the great increase in our debt coupled with altogether insufficient provision for repayment. He did not pretend that the problem of unemployment arose only from the expenditure of money by the government; but it was to Mr. Balfour and Mr. Chamberlain, who had lavishly squandered the treasure of this country by vast increases in armaments and doles to favoured classes – it was to those twin brethren of extravagance and profusion that the sufferings of many were in a certain proportion due. His third charge against the late administration was the gravest constitutional misdemeanour. They had scorned and mocked at the liberties of parliament, and they had shown in dealing with the fiscal question a want of candour. They had witnessed an increased arrogance on the part of the executive government, coupled with an increasing subservience and servility towards the great vested interests on which the party depended. Last of all he charged them with having ruled for two years without the confidence of the country or the respect of the house of commons . . . if returned it would be as a protectionist government, pledged to tariffs and with Mr. Chamberlain at its head. At present the harvests of the whole world were open to the purchasing power of our people, and when they saw the ambitious hands of statesmen struggling for political mastery laid recklessly on the vitals of national existence they ought to say, with a very ugly tone in their voice, 'hands off'. Great combines and trusts in America had succeeded in enormously raising the price of articles produced within the circle of protective tariffs, greatly to the disadvantage and even to the cruel injury of the people of that country, not only as consumers, but also in respect of their productive powers in regard to other manufactures. If protection were given, if only ten per cent for home industries, everything would cost a little more, and in this country there was a very great number of people who had only a slender margin between them and absolute starvation. Everyone would then buy a little less, and the shrinkage in the great home market would begin, which would inflict suffering on the people on a scale they had never experienced since the dark and evil days from which they were rescued by the patient courage of Mr. Cobden and by the genius of Sir Robert Peel.

Document 9

The rhetoric of the new prime minister, Campbell-Bannerman, was a degree more restrained, with its emphasis on the traditional, even conservative, merits of Liberalism. There is an irony in the following extract, in that Campbell-Bannerman's dreams of low taxation and low expenditure were based on the hope of a new international order in the wake of the Anglo-French entente and the Russo-Japanese war – dreams that would all too soon be dispelled by the serious intensification of Anglo-German naval rivalry.
From a speech by Campbell-Bannerman at Liverpool, *The Times*, 10 January 1906.

. . . Suppose that by a settled and pacific policy, accompanied by the growth of good feeling between the nations of the world (Cheers), a state of things was so established in which our present scale of armaments and the scale adopted by our neighbours was generally regarded as superfluous. Supposing, again, that the navy of a power which had been reckoned a potential foe is wiped out, and that the navies of such powers, whose relations with us had hitherto been uncertain, cease to be a possible menace, because of treaties or arrangements of amity and friendship (Cheers). Suppose, again, that by the development of tribunals of arbitration (Cheers) the causes and occasions of war were sensibly reduced (Hear, hear) would it be statesmanship, would it be commonsense in such an event to say 'Oh, we cannot dream of any reduction in our expenditure on armaments'?

Document 10

Churchill, in contrast to Chamberlain in his decline, was a rising star in the political firmament and the most forceful and coherent exponent of the new Liberalism until admiralty affairs engrossed his attention after 1911. The extent of his youthful radicalism is revealed in the following passage, in which he anticipates subsequent government policies and adroitly marries the concerns of the older Liberalism to the new.
The Times, 22 April 1908. (Speech at Drury Lane Theatre).

Mr. Churchill . . . said they had pulled the curtain up upon a piece that was going to have a good long run. They were there to consider what was the most important and certainly the most fundamental part of the constructive Liberal social policy and they had to face all the resources of a great monopoly so ancient that it had become almost venerable. They saw first of all that this island alone among civilised states presented the melancholy spectacle of a landless peasantry. Side by side with that, and arising, as they contended, directly out of it, they saw a blighted and restricted agriculture. The rural population was melting fast into the great cities, and whether they looked at the reports on physical deterioration or at those dealing with the supply of men for the army, no one could doubt that there was grave reason for alarm in the physical deterioration which was taking place in many of the great cities to which the rural population had been drawn . . . the local taxation system of our country was wholly unreformed; it was archaic and chaotic, vexatious, unhealthy and unjust. It bore no relation to modern requirements and exhibited just the same sort of vices as the old protectionist system; it hampered enterprise, it oppressed effort, it rewarded inertia. They must go forward and repeat in the arena of local taxation the same sort of triumphs as were won sixty years ago in the arena of national taxation when the corn laws were repealed . . . Under the old system people had dear food, under the present system they had dear houses . . . The movement for land reform aimed, not at the redistribution of existing wealth, but at the discovery of new springs of production, at an equitable partition of corporate and individual increments from day to day and from year to year through the operation of just laws regulating the acquisition of wealth.

Document 11

The question of votes for women, a leading theme of the Edwardian period, generated a considerable degree of controversy, some of which carries distinct echoes to this day. The following extracts are taken from correspondence published in *The Times* in 1912 on the occasion of the Conciliation Bill's failure to pass the House of Commons. Sir Almroth Wright's notorious letter, not surprisingly, provoked considerable offence, but it expresses, albeit in extreme form, a widespread male, and to some extent female, prejudice, that the distinction between the sexes should be preserved as fully as possible, and that women are too delicate for the rough and tumble of political life.

(*a*) From a letter from Sir Almroth Wright, distinguished physician, *The Times*, 28 March 1912.

. . . For man the physiology and psychology of woman is full of difficulties. He is not a little mystified when he encounters in her periodically recurring phases of hypersensitiveness, unreasonableness, and loss of the sense of proportion. He is frankly perplexed when confronted with a complete alteration of character in a woman who is child-bearing. When he is a witness of the tendency of woman to morally warp when nervously ill, and of the terrible physiological havoc which the pangs of a disappointed love may work, he is appalled. And it leaves on his mind an eerie feeling when he sees serious and long-continued mental disorders developing in connexion with the approaching extinction of a woman's reproductive faculty . . . No doctor can ever lose sight of the fact that the mind of woman is always threatened with danger from the reverberations of her physiological emergencies. It is with such thoughts that the doctor lets his eyes rest upon the militant suffragist. He cannot shut them to the fact that there is mixed up with the women's movement much mental disorder; and he cannot conceal from himself the physiological emergencies which lie behind. The recruiting field for the militant suffragists is the half million of our excess female population – that half million which had better long ago have gone to mate with its complement of men beyond the seas . . .

If women's suffrage comes in here, it will have come as a surrender to a very violent feminist agitation – an agitation which we have traced back to our excess female population and the associated abnormal physiological conditions. If ever parliament concedes the vote to women in England, it will be accepted by the militant suffragist, not as an eirenicon, but as a victory which she will value only for the better carrying out of her fight *à outrance* against the oppression and injustice of man.

(b) From two letters in reply, in *the Times*, 29 March 1912.

(Mr. Silvanus Thompson) Sir Almroth Wright's trenchant letter would carry more weight if it did not ignore or deny the one thing which has made into advocates of the suffrage many women who are bitterly opposed to the deplorable tactics of the Pankhurst rabble. That thing is the continued violation by law and under the aegis of law of the very 'covenant' which Sir Almroth Wright declares to be 'within the frontiers of civilisation'. There is in fact continued failure, both of the law as administered and of the unwritten code of social law, to put an end to crimes against the person of women. The absurdly low sentences against men convicted of assault, the utterly inadequate protection against seduction, the tolerance by society of a double standard of morals in the premarital state, the advocacy, even by an eminent Judge, of an inequality between man and woman in the laws of divorce – these are the things that give the lie to Sir Almroth Wright's complacent assumption that 'under this convenant a full half of the programme of Christianity has been realised'.

(Lady Emily Lutyens) Sir Almroth Wright, in the very comprehensive history he gives in your issue of today of the types of women who figure prominently in the ranks of suffragists, has omitted to mention one class who are very largely represented in this movement. I refer to the happy wives and mothers who, having everything that this world can give, have yet been willing to face insult, imprisonment, and even death if necessary, because by so doing they hoped to bring a little nearer the day when their sisters would no longer toil in sweated industries or be driven on to the streets for a livelihood.

(c) From a letter, by Vera Collum, *The Times*, 28 March 1912.

The voteless woman worker found at the outset that, although union and organisation to a great extent minimised the ill effects of illegitimate competition among the women workers of a given trade or profession, it was powerless to help her when it came to a struggle between employers and employed, between sweated producers and consumers . . . This leverage of the vote is keenly desired by and for working women, for without it they will always have to fight a losing battle when their own legitimate interests come into collision with those of voters. That, to a large section of suffragists, is the strongest argument for the enfranchisement of women. It is not, of course, a romantic argument. Instead of regarding the parliamentary franchise as the badge of emancipation, it simply looks upon it as a useful lever which it is unfair to withhold from women workers when it is given to their male competitors and employers.

Document 12

Naval rearmament loomed large in the politics of the decade prior to 1914. It strengthened considerably the sense of antagonism towards Germany which took Britain into war. Domestically its consequences were hardly less profound. It was a main reason for the people's budget, and, in subsequent years, its mounting cost prevented the Liberals from introducing social reforms or tax-cutting measures which might have helped to maintain their popularity. This was very much the case with the budget of 1914, the same year from which these extracts, from the House of Commons debate on the naval estimates on 18 and 19 March, are taken. Churchill's masterly rhetoric is matched with a sharp rejoinder from Snowden, a Labour member who expressed the anxieties of many backbench Liberals.
Parliamentary Debates, fifth series, LIX 1896–1938 and 2126–2142 (18 and 19 March 1914).

(Mr. Churchill) We must begin by recognising how different is the part played by our Navy from that of the navies of every other country. Alone among the great modern states, we can neither defend the soil upon which we live nor subsist upon its produce. Our whole regular army is liable to be ordered abroad for the defence of India. The food of our people, the raw material of our industries, the commerce which constitutes our wealth, have to be protected as they traverse thousands of miles of sea and ocean from every quarter of the globe. Here we must consider the disparity of risks and stakes between us and other naval powers.

Defeat to Germany at sea means nothing but loss of the ships sunk or damaged in battle. Behind the German 'Dreadnought' stands four and a half million soldiers, and a narrow sea-front bristling with fortresses and batteries. Nothing we could do, after a naval victory, could affect the safety or freedom of a single German hamlet.

Behind the British line of battle are the long, lightly-defended stretches of the east coast, our endless trade routes and food routes, our small army and our vast peaceful population, with their immense possessions. The burden of responsibility laid upon the British navy is heavy, and its weight increases year by year. All the world is building ships of the greatest power . . . In every country powerful interests and huge industries are growing up, which will render any check or cessation in the growth of navies increasingly difficult as time goes by . . . None of these powers need, like us, navies to defend their actual independence or safety. They build them so as to play a part in the world's affairs. It is sport to them. It is life and death to us . . . Our naval strength is the one great balancing force which we can contribute to our own safety and to the peace of the world.

(Mr. Snowden) If there was one thing more than another on which this government was returned to power in 1906, it was on a pledge of peace and retrenchment . . . The first year for which the present government were responsible for the estimates – 1906–7 – the naval expenditure stood at, roughly, £31,000,000. The house is now asked to vote £51,000,000 . . . I can well remember the time when a Tory chancellor of the exchequer resigned office rather than be responsible for providing £13,000,000 per year for naval expenditure. We now have the son of that Tory minister, practically without apologising to the house – nay, glorying in the magnitude of the estimate – proposing, in the name of a Liberal government, an expenditure of more than £51,000,000 . . . I said that our party was not going to take 'Dreadnoughts' as a substitute for social reform . . . If it had not been for this £20,000,000 increase in naval expenditure, what could we not have done? This government, during its ten years of office, has spent £360,000,000 upon the navy. With half of that sum we could have established a utopia in this dear land of ours. With that £20,000,000 alone we could have wiped out the tea tax, the sugar tax, and all the food taxes, and still have had a sum left which would have enabled you to attempt something in the way of better housing, better education, and so on, for our people. As a matter of fact, we are the most heavily taxed nation for war purposes in Europe . . . By the expenditure of this money you are withdrawing labour from remunerative and far more productive employment . . . From the economic point of view, and I would add, from the point of view of social economy, it would be just as wise, well, and profitable for the community to spend the same amount of money to employ the same labour to make fireworks and let them off.

Document 13

The people's budget of 1909 was a major instalment of the new Liberalism. As such it was opposed in the House of Lords by an overwhelming majority of peers, including a former Liberal prime minister, the Earl of Rosebery, whose speech is quoted at some length here. Typically Rosebery could not bring himself actually to vote against the budget, rightly foreseeing that to do so would call the powers of the upper chamber into question.
Parliamentary Debates (House of Lords) fifth series, 942–966 (24 November 1909).

Your lordships are accused by your enemies of owning some enormous proportion of land in England . . . But what have we to say about no taxation without representation. This one fifth, one third, or this entirety if you like of the land of England held by the unfortunate people who sit in this house is to be taxed freely, abundantly, and increasingly without its having a word or a vote . . . The budget has already done incalculable mischief. It has already destroyed confidence in a remarkable degree. This country was not long ago the strong-box and the safe of Europe, to which every man outside this country sent his savings that they might be secure. I venture to ask whether those millions have not already disappeared from this country. Those have been wantonly cast away. What is following? Many millions from the people of this country as well . . .

Remember, that in hanging up or in rejecting the budget the house of lords is doing exactly what its enemies wish it to do . . .

I should have liked to see the house of lords pass this finance bill, not because I have a good opinion of it but because I have such an excessively bad opinion of it. I have such confidence in its demerits that I should wish it to be judged by its performance after six or eight months of experience, and not by its promise as it will be held out at the polls. I believe that if you chose to allow the budget bill to take effect, and when the country had had a sufficient experience of its intolerable inquisitions, its intolerable bureaucracy, and, above all, the enormous loss of employment and capital which it must involve – a loss of employment which must add enormously to the hideousness of the problem which the budget will do nothing to solve – the problem of unemployment . . . you would achieve a victory when you next approach the polls which would surprise yourselves . . . We should then have an anti-Socialist government, a luxury which I cannot say we possess now . . . I am sorry that I cannot give a vote against the budget on this occasion. My interest in this matter is mainly that of the second chamber, and I cannot stake all my hopes of its future utility and reform on the tumultuous hazard of a general election.

(Lord St. David's of Roch Castle) The noble earl who has just sat down talked of unemployment. He said that the budget was going to cause great unemployment, and that if noble Lords would only let it pass, it would cause so much more unemployment that some day or other noble Lords would get a majority in the other House of their own way of thinking. Why cannot the noble earl give us some statistics for that statement? There has been a good deal of talk of unemployment in this House, but after all these are the statistics . . . If you compare the state of things before the budget with the state of things after the budget, it works out thus: In October this year, after the budget, the figure for unemployment was 7.1, whereas in October last year before the budget it was 9.5. Let that be a little check on some noble Lords who have no personal experience in the matter.

Document 14

The general election of December 1910 has tended to become submerged in the wider constitutional conflict of the years 1909–11. In fact, it was probably as significant as any election of the century. Had the Liberals lost, there would arguably have been no Parliament Act, no National Insurance Act, and no third Home Rule Bill. Out of office, the Liberals might well have avoided some of the embarrassments and the fatal split occasioned by the first world war. Ironically, defeat in December 1910 might have meant long-term survival as a party of government. Instead the election marked perhaps Asquith's most signal triumph, as he claimed the centre ground while manoeuvring the Unionists into appearing a party of dangerous radicalism and reckless constitutional innovation.

(a) Speech by Balfour at the Albert Hall, *The Times*, 30 November 1910.

A dissolution, as many of the tradespeople of London know to their cost, is not only very expensive but it is very disturbing. The advantage of the referendum is this – that the issue is quite clear and quite precise. It is not one of the mixed issues put before the constituencies at a general election . . . it does not involve all the personal bitterness inevitably involved in a contest between the two competitors for a seat; it does not carry with it a change of government; and it does get a clear verdict from the people. I should have thought that with this method of dealing with deadlock or collisions of opinion between the two houses of parliament the whole radical party would have competed in their anxious desire to make the project their own, and to say 'Here at last is our ideal of government by the people and for the people really carried into effect' (cheers).

. . . Surely no mystery was ever so mysterious as that of a chancellor of the exchequer who trembled at the idea of consulting the people because of its cost, but who regarded it as a great reform that every one of the people's representatives should for the first time for many centuries of British history be paid a salary out of public funds (laughter and cheers). As a member of parliament I see great merit in the last proposal (laughter). I daresay it would be much more agreeable to receive a salary than to pay for a referendum, but, frankly, which is the more democratic? (loud cheers).

(b) Speech by Asquith at Wolverhampton, *The Times*, 2 December 1910.

We live in a time of rapid movement . . . Contrast the position held by the Tory party twelve months ago with the position which they hold today. There were, to use the common phrase, two planks in their platform. The first was the vindication of the house of lords . . . And what was the other plank? Tariff reform . . . Well, how do we stand today? Why both these positions have been precipitately abandoned. In the course of little more than a fortnight, we have seen on paper – on paper, do not forget that – the hereditary house of lords abolished, a revolutionary cardboard structure run up in its place, parliamentary government, as we have hitherto understood and practised it, abandoned, practically abandoned, in favour of government by plebiscite; and last, but not least, tariff reform postponed to the uncertain chance of a remote and indefinite future . . . I think it is the largest and most variegated experiment in vote-catching of which I have ever heard . . . unique in its almost colossal indecency.

I think we ought to look rather closely at the language which is being used . . . The first question I want to ask is this. At what stage is the proposed reference to the people going to take place? Is it before you introduce your budget, or after the budget has been through the house of commons? . . . Then again, who is going to vote? . . . Suppose the country says 'no'. What is going to happen then? Apparently they are going to sit on, the government and the Tory house of commons, sit on placidly at Westminster as though nothing had happened, holding power, administering the affairs of the empire, framing, for aught I know, new budgets or a fresh reform year after year, in a discredited house of commons, an adverse verdict of the country upon a most national issue staring them all the time in the face (hear, hear). If any one a week ago had asked a sane and responsible statesman to contemplate such a transformation of parliamentary institutions, you would have said the man had escaped from Bedlam and ought to be returned there as quickly as possible (laughter and cheers).

Document 15

The December 1910 election led directly to the Parliament Act of 1911, whose eventual passage, overshadowed by the threat of large-scale peerage creations, split Unionists in the House of Lords into moderates and diehards. A leading member of the latter is quoted here.
Parliamentary Debates (House of Lords), fifth series, IX 930–937 (9 August 1911).

(Lord Willougby de Broke) The radical caucus challenged the British constitution when they manoeuvred the house of lords into rejecting the budget . . . A Liberal government was returned to office in 1906 with one of the most magnificent majorities by which any party has ever been returned to the house of commons, and they proceeded to legislate, not for the welfare of the people, but underlying the whole of their policy was the purpose of making war upon the constitution of this country, partly because inveighing against the *personnel* of the house of lords suited their general plan of campaign of setting class against class, and partly because they knew that sooner or later they were bound to be faced with the problem of getting a home rule bill through parliament without an appeal to the people . . . The rejection of the budget, if I may put it this way, is the very reason why your lordships should stick to your guns now. It is all part and parcel of the same policy

. . . And when we are told that the time has come for throwing up the Constitution, our answer to that is 'Never'. We do not intend to allow the ancient tradition of parliamentary practice to be applied to a class of measures which has never been before parliament in the recollection of I do not know how many generations. During the last eighteen months we have heard nothing else up and down the country but loud-mouthed denunciations of the parliament bill by Lord Curzon and others because it would establish a system of single-chamber government in this country. Yet now at the very last minute we are told that we must assent to the passing of the bill because, after all, it still leaves the house of lords a certain amount of power which is worth keeping. Noble lords who make use of that argument cannot possibly have it both ways. This bill either means single-chamber government or it does not. If Unionists peers say it does not, then they are adopting the Radical argument . . . that noble lords opposite are always using in order to rope in the moderate men on their own side. If, on the other hand, the bill does mean single-chamber government, then we who belong to the Conservative and Constitutional party have no right to assent to its passing in any shape or form.

Document 16

Bonar Law's speech at Blenheim Palace in mid-1912 remains one of the more notorious utterances of a British political party leader. On one level it can be read as a repudiation of the 'gospel of class hatred' said to be being practiced by the Liberals, and as a refusal to try to outbid them by promises of social reform. On another level it reads as an appeal to ancient animosities and as a dangerous intensification of the Irish problem, partly induced by bitter resentment at the constitutional changes of 1911.

(a) From a speech by Bonar Law at Blenheim Palace, *The Times*, 29 July 1912.

How was the parliament bill carried? It was carried because Her Majesty's ministers pretended that they were not in favour of single-chamber government, when they were deliberately arranging an autocratic power for a single chamber. It was carried by means of a declaration, by a pledge as clear and as solemn as was ever given by any man, that the destruction of the power of the house of lords would immediately be followed by a reform of the house of lords. That pledge has been broken. The parliament bill was not carried for nothing. It was carried in order that the government might be able to force through parliament home rule proposals which at the election were carefully hidden from the people of this country – proposals which they are trying to carry, not only without the consent, but, as we know and as you know, against the will of the people of this country . . . We do not recognise that any such action is the constitutional government of a free people. We regard them as a revolutionary committee, which has seized by fraud upon despotic power (cheers). We shall use any means (loud cheers) to deprive them of the power which they have usurped and to compel them to face the people whom they have deceived.

. . . Mr. Asquith denies that there are two nations in Ireland. How can he deny it with the fact staring him in the face? . . . There are those two nations separated from each other by a gulf far greater than that which separates Ireland as whole from the United Kingdom . . . Under such circumstances, surely the only sane method is to make the British people arbiters between them, to have both subject to the British house of commons, in which both are represented (cheers). The government, in spite of the declarations of two of their ministers, at the bidding of Mr. Redmond (groans) have refused even to consider separate treatment for Ulster. Well, they must take the consequences (cheers). In Belfast and the surrounding counties there is a population of more than a million people – more than a quarter of the whole population of Ireland, a number almost as great as the whole white population of South Africa. These people say that under a government dominated by men who control the Ancient Order of Hibernians . . . neither their civil nor their religious liberty will be safe.

. . . These men will not submit to home rule. How are they going to be made to submit to it? Does anyone imagine that British troops will be used to shoot down men who demand no privilege which is not enjoyed by you and me and no privilege which any one of us would ever surrender? The thing is unthinkable . . . No nation will ever take up arms to compel loyal subjects to leave their community (cheers). I do not believe for a moment that any government would ever dare to make the attempt, but I am sure of this – that, if the attempt were made, the government would not succeed in carrying home rule. They would succeed only in lighting fires of civil war which would shatter the empire to its foundations. . . . If an attempt were made without the clearly expressed will of the people of this country, and as part of a corrupt parliamentary bargain, to deprive these men of their birthright, they would be justified in resisting by all means in their power, including force

193

(cheers). I say now, with a full sense of the responsibility which attaches to my position, that I can imagine no lengths of resistance to which Ulster will go in which I shall not be ready to support them and in which they will not be supported by the overwhelming majority of the British people. (The audience rose from their seats and cheered this declaration for some minutes).

(b) From Rudyard Kipling's poem, 'Ulster 1912'.

The dark eleventh hour
Draws on and sees us sold
To every evil power
We fought against of old.
Rebellion, rapine, hate,
Oppression, wrong and greed
Are loosed to rule our fate,
By England's act and deed . . .

We asked no more than leave
To reap where we have sown,
Through good and ill we cleave
To our own flag and throne,
Now England's shot and steel
Beneath that flag must show
How loyal hearts should kneel
To England's oldest foe.

Document 17

Ulster naturally assumed pride of place in the Unionist campaign against the third Home Rule Bill, but it should not be allowed to distract all attention from more long-standing objections to home rule, which were now urged as strongly as they had been in 1886 and 1893. A good example is provided by a speech in the House of Lords, by the Unionist elder stateman and leading financial authority, Viscount St Aldwyn, formerly Sir Michael Hicks Beach.

Parliamentary Debates (House of Lords) fifth series, XIII 518–534 (28 January 1913).

We have been asked to hope that this bill will establish friendly relations between Great Britain and Ireland, that it will, in the words of the noble marquess opposite (Crewe), remove the intolerable burden of Irish debate in the house of commons, and that it will give to the British taxpayer a certain knowledge of his future liability to contribute for Irish purposes . . . I think it has recently come into Mr. Redmond's mind that for many years past he and his friends have held out to the people of Ireland expectations of a millennium of material advantages to be derived from home rule . . . Yesterday the noble marquess gave us some very plausible reasons why forty-two Irish members should be retained in the British house of commons. He said that taxation and representation ought to go together . . . No, my lords, the real reason for the presence of Irish representatives in the British parliament is this: they are to act as agents of the Irish government with the British treasury. The noble marquess spoke of them as a microcosm of Ireland. I think he mistook the word. He meant an Irish microbe devastating the British constitution.

What will these agents do? There will be no division of parties. One and all will vote together in a raid on the British treasury. They will simply go to the prime minister of the day and say, 'We want further aid and you must give it to us . . . There is a critical division coming on; forty-two votes will make a lot of difference, and if you do not give it us there may be unpleasant results.' That will initiate a series of blackmailing acts on the British exchequer and the British parliament which I venture to say will be the worst form of political corruption. Here will be these men, having a government of their own with which British members will have nothing to do, supporting a government in power at Westminster which may be odious to the majority of the British electorate.

Document 18

Naturally, a rather different view of the Ulster question was taken by the Nationalist leader of the Irish parliamentary party, John Redmond. He maintained that Ulster's opposition to home rule was a matter of bluff, which would subside as easily as had earlier agitations against Catholic emancipation and Irish church disestablishment. The following extract is taken from Redmond's speech against Agar-Robartes's amendment, an initial attempt to partition Ireland.
Parliamentary Debates, fifth series, XXXIX 1078–1089 (18 June 1912).

This idea of two nations in Ireland is to us revolting and hateful. The idea of our agreeing to the partition of our nation is unthinkable. We want the union in Ireland of all creeds and of all classes, of all races, and we would resist most violently as far as is within our power the setting up of permanent dividing lines between one creed and another and one race and another . . . To attempt to cut off the Protestants under the two-thirds theory from the national tradition and aspiration of the Irish race sounds to many of us something like sacrilege. Yes, many of the most revered of our national saints and martyrs in the national struggle have been Protestants. Grattan's parliament, which possesses today the enthusiastic and affectionate remembrance of the Irish people, was a parliament in which no Catholic could sit; for election to it no Catholic was allowed to vote. I say to you here that most of the Catholics in Ireland would prefer tomorrow to take back Grattan's parliament with all those disqualifications than to consent to be governed under the union or consent to the partition of the Irish nation.

Why is Ireland to be the only country in the world where religious animosity is permanently to divide the people? We demand that under home rule we in Ireland shall be given the same chance as was given to the Catholics and Protestants in Canada, to the Boers and Britons in South Africa, the same chance to sit down side by side and to endeavour to administer jointly the affairs of our common country . . . Let me read what Mr. Parnell said about this subject in 1886. 'No, Sir, we cannot give up a single Irishman. We want the energy, the patriotism, the talent, and the work of every Irishman to ensure that this great experiment shall be a successful one . . . We have heard of the dangers that will result from an untried and unpractised legislature being established in Ireland. Now I regard variety as vitally necessary for the success of this trial. I want, Sir, all creeds and all classes in Ireland. We cannot admit that there is a single one of them too good to take part in the Dublin parliament.'

Document 19

Redmond however was obliged to yield to circumstances. By early 1914 the government had determined to try for a compromise on Ulster based on temporary partition. Redmond found himself as much beholden to the Liberals as they were to him. As the following extracts show, the county option proposals did not dispel controversy, and they also exposed Redmond to a backlash from some of his supporters who felt home rule on such terms to be no longer worth having.

Parliamentary debates, fifth series, LIX 906–948 (9 March 1914).

(The Prime Minister) . . . Any county in the province of Ulster is to be excluded for a certain period, if on a poll being taken of the parliamentary electors in the county before the bill comes into operation, a majority – a bare majority vote in favour of exclusion . . . Assume that the bill passes into law in the month of July in the present year – that is, July 1914. The meeting of the Irish legislature might be accelerated, but in all probability, and according to the intentions of the bill, it would be a year after that. I am assuming that the Irish legislature meets in July 1915. A general election in this country must take place – I mean a dissolution of the present parliament, if it is prolonged to the last possible moment of its constitutional existence – in October or November, 1915 . . . Then if these counties, after the passing of the act in July 1914, have taken polls and voted for exclusion, that exclusion for six years dates from July 1915. Therefore it cannot come to an end until July 1921. The house will see from the timetable, in which I have taken every date as adversely as I possibly can, that before inclusion becomes operative there must be two general elections in this country, one in 1915 and another in 1920. And before the second of those general elections takes place, the electorate of this country and of Ireland will have had between five and six years' actual experience of the working of the Irish parliament and of the Irish executive. We believe that this is a fair and equitable arrangement. It gives to these counties, it gives to the whole of Ulster, in the first instance, the option to say whether they will come within the bill, and if they vote for exclusion they cannot be brought back into it unless with the assent, at a general election, of a majority of the electorate of the whole of the United Kingdom.

(Sir Edward Carson) . . . We do not want sentence of death with a stay of execution for six years . . . Knowing these men as I do, I believe that they would rather you would bring this matter to close quarters tomorrow, than leave them in this state of having it dangled before them that they are to be a pawn in your political game for the next six years . . . You know very well that once your bill has passed you will not get the electors of the country to give their attention back again to this question, and your whole pre-tence of parliament intervening is a sham . . . To my mind this period of six years is fantastic. You are going to set up a whole system of government for Ulster, or for the counties that go out, a whole financial system; and, in passing, I would like to know how the finance of this bill is to be regulated when you do not know how much of Ulster is to be in and how much is to be out. Are you going to set up all this system of government for a period of six years alone? Why, you will hardly have settled down in your government before you are turning into another one.

(Mr. T. M. Healy) . . . This question is our lives. It is not a question to be measured on the half-a-loaf principle. We insist on all Ireland and I prefer no bill to the bill declared for by his majesty's government . . . It is to me perfectly plain that just as the right honourable gentleman the first lord has accepted the principle of exclusion, so his obedient acolyte behind me, the hon. member for Waterford (Mr. John Redmond), will swallow the principle of perpetual exclusion . . . On every occasion when it was necessary for the convenience of the ministry the member for Waterford fled from his principles and declared in favour of the convenience of the Liberal party . . . Came the budget, which he voted against in 1909 and swallowed in 1910 . . . Then again, there was the insurance act, which the entire and united hierarchy of Ireland said meant disaster to the country. For the convenience of the chancellor of the exchequer the member for Waterford immediately endorsed the insurance act, and it was put in the first place instead of home rule. It is an act which has abstracted £1,400,000 of the money of the Irish people, and has not given them £100,000 in exchange . . .

We now come to this 'very slight concession' for which the member for Trinity College (Sir Edward Carson) asked. Would any sane Britisher go to civil war for the difference between six years and 666 years? Is there any sane man amongst you who would let loose the fires of civil war for such a mere form? Why cannot the member for Waterford give that up as he has given up everything else? The remains of his principles ornament every step of this gangway. Accordingly, I take it as absolutely certain that exclusion will be made permanent. Let me tell the house what that means. I say I prefer no bill to it . . . The time has come when it is necessary to make plain to the house that this bill, already so restricted, with perpetual exclusion in it, is the worst possible endowment you can confer on our country. What will happen? These four counties so excluded will become a target for the rest of Ireland. Their inhabitants will be boycotted by every Catholic outside, and not only that, but this will breed among Protestants in the south of Ireland a feeling of irritation and annoyance, as well as a feeling of sympathy with those beleaguered in what my hon. friend called 'the Orange Free State'. You will have every day, every week, and every month of the year, reprisals and repression as well as boycotting. You will have Catholics set against Protestants, and

Protestants set against Catholics within the new enclave and outside it. And what about our countrymen abroad? You have recognised after all their power even in the matter of the Panama canal.
How long will it be before there is a movement in the American
congress to put a tariff on Belfast linen? . . . Do you think that
these changes in the bill are things to be thrown off at a moment's
notice by a man at that box opposite, when we who have been
thinking of Ireland ever since we were children, whose hearts
throb with every vibration of Irish feeling, are going to be cut off
from the country of Hugh O'Neill and Owen Roe, the country
where St. Patrick lies buried, the country where his great cathedral
was founded, the hills where he laboured as a slave . . . For what
purpose are we here? We are here to state, as we have stated for
thirty-three years, the evangel of Ireland as it has come down to us
from our forefathers for 700 years.

Document 20

The widespread industrial unrest of the years immediately before
the first world war, like the last-ditch resistance in the House of
Lords, Ulster's intransigence, and suffragette militancy, seemed
to many evidence of a crisis in Edwardian society. The tidal wave
of strikes offers parallels with 1968 in France, along with the
paradox of protest at a time of unprecedented prosperity. The
House of Commons was both disturbed and intrigued when it
debated, on 8 May 1912, a motion for an investigation into the
causes of industrial unrest. All the political parties had their own
explanations – the Unionists blaming free trade and Lloyd
George's exploitation of class conflict – but the debate is anyway
worth following for the light which it throws on one of the more
significant developments of the years immediately before the first
world war.
Parliamentary Debates, fifth series, XXXVIII 487–534 (8 May 1912).

(Lord Robert Cecil) People are more and more growing to distrust
the legislature and to think that they have not a chance of obtaining
justice from the legislative machine. You see it from passive
resistance – a feeling among Nonconformists that they had not
been fairly represented in this house . . . So it is with the
suffragettes. Many honorary members are very angry with the
action of these women; but ultimately what is it that moved the
women to do these things? They complained that they were not

fairly treated by this house: that they were treated with chicanery and trickery, and that this house has no real authority to do what it does. I take another example, namely the example of Ulster . . .

As to the industrial side of it, in my judgment the only hopeful remedy suggested is co-partnership . . . With regard to the other matter of giving the public greater confidence in this house, I have no doubt that you must bring the electorate into closer relationship with this house. I have always been a strong supporter of the policy of the referendum for that reason.

(Mr. Keir Hardie) It is all very well for us to discuss here academically what should be done, and to appoint nice respectable committees; but outside there is seething unrest, and the appointment of these committees will simply accentuate it. There have been several expressions of opinion as to the causes of unrest. The poverty cause is well known. The late leader of the Liberal party (Sir Henry Campbell-Bannerman) at the general election of 1906 put his imprimatur upon the statement that one third of the population of Great Britain were living either in poverty or on the poverty line. The last ten years have accentuated every evil that then existed. Let me give the house these figures. During these ten years, the first ten years of this century, the cost of living, according to the board of trade returns, has increased by twelve and a half per cent, or 2s 6d in the pound, but the increase in wages obtained by the working classes comes on an average to only 1d per week.

The workers have been crying out for a fuller share of life . . . but, while there has been this increase in the demand, there has been a lessening of the power to satisfy the demand. Various reforms have been proposed, but all these things have been tinkering with effects without touching causes. Let me enumerate very briefly what has been done. Pensions have been given to the aged over seventy, but the need for pensions is due to the poverty-stricken life, owing to low wages, which the workers have to endure until they are seventy. Insurance! There is attached to it irritating conditions and a burdensome payment for which there was not the slightest necessity, since a small addition to the income tax or to the tax on land values would have found all the money necessary to pay for the cost of insurance. I come now to the reform most referred to tonight, the miners' minimum wage, and I cite this as a sample of the way the house plays with this question . . . At the present time every improvement in the condition of the workers is made a fresh pretext by the capitalist class for enriching themselves. The minimum wages act passed this house a few weeks ago. It meant an increase in the cost of getting coal of 2d.

and, in some districts, 3d. per ton. What has happened? Already here in the city of London the consumer is told that, because of the cost of getting the coal, due to the minumum wage act, there is to be a permanent increase of 2s. 6d. per ton in the price charged to the consumer! So, although that act was passed ostensibly for the benefit of the miner, it will be the mineowner who will be enriched . . .

We can see no solution of the industrial problem short of Socialism. There is no good giving working men rises in wages if the landlord, the colliery owner, and the middleman are going to take it for themselves and for their own benefit. The only remedy for that is to have the mines, the land, and industries generally the property of the community as a whole, so that the whole of the wealth created will belong to the community, and the present order would be reversed by which those who do really useful and hard work receive the smallest portion of that which their labour produces.

(Mr. Lloyd George) During the last year or two we have had more serious strikes than during any previous period for some years. I think that is due to the fact that when you have a certain accession of prosperity the working classes are apt to complain, and I think often with a good deal of reason, that there is a tardiness in allocating to them their share of the increased profits. That is why you probably get more serious strikes during periods of increasing prosperity. The symptoms are manifested in all the industrial countries in the world. There have been serious strikes in Germany. The result of the last general election there is an indication of very deep social and economic unrest on the part of the working classes . . .

I was rather surprised to hear the noble lord say that in his judgment the conditions of labour in the agricultural districts of this country were on the whole more favourable than those in the industrial districts. I think he will find that it is quite the reverse, and that a good deal of the trouble in the industrial districts is due to the fact that the conditions of labour in the agricultural districts are so unfair to the workers . . . That undoubtedly is a matter which ought to be inquired into, and I am certain that it does have a very serious effect in depressing wages in the labour market in the industrial districts and towns of this country.

Bibliographical essay

Biographies offer a rich source for the political history of this period. Two leading politicians have been particularly favoured: Joseph Chamberlain and Lloyd George. For the former, J. L. Garvin and J. Amery, *A Life of Joseph Chamberlain*, vols 4–6 (London, 1931–69) provides a fairly comprehensive survey. Among other useful, shorter studies are P. Fraser, *Joseph Chamberlain: radicalism and empire 1868–1914* (London, 1966) and R. Jay, *Joseph Chamberlain: a political study* (Oxford, 1981). Works of scholarship about Lloyd George include J. Grigg, *Lloyd George: the people's champion, 1902–1911* and *Lloyd George: the road to war, 1912–1916* (London, 1978 and 1985) and also B. B. Gilbert, *Lloyd George: the architect of change 1863–1912* (London, 1987). There are useful biographies of the prime ministers of the day, for instance J. Wilson, *C.-B.: a life of Sir Henry Campbell-Bannerman* (London, 1973) and S. Koss, *Asquith* (London, 1976). Interesting essays on Churchill are contained in R. Blake and W. R. Louis eds, *Churchill* (Oxford, 1993). D. Marquand, *Ramsay MacDonald* (London, 1977) deals with a principal personality of the young Labour movement. J. Campbell, *F. E. Smith: first earl of Birkenhead* (London, 1983) vividly brings to life a whole political era.

Military histories of the south African war are plentiful, among the best being T. Pakenham, *The Boer War* (London, 1979) and P. Warwick ed., *The South African War* (London, 1980). Much less in evidence are accounts of the domestic impact of the war in Britain, though a particular viewpoint is expressed in R. Price, *An Imperial War and the British Working Class* (London, 1972). Rather more attention has been given to the war's aftermath in terms of the tariff reform campaign, for instance in A. Sykes, *Tariff Reform in British Politics* (Oxford, 1979) and R. A. Rempel, *Unionists Divided: Arthur Balfour, Joseph Chamberlain and the Unionist Free Traders* (Newton Abbot, 1972). Also useful here is N. Blewett, 'Free fooders, Balfourites, whole hoggers: factionalism within the Unionist party, 1906–1910', *Historical Journal*, 1968. A main landmark is examined in A. K. Russell, *Liberal Landslide: the general election of 1906* (Newton Abbot, 1973).

The political history of the ensuing years, down to 1914, has been intensively covered in P. Rowland, *The Last Liberal Governments: the promised land, 1905–1910* (London, 1968) and *The last Liberal Governments: unfinished business* (London, 1971). Key episodes have attracted particular analysis. The crisis brought about by financial innovation is examined by B. K. Murray, *The People's Budget, 1909–1910* (Oxford, 1980) and N. Blewett, *The Peers, the Parties and the People: the British general elections of 1910* (London, 1972). Note also R. Jenkins, *Mr. Balfour's Poodle* (London, 1954). Home rule and the accompanying Ulster crisis have been the subject of a number of monographs, among them P. Jalland, *The Liberals and Ireland: the Ulster question in British politics to 1914* (Brighton, 1980) and A. T. Q. Stewart, *The Ulster Crisis: resistance to Home Rule, 1912–1914* (London, 1967).

The fortunes of the political parties in this period have received a good deal of attention. Conservatism is analysed in J. A. Ramsden, *The Age of Balfour and Baldwin* (London, 1978) and M. Fforde, *Conservatism and Collectivism, 1886–1914* (Edinburgh, 1990). The new force on the left is examined in K. D. Brown ed., *The First Labour Party, 1906–1914* (London, 1985). Liberalism and radicalism are the subject of a number of studies, among them H. V. Emy, *Liberals, Radicals and Social Politics, 1892–1914* (Cambridge, 1973), G. L. Bernstein, *Liberalism and Liberal Politics in Edwardian England* (London, 1986), A. J. A. Morris, *Radicalism Against War 1906–1914* (London, 1972). The historiography of Liberalism at this time is closely tied up with the long-running debate about the likely destiny of the Liberal and Labour parties before 1914, a debate which was in its way started by the publication of the suggestively entitled G. Dangerfield, *The Strange Death of Liberal England* (London, 1935). Significant contributions to this debate have included P. F. Clarke, *Lancashire and the New Liberalism* (Cambridge, 1971), R. McKibbin, *The Evolution of the Labour Party* (Oxford, 1974) and D. Tanner, *Political Change and the Labour Party* (Cambridge, 1990). Among relevant articles are P. F. Clarke, 'The electoral position of the Liberal and Labour parties, 1910–1914', *English Historical Review*, 1975, and 'Liberals, Labour and the Franchise', *English Historical Review*, 1977, and H. C. G. Matthew, R. I. McKibbin and J. A. Kay, 'The franchise factor in the rise of the Labour party', *English Historical Review*, 1976. A different twist to the whole debate is to be found in E. H. H. Green, 'The strange death of Tory England', *Twentieth Century British History*, 1991. Two works covering a wider period of history, but which deal significantly with this area, are M. Pugh, *The Making of Modern British Politics, 1867–1939* (Oxford, 1982) and G. R. Searle, *The Liberal Party: triumph and disintegration, 1886–1929* (London, 1992).

Social and economic developments which had an important bearing on political history in this period are investigated in a number of works. Welfare policy is the subject of B. B. Gilbert, *The Evolution of National Insurance in Great Britain* (London, 1966) and J. Harris, *Unemployment and Politics: a study in English social policy 1886–1914* (Oxford, 1972). The impact of feminism is examined in D. Morgan, *Suffragists and Liberals: the politics of women's suffrage in Britain* (Oxford, 1975) and S. S. Holton, *Feminism and Democracy: women's suffrage and reform politics in Britain, 1900–1918* (Cambridge, 1986). Trade unionism is investigated in R. Gregory, *The Miners and British Politics 1906–1914* (Oxford, 1968) and H. A. Clegg, A. Fox and A. F. Thompson eds., *A History of British Trade Unions Since 1889* (Oxford, 1964). The other side of the social and economic divide is explored in A. Offner, *Property and Politics, 1870–1914* (Cambridge, 1981) and K. D. Brown ed., *Essays in Anti-Labour History* (London, 1974). An additional appraisal is to be found in G. R. Searle, 'The Edwardian Liberal party and business', *English Historical Review*, 1983, an article which returns one once again to the whole debate over Liberal England, usefully summarised in J. A. Thompson, 'The historians and the decline of the Liberal party', *Albion*, 1990.

Index

205

Index

Index